Springer Texts in Business and Economics

More information about this series at http://www.springer.com/series/10099

Maximilian Fandl

Monetary and Financial Policy in the Euro Area

An Introduction

Springer

Maximilian Fandl
Frankfurt am Main, Germany

ISSN 2192-4333 ISSN 2192-4341 (electronic)
Springer Texts in Business and Economics
ISBN 978-3-030-10243-2 ISBN 978-3-319-72643-4 (eBook)
https://doi.org/10.1007/978-3-319-72643-4

Printed on acid-free paper

This Springer imprint is published by the registered company Springer International Publishing AG part of Springer Nature.
The registered company address is: Gewerbestrasse 11, 6330 Cham, Switzerland

Preface

About 10 years ago, cracks started to appear in the monetary and financial system. In the fall of 2008, the global financial crisis brought the system to the verge of collapse. Citizens and policymakers alike were taken by surprise how this could have happened. Sufficient safeguards were thought to be in place: Central banks that would provide emergency liquidity when needed, supervisors that would prevent banks from taking excessive risks and a deposit guarantee system that would protect depositors from losses. In the fall of 2008, the confidence in the stability of the system was shattered by an unprecedented crisis only few people had seen coming.

Crisis management dominated monetary and financial policy in the euro area in the years that followed. Unlike the Great Depression of the 1930s, central banks reacted with a bold monetary policy response, significantly increasing the liquidity provision to the banking system through conventional and unconventional measures. Governments provided unprecedented fiscal support to the banking sector in the form of public bailouts and other measures. Many observers share the view that the monetary and fiscal policy response prevented the financial system from collapsing. Nonetheless, the European financial crisis deepened in the years thereafter and morphed into a sovereign debt crisis in several countries, followed by public bailouts and lengthy economic adjustments.

As of the time of writing, the euro area remains in an environment of low growth, low inflation, high unemployment and crisis legacies. Euro area member states are also confronted with new policy challenges and adverse global developments, such as increased geopolitical tensions or the slowdown in some emerging markets. In the field of monetary and financial policy, the last 10 years have been characterized by a myriad of changes. Yet, the question remains whether current policies provide us with adequate comfort to overcome both the current and the structural challenges in the euro area.

A proper understanding of the monetary and financial system is essential to form an educated opinion about some challenges we face in the euro area. Many observers acknowledge the central role the monetary and financial system plays for an advanced economy such as the euro area. Nonetheless, the subject is still not covered adequately in many economics curricula at universities. In addition, the number of policy-oriented books that provide a useful overview of the 'nuts and bolts' of the system stands in stark contrast to their relevance for the broader economy.

This book provides an introduction to monetary policy, banking supervision and financial stability in the euro area from a policy perspective. In line with this purpose, it has a focus on:

1. *Real-world observations* instead of theories or formulas. The reason is to separate the process of making observations from proposing solutions to perceived problems. While the latter is obviously important, it is not the focus of this book. At the same time, the book may facilitate the process by pointing to various alternative policy choices and raising questions along the way, which are meant as 'food for thought'.
2. *Descriptions in plain English*, while explaining technical terms where needed. The reason is simply to provide a guidebook for a broad audience, including university students, journalists, finance professionals and the interested public that may not have an academic background in economics or finance.
3. *Euro area policies*. The book does not discuss monetary and financial policy in non-euro area countries in Europe or other parts of the world. Nonetheless, it also covers the international dimension of the three policy areas from the perspective of the euro area.

The book is structured as follows: Chap. 1 provides the 'lay of the land' for the monetary and financial system in the euro area. Chapters 2, 4 and 5 discuss the three stated policy areas: monetary policy, banking supervision and financial stability. As the policy framework for the latter two was revamped due to the crisis, their discussion is preceded by an overview of the main crisis episodes in the euro area since 2007 (Chap. 3). Chapter 6 integrates the main findings and discusses the interaction of the three policy areas (see Fig. 1).

This book benefited from comments and helpful thoughts by various people. In particular, I would like to thank Veronika Arnold, Gregor Eperjesi, Stefan Schmitz, Ralph Spitzer, several anonymous reviewers in the field of central banking and my brothers Albert, Konrad and Ulrich, all of whom read and commented on various chapters. Special thanks go to Kevin Kalaugher for his kind permission to use some of his cartoons in the book. I am also grateful to Rocio Torregrosa, Irene Barrios-Kezic and other colleagues at Springer International Publishing for showing confidence in my work and for their patience and help. Any remaining errors and omissions are my sole responsibility. While the book is mainly based on real-world observations, any views expressed are solely those of the author and do not necessarily reflect those of the European Central Bank or the Eurosystem.

Most issues in the field of monetary and financial policy are interconnected. Suitable policies therefore need to be based on a thorough understanding of the objectives and interaction of the various policy functions. The book can hopefully provide some clarity on this issue to readers who are new to the field. As regards taking the next step and developing new policies, a lot of analysis still needs to be done. There are no shortcuts in developing well-thought-out policy alternatives, despite the tempting calls by some people that offer simple panaceas or grand solutions. With sufficient openness, understanding and diligence, I am sure that

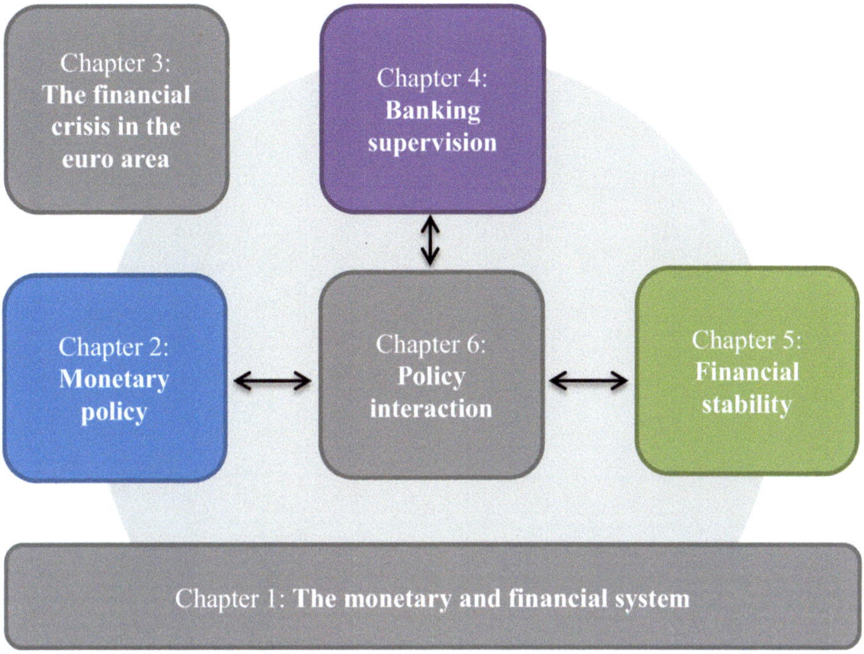

Fig. 1 Structure of the book

readers will have an intellectually fascinating and liberating experience to investigate further the policies that would be needed to shape the monetary and financial system of the future in an appropriate manner.

Frankfurt am Main, Germany M. Fandl
August 2017

Contents

List of Abbreviations

ABS	Asset-backed security
ABSPP	Asset-backed securities purchase programme
ATM	Automated teller machine
Basel I–III	Basel Capital Accord I–III
BCP	Basel Core Principles for Effective Banking Supervision
BCBS	Basel Committee on Banking Supervision
BIS	Bank for International Settlements
BRRD	Bank Recovery and Resolution Directive
CAC-40	Main French stock exchange index
CBM	Central bank money
CCyB	Countercyclical capital buffer
CCP	Central counterparty
CET1	Common Equity Tier 1
CD	Certificate of deposit
CDS	Credit default swap
CGFS	Committee on the Global Financial System
CHF	Swiss franc
CRD IV	Capital Requirements Directive IV
CRR	Capital Requirements Regulation
CSD	Central securities depository
CSPP	Corporate sector purchase programme
DAX	Main German stock exchange index
DGS	Deposit guarantee scheme
DGSD	Deposit Guarantee Scheme Directive
EAPP	Extended asset purchase program
EBA	European Banking Authority
EC	European Commission
ECB	European Central Bank
ECOFIN	Economic and Financial Affairs Council
EFC	European and Financial Committee
EFSF	European Financial Stability Facility
EIOPA	European Insurance and Occupational Pension Fund Authority
ELA	Emergency liquidity assistance

EMS	European Monetary System
EONIA	Euro Overnight Index Average
EP	European Parliament
ESAs	European Supervisory Agencies
ESM	European Stability Mechanism
ESMA	European Securities and Markets Authority
ESRB	European Systemic Risk Board
EU	European Union
EUR	Euro
Euribor	Euro Interbank Offer Rate
EWG	Eurogroup Working Group
FSAP	Financial Sector Assessment Program
FSB	Financial Stability Board
FSC	Financial Stability Committee
FVC	Financial vehicle corporation
FX	Foreign exchange
G-7	Group of Seven
G-20	Group of Twenty
G-SII	Globally systemically important institution
GBP	British pound
GDP	Gross domestic product
HICP	Harmonized Index of Consumer Prices
HUF	Hungarian Forint
IASB	International Accounting Standards Board
IBAN	International Bank Account Number
ICAAP	Internal Capital Adequacy Assessment Process
IFRS	International Financial Reporting Standards
IMF	International Monetary Fund
JPY	Japanese yen
JST	Joint supervisory team
LCR	Liquidity coverage ratio
Libor	London Interbank Offered Rate
LSI	Less significant institution
LTRO	Long-term refinancing operation
LTV	Loan-to-value
M1–3	Monetary aggregates 1–3
MEP	Member of the European Parliament
MLF	Marginal lending facility
MOC	Market Operations Committee
MPC	Monetary Policy Committee
MREL	Minimum requirement for own funds and eligible liabilities
MRO	Main refinancing operation
NCA	National competent authority
NDA	National designated authority

NPE	Non-performing exposure
NPL	Non-performing loan
NSFR	Net stable funding ratio
O-SII	Other systemically important institution
OMT	Outright monetary transactions
OTC	Over-the-counter
P&L	Profit and loss
PSPP	Public sector purchase programme
RWA	Risk-weighted asset
SEPA	Single Euro Payments Area
SI	Significant institution
SIFI	Systemically important financial institution
SMP	Securities Markets Programme
SPV	Special purpose vehicle
SRB	Single Resolution Board, Systemic risk buffer
SRF	Single Resolution Fund
SREP	Supervisory review and evaluation process
SRM	Single Resolution Mechanism
SSM	Single Supervisory Mechanism
SWIFT	Society for Worldwide Interbank Financial Telecommunication
TARGET2	Trans-European Automated Real-time Gross Settlement Express Transfer 2
TBTF	Too-big-to-fail
TLAC	Total loss-absorbing capacity
TLTRO	Targeted long-term refinancing operation
US	United States
USD	US dollar

List of Figures

List of Tables

List of Boxes

1 The Monetary and Financial System

This chapter explains the functioning of the monetary and financial system in the euro area. As such, it establishes the basis for the discussion of monetary policy, banking supervision, and financial stability in the following chapters. The overview is deliberately brief and leaves technical details aside, while using everyday life examples to facilitate the understanding of otherwise rather generic concepts. The section first discusses the main elements and functioning of the monetary system, including the three types of money in the euro area. Afterwards, we sketch out the structure of the financial system and its three main components: financial institutions, markets, and infrastructure (see Fig. 1.1).

The system-wide overview will be anchored in the micro-setting of an individual taking part in the system. For this purpose, we will use a random euro area citizen called Marie as an example throughout the section. Marie takes part in the monetary and financial system on a daily basis, as almost all individuals in the euro area do (if they like it or not).

We have some basic information about Marie's current situation, which we will get back to throughout the section:

- Marie has an office job with a salary that allows her to pay her bills and save a little bit each month. She cares about her financial situation but is not particularly keen on actively managing her personal finances.
- Marie has a bank account for her salary and for making regular electronic payments, such as for paying her electricity bills. She uses her debit card to withdraw cash from ATMs and to pay in shops. In addition to her debit card, she always keeps some cash for small-value purchases in her wallet, yet the total amount rarely exceeds 100 euros.
- Marie keeps some savings in a savings account at her bank. In addition, she invested in a mutual fund a few years ago, which she still holds at the security portfolio of her bank.
- She recently bought a small apartment and for this purpose took out a loan from her bank. The bank provided the loan after assessing her financial situation and

M. Fandl, *Monetary and Financial Policy in the Euro Area*, Springer Texts in Business and Economics, https://doi.org/10.1007/978-3-319-72643-4_1

registering a mortgage on the apartment. At the same time, she also obtained a life insurance policy and took out property insurance for her apartment, following the advice of her bank.

1.1 The Monetary System

Despite being essential to the way our societies are organized, the functioning of the monetary system is still not widely understood by the general public. Whatever the reasons are for this shortcoming, it has implications for the public discourse on monetary or financial issues. The discourse could be much richer if it was not confined to a small group of central bankers, international experts, commercial bankers, and academics, as it is currently the case.

The obvious starting point of the discussion is the question what constitutes money in the euro area and for which reason. A key characteristic that sets money apart from other assets (which means anything that individuals can own and exchange with others) is that it can be used as a means of payment. To maintain this function over time, money has to meet certain criteria.

- *Firstly, it has to broadly maintain its value in terms of purchasing power.* A unit of money should allow you to buy a roughly similar set of goods and services today and 1 year from now. In situations, where the amount of money in circulation experiences excessive growth, it risks losing its function as a store of value and may ultimately cease to be used as a means of payment. This is particularly the case if suitable alternatives are available. For instance, the African country of Zimbabwe experienced hyperinflation in the early 2000s, which rendered its banknotes practically worthless by 2009. Citizens stopped using the local currency as money and the central bank discontinued banknote production. Ever since, payments in Zimbabwe are made in US dollar or other foreign currencies. What used to serve as money for many years ceased to be money due to the loss in value.
- *Secondly, another characteristic of money is that it is typically denominated in a certain currency (such as the euro or the US dollar) and has a numerical function in the economy.* This means that by convention the price of goods and services in an economy are given in monetary units. The price of different goods in supermarkets in the euro area is stated in euro and not in terms of other assets

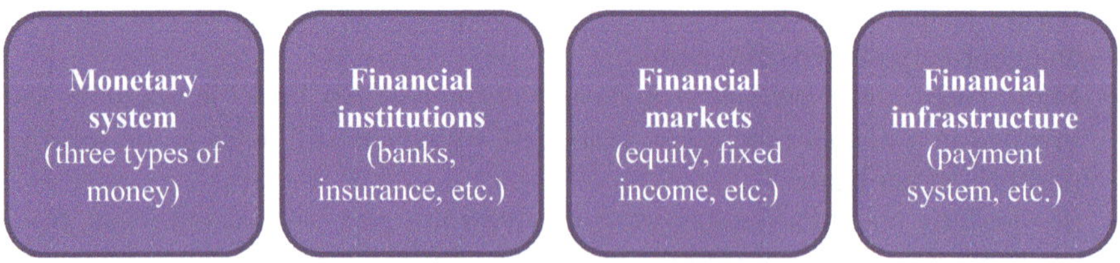

Fig. 1.1 Key components of the monetary and financial system

that may be used as money. Associated with this function, money must be easily dividable into smaller units. It would be very difficult, for instance, to pay in gold bars at the supermarket (or at least to expect to get appropriate change).

We can distinguish three types of money in the euro area:

1. **Cash:** These are the banknotes and coins in circulation.
2. **Commercial bank money:** These are created when readily available funds are placed in banks, which we will discuss further below.
3. **Central bank money:** These are reserves of banks held at accounts at the central bank.

Let us look at the key characteristics of these types of money and the way they are created.

Cash

Cash is a fundamental means of payment in everyday life. In the euro area, it is used for a high proportion of all payments below 20 euros. Cash mostly takes the form of banknotes, which are issued by central banks that have a monopoly position in their supply. Despite being intrinsically worthless pieces of paper, they can be used to purchase valuable goods and services in an economy. What gives banknotes their value is primarily the social convention to be generally accepted as a means of payment. This convention is supported by the fact that banknotes are issued by an independent public authority—the central bank—that aims at maintaining their function as a store of value. The credibility of this promise is important, as it implies that the central bank as the monopoly supplier of cash will pay attention to the amount of goods or services that a given amount of cash can buy. Whenever needed, the central bank should react to the potential erosion in the value of banknotes. How this is done will be explained in Chap. 2.

Cash is put in circulation through services offered by the banking system. The specific channels are bank branches and ATMs, which allow individuals to withdraw cash from their bank accounts. This is, for instance, also the way Marie in our example typically obtains cash for everyday payments. Banks also offer cash services to shops and other businesses that need to maintain an inventory of cash for retail transactions. Hence, it is worth bearing in mind that, even though the central bank is the issuer of banknotes, it almost never occurs that individuals receive cash directly from the central bank. In almost all instances, individuals obtain cash either through banks or through transactions with businesses and other individuals (e.g., when a friend returns borrowed cash to Marie).

Central banks are in charge of ensuring sufficient cash availability in an economy to facilitate transactions. This implies the responsibility for three processes: Cash production, distribution, and replacement. All these activities take place largely unnoticed by the general public as long as they function properly.

- To start with production, euro banknotes are produced by different central banks in the euro area, other public institutions (such as the "*Bundesdruckerei*" in Germany), and private specialist firms (such as the UK-based banknote manufacturer De La Rue). All banknote manufacturers have to meet high security standards and need to be certified by the European Central Bank (ECB). The fact that banknotes are also produced by private companies may be surprising to some readers, but it is a fact that banknote production has become an international market in recent years with both public and private players competing for market share. The amount and denominations of banknotes to be produced by each of these entities are centrally coordinated by the ECB within the euro area. The simple reason for coordination is that central banks need to maintain the purchasing power of banknotes and thus need to carefully manage the produced quantities.
- Following their production, banknotes are held in vaults by central banks. Banks can submit orders to the central bank, provided they hold sufficient central bank money, the third type of money, which we will describe further below. In practice, banks order a sufficient quantity of banknotes to maintain a stock of cash (banknotes and coins) at all times. These are held in ATMs ("vault cash"), branch vaults, and central vaults (e.g., for a certain region). Cash reserves are an important precautionary measure by banks, given that banks are expected to make cash payments as needed (e.g., when customers want to withdraw their deposits). Similarly, central banks maintain logistical reserves to address the seasonality in cash demand (e.g., higher demand for banknotes in the weeks before Christmas) and strategic reserves for emergency situations. The bulk of banknotes is in circulation and used for transactions in the economy or, to a minor extent, for savings purposes (so-called mattress money).
- After having circulated for some time, the physical quality of banknotes deteriorates. When they have reached that point, banknotes are replaced by banks, which exchange them for new banknotes at their central bank. The latter eventually takes care of their physical destruction. Figure 1.2 illustrates the cycle that starts with cash production and ends with cash destruction in a stylized way.

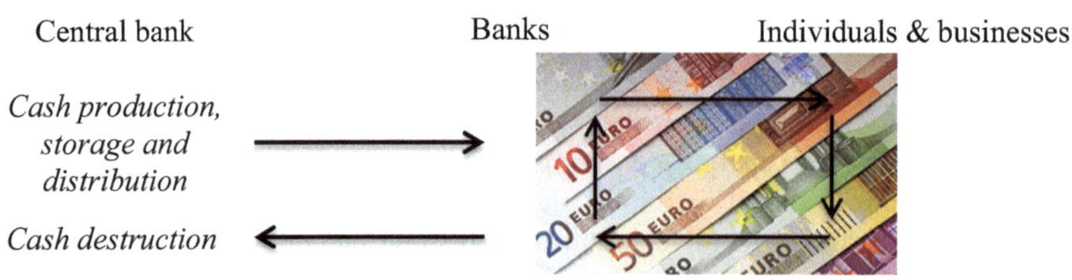

Fig. 1.2 Cash circulation

Cash payments have several advantages over other forms of payments:

- *Firstly, they allow the final settlement of transactions, unlike card payments or electronic transfers.* To use a practical example, imagine buying a new pair of shoes for 100 euros in a shop. If you choose to pay in cash, the transaction will immediately be final once you have handed over 100 euros in cash to the sales person in exchange for the pair of shoes. If you instead pay by debit or credit card, a series of transactions is triggered that will only in a subsequent step lead to a final payment to the shop. More precisely, if you use the debit card, confirming the payment using the shop's payment device sends an instruction to your bank to transfer 100 euros from your account to the account of the shop. Only once your bank has indeed transferred the funds, the payment is considered final (obviously, the shop will check through the payment device whether your account is sufficiently covered before accepting the card payment). If you pay by credit card, the payment is not made from your own account but from the account of your credit card company to the account of the shop. At the same time, a credit is recorded between the credit card company and you, which you eventually have to repay. Hence, paying for your pair of shoes by credit card does not constitute an immediate final payment either. Only cash allows the final payment at the counter.
- *Secondly, cash allows for transactions in which the counterparts remain anonymous and that are difficult to track.* This may at first sight seem an odd reason to use money for payments but in everyday life there are many transactions that individuals prefer to remain private. For instance, cash is widely used as a means of payment for not entirely legal activities. To give a specific example, some households in Europe cheat on taxes or social security contributions when paying cleaning or construction workers. It is probably no coincidence that these transactions are typically made in cash and not via electronic transfer, even if they are recurring. More generally, individuals often prefer anonymity in their private transactions. Anonymity in payment transactions supports the freedom of individuals in their everyday activities compared to a world in which all transactions are recorded.

Box 1.1 Euro Banknotes of the "Europa Series"

Central banks are in the process of introducing a new series of euro banknotes from 2013 to 2018. The new banknotes are part of the so-called Europa series. The circulation of new 5 euro banknotes started in 2013. It was followed by new 10 euro banknotes in 2014, 20 euro banknotes in 2015, and 50 euro banknotes in 2017. The 100 euro and 200 euro banknotes of the Europa series are scheduled to be introduced in 2018. The production of the 500 euro banknote will be discontinued in 2018. All banknotes of the previous euro banknote series, including the 500 euro banknote, will remain valid. National

(continued)

Box 1.1 (continued)

central banks have promised to exchange 500 euro banknotes for an unlimited period of time (ECB 2016c).

The Europa series introduces new security features for euro banknotes, which should make it more difficult to counterfeit them. For instance, the front side of each banknote includes a portrait hologram (on the right-hand side), and the banknote denomination is indicated in a special color (emerald) on the bottom left-hand side. The use of different materials should make banknotes with low denominations (5 euro and 10 euro), which are used for most daily transactions, more durable than the previous ones. As a consequence, banknotes need to be replaced less often than in the past, which reduces the associated costs.

Commercial Bank Money

Commercial bank money is a type of money that has significantly gained in popularity in recent years. It essentially covers current accounts and bank deposits that can be readily used for transactions by customers. Unlike cash, commercial bank money is not created by the central bank but results from private transactions between banks and their customers, as illustrated in a stylized manner in Fig. 1.3.

Most individuals in the euro area use commercial bank money on a daily basis. As an employee of her company, Marie receives her salary every month by electronic transfer to her bank account. She can use these funds to make her everyday payments by withdrawing cash from ATMs, which essentially converts bank deposits into cash, i.e., one type of money into the other. She can also make direct payments without converting the funds on her bank account into cash, for instance by paying her monthly electricity bill through standing order or by using her debit card in a shop to purchase a pair of shoes. While there are differences in the use of card payments and electronic transfers within the euro area, recent years have seen cashless payments become more common in the euro area as a whole.

Most money in circulation takes the form of commercial bank money rather than cash. At the end of 2016, the total value of cash in circulation was approximately 3200 euros per euro area inhabitant, while the total amount of broad money in circulation, which includes bank accounts and other deposits by the nonbank public, was about nine times higher at approximately 28,000 euros per inhabitant (see

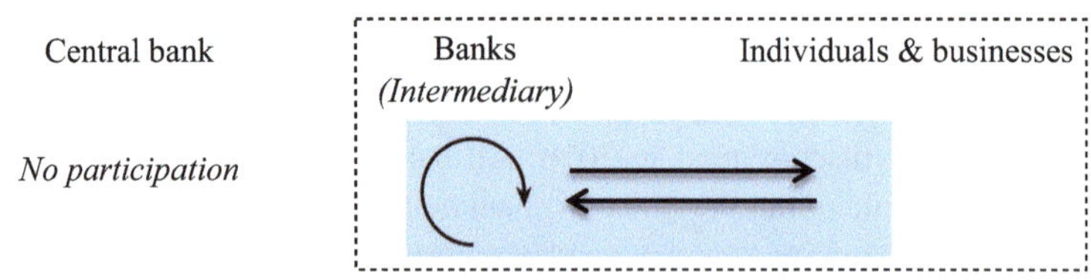

Fig. 1.3 Commercial bank money in circulation

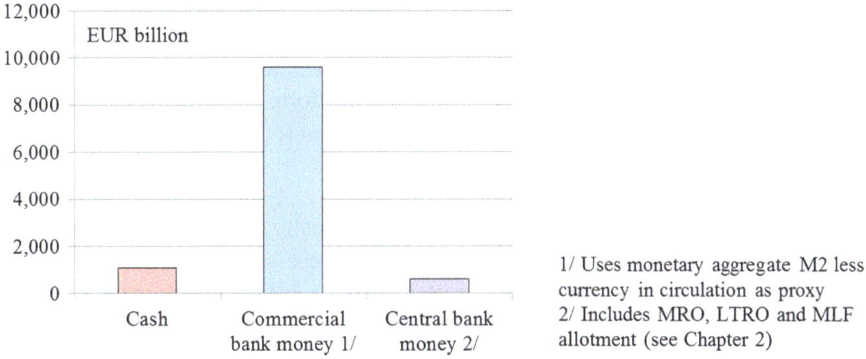

Fig. 1.4 Cash, commercial bank money and CBM in the euro area (end-2016). Source: ECB (2017d), author's calculations

Fig. 1.4 for the total amount of cash, commercial bank money, and central bank money in circulation as of end-2016). Obviously, most people hold more money on their bank accounts than in the form of cash. This simple observation is fundamental to the understanding of the monetary system in the euro area: Most money is not created by the central bank but by commercial banks. This fact suggests that banks play a special role in the financial system due to their money creation powers. At the same time, it leads to the obvious question why commercial bank money is used as money in the first place, given that it was not created from a public institution, i.e., the issuer's promise of its safety and acceptance as a means of payment might not be equally strong as the promise by the central bank for cash in circulation.

The reasons for the widespread acceptance of commercial bank money are related to public trust, social conventions, safety, and convenience.

- *Firstly, trust is crucial for commercial bank money.* Bank customers will use their bank accounts as a means of payments as long as they trust in banks to be able and willing to convert it into cash when needed (or alternatively to turn it fully into a deposit in a safer institution). This trust is stronger in case of assurances by other institutions, for instance when the account is covered by a deposit guarantee scheme, which we will discuss further below and in Chap. 5.
- *Secondly, using commercial bank money for payments is a social convention.* A number of payment transactions essentially require the use of commercial bank money. Just think of the situation in which Marie moves to another city. Most likely she will not manage to conduct all her payments in cash, so she will need to rely to some extent on commercial bank money. It would for instance be difficult to convince her new employer to pay her salary in cash rather than via bank transfer.
- *Thirdly, using commercial bank money is often safer and more convenient than cash transactions.* For instance, receiving her monthly salary in cash would probably increase the risk of Marie being robbed on her way back from work. Using bank services makes such transfers not only safer, in particular if they

involve higher amounts, but also more convenient. Practically speaking, Marie's employer does not have to order cash for all salaries each month and arrange the handovers. Most customers also perceive commercial bank money as a safer storage of money compared to cash held in the form of mattress money or in vaults, as money on bank accounts cannot be stolen (or at least not in a similarly straightforward way as cash).[1]

On the last point, it is worth adding that banks actually do not "store" money that is deposited with them but rather use the funds they receive for other purposes. This feature sets banks apart from savings boxes or piggy banks, which are commonly used by children for savings purposes. Commercial bank money is not stored in safe or liquid instruments but is ultimately nothing else than a claim against the bank. The reasons for its widespread use in the monetary system are closely related to payment systems to which banks offer customers access through this type of money. For instance, Marie can make electronic transfers to pay her utility bills only if she owns a bank account.

Commercial bank money is created in the context of providing bank credit. One important function of banks, which is discussed in more detail further below, lies in providing the broader public with the possibility to deposit funds that can subsequently be used as money. For instance, Marie holds some of her money on her bank account and uses it for electronic payments via debit card transactions or bank transfers. In principle, these deposits may be created in two ways: either by bank customers (individuals or businesses) physically depositing cash in their bank, which then credits their account by an equal amount, or by bank transactions that do not involve cash. The second case is the predominant one for deposit creation in the euro area, given that providing bank credit and creating deposits are two sides of the same coin (see Box 1.2).

As an example, let us consider the mortgage loan taken out by Marie to purchase her apartment. In this transaction, the bank deposited the loan amount to Marie's account, from where Marie transferred it to the seller's account to finalize the purchase of the apartment. From a broader perspective, the credit provided by the bank to Marie created new commercial bank money in the system. Importantly, this type of money creation does not involve the central bank but results from transactions between banks and their customers. This feature sets commercial bank money apart from cash and central bank money, for which the central bank is the monopoly supplier.

[1] In theory, another advantage of holding money in a bank rather than in cash is linked to interest that is earned on bank deposits. However, in practice, interest earned on current accounts and sight deposits is minimal, if positive at all after deducting fees. Interest earnings are more of a motivation for less liquid forms of bank deposits, which need to be converted into commercial bank money first before they can be used as a means of payment.

Box 1.2 How Do Banks Create Commercial Bank Money?
Banks create money through providing credit. Nonbanks do not have this power due to a small but important difference between bank and nonbank credits. Let us use a simple example for illustration. Suppose a company would like to obtain a loan to fund an investment project. It has the choice of taking out a loan from another company (a nonbank) or a bank. What is the difference between the two transactions?

In the first case, the company obtains a loan from the nonbank. The first figure shows the financial position of both entities before and after the loan is provided. The transaction is straightforward: The nonbank, which had money holdings in the form of commercial bank money before providing credit, lends money to the business. After the transaction, the business has a liability to the nonbank (i.e., it has to repay the credit upon maturity), and the nonbank has a corresponding claim.

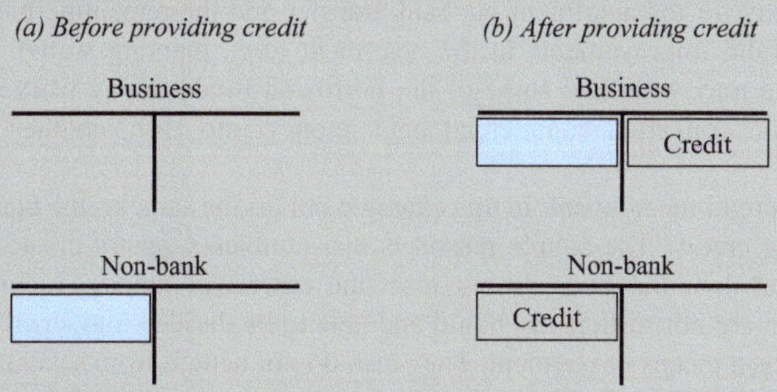

In the second case, the company obtains a loan from the bank. The figure again shows the financial position of both entities before and after the loan is provided. Similarly to the first case, the lending transaction creates a liability for the business and a claim for the lender. However, there is an important difference: The bank does not use money holdings it had before providing credit but instead creates new commercial bank money at the time of the lending transaction. In other words, the bank lends money to the businesses that had not existed before. The provided credit leads to an extension of the bank balance sheet (creating both assets and liabilities at the same time), unlike in the first case where the provided nonbank credit led to a substitution of assets on the balance sheet of the lender.

(continued)

Box 1.2 (continued)

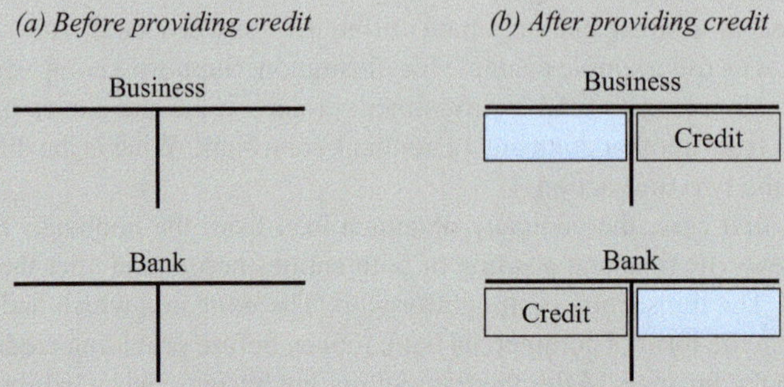

In both cases, the borrower may convert commercial bank money it received into cash. For instance, Marie may use a large part of her mortgage loan to pay for the apartment via bank transfer and the remaining part of the loan to fund improvements in the apartment (e.g., painting walls). For the latter, she may withdraw some of the borrowed funds to pay workers. This transaction converted commercial bank money into cash, another type of money.

Why could the nonbank in this example not do the same as the bank when providing credit? The simple reason is that nonbanks cannot create money, given that their liabilities do not meet the criteria of money. Liabilities to nonbanks are not sufficiently liquid and able to be divided into small units to be used as a means of payment. They also do not benefit from several special arrangements, such as deposit insurance or emergency liquidity assistance, which are only available to banks in the current setup of the monetary and financial system.

Access to commercial bank money requires the use of bank services. Individuals and businesses in the euro area can convert their holdings of commercial bank money into cash by using ATMs, bank branches, or electronic payment systems. In crisis situations, when public trust in banks and the safety of commercial bank money decreases, many individuals may wish to take out their commercial bank money and other savings from banks. Such development may put significant pressure on the liquidity situation of banks and worsen the crisis situation.

To give a practical example, the Greek banking system witnessed a severe liquidity crisis in the first half of 2015. Roughly a quarter of the deposits left the banking system due to heightened uncertainties about their safety. At the end of June 2015 a bank holiday was declared, which meant that bank branches were temporarily closed. Withdrawals from ATMs were limited to 60 euros per day and account. In addition, electronic transfers to accounts outside Greece were restricted. Under such circumstances, it made a great difference whether an individual held money in the form of cash or commercial bank money. It also mattered whether one had a debit card or not (i.e., to be able to obtain at least 60 euros in cash from ATMs per day).

Banks also offer payment services to other banks, in addition to individuals and businesses. These services are known as correspondent banking and grew in importance with the increase in cross-border payments. For instance, a bank located in the euro area may hold its Japanese yen liquidity (in case it has payments in that currency) in an account at a Japanese banking group. Correspondent banking is also widely used among smaller banks in the euro area which use the correspondent services provided by larger banks instead of participating directly in payment systems that settle in central bank money. This brings us to the third type of money in the euro area that plays a key role in the implementation of monetary policy.

Central Bank Money

Central bank money serves as the ultimate means of payment between banks. This type of money is used by banks to transfer funds to other banks. The transfers may either result from their own activities, such as from an interbank loan, or from transactions by their customers. For instance, when Marie pays her monthly electricity bill via online banking, her bank makes a payment to the bank of the electricity company. This interbank transaction is settled in central bank money (CBM), as illustrated in Fig. 1.5. The receiving bank then credits the amount to the account of the electricity company in commercial bank money. The reason for conducting the interbank payment in central bank money lies in the bundling and netting of retail payments by banks, which we will get back to in the section on financial infrastructure.

This third type of money is created in transactions between the central bank and commercial banks. The details of CBM creation will be discussed in Chap. 2 in the context of monetary policy operations. The main points for the purposes of this overview are the following:

- *Firstly, commercial banks hold CBM on their accounts at the central bank.* This is analogous to individuals holding commercial bank money at their accounts at the commercial banks. In other words, the central bank acts as the bank of commercial banks. Individuals and nonbank corporations do not have the possibility to hold central bank money, which may also explain the limited public knowledge about this type of money and its relation to the other types.

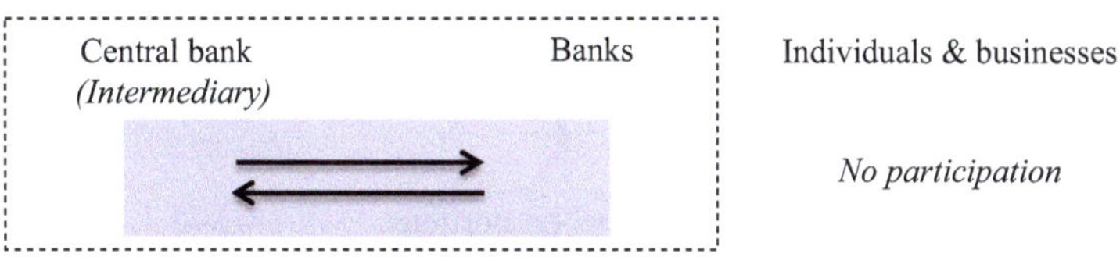

Fig. 1.5 Central bank money in circulation

- *Secondly, the central bank is the monopoly supplier of CBM.* Banks in the euro area can only hold euro-denominated CBM on their accounts at the Eurosystem. A bank that has no establishment in the euro area has no access to CBM denominated in euro, as the ECB does not allow it to open an account. As an alternative, such foreign banks may turn to other commercial banks to obtain euro liquidity in the form of commercial bank money, using correspondent banking services as discussed above.
- *Thirdly, CBM can only be used for transactions between banks or for their conversion into cash.* Both functions are of crucial importance for the functioning of the monetary system in the euro area. As already mentioned, interbank transactions within the euro area are typically settled in CBM. Banks are, however, not required to do so. Alternatively, they can use the services of other banks and settle transactions in commercial bank money. For foreign currency transactions, banks in the euro area most often do not have access to CBM of foreign central banks but instead rely on other commercial banks. For instance, euro area banks obtain US dollar liquidity from other commercial banks and not from the US Federal Reserve System, unless they also have operations in the United States.

Total central bank money in the euro area is significantly lower than the outstanding volume of commercial bank money. As of end-2016, it amounted to 1073 billion euros, compared to 9614 billion euros held as commercial bank money (see Fig. 1.4). Despite the difference in size, CBM plays a crucial role for the way monetary policy is operationalized in the euro area (see Chap. 2). Its allocation within the system may also give rise to liquidity risks for individual banks and the system as a whole (see Chaps. 4 and 5).

Interrelation Between the Three Types of Money

How do the three stated types of money relate to each other? Figure 1.6 summarizes the use of the three types of money by various parts of the economy. The central bank acts as the monopoly supplier of cash and central bank money, which are liabilities from its perspective. Banks use central bank money for interbank payments and hold an inventory of cash to meet customer demand. Both are on

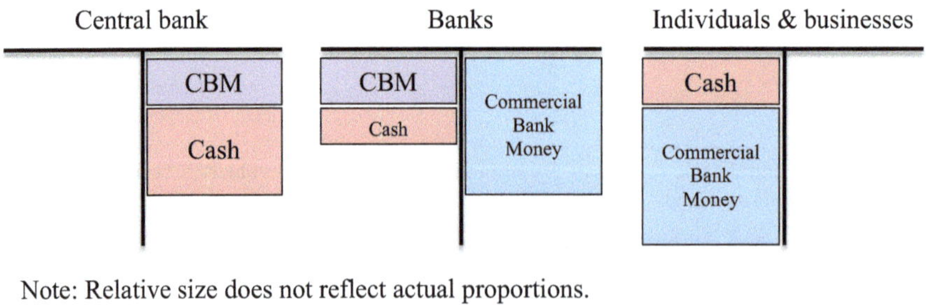

Fig. 1.6 Money as assets and liabilities

Table 1.1 Key differences between the three types of money

	Cash	Commercial bank money	Central bank money
Issuer	Central bank (monopoly supply)	Banks	Central bank (monopoly supply)
Distribution	Banks	Banks	Central bank
Means of Payment	Individuals/ businesses	Individuals/ businesses, banks	Banks
Intermediary to settle payments	None (bearer instrument)	Banks	Central bank

the asset side of bank balance sheets. On the liability side, commercial bank money is recorded that is held by individuals and businesses in the economy. In addition, the nonbank sectors also hold cash, primarily used as a means of payment. On a system level, monetary assets and liabilities always have to match, as illustrated in Fig. 1.6.

Table 1.1 provides an overview of the differences between the three types of money with respect to their creation and use, summarizing the main elements of the discussion above.

Under normal circumstances, the three types of money should be convertible at par, given that they are part of a single currency. The public should be able to use the different types of money interchangeably when making payments. Individuals and businesses may pay a bill of 100 euros either by 100 euros in cash or by the same amount in commercial bank money. Similarly, banks should be able to shift holdings of central bank money into equal holdings of cash. Full convertibility at par means the possibility to switch from one type of money holding to the other at an exchange rate of one. This requires, among others, sufficient availability of all three types of money. This is one of the main objectives of the central bank as the public institution that bears the ultimate responsibility of maintaining trust in the currency. How it can be achieved and by which means the process of money creation can be steered will be discussed in Chap. 2.

The monetary system is ultimately based on trust. In situations where this trust is lost, some types of money may cease to be used as such and other assets may take over their functions. This may for instance be caused by irresponsible behavior of the institutions that create money. The risk is particularly inherent in so-called fiat money systems, as opposed to commodity-based money systems, such as the gold standard. While the latter is based on precious metals or other valuable assets, fiat money is created out of nothing (fiat is Latin for "it shall be").

Commodity-based money was the historical norm until the 1970s. Ever since, we live in a world of fiat money systems. Fiat money has no intrinsic value and there are no strict limits in its production. Very large quantities of cash, commercial bank money, and CBM could theoretically be produced and injected in the system. Fiat money is only backed by a promise by the issuer to honor it as a means of payment.

Sometimes, it is accompanied by some type of enforcement, for instance by declaring it legal tender or requiring taxes to be paid in the form of fiat money.[2] All major currency areas are fiat money systems, including the euro area.

Let us now move on to the financial system, in which public trust plays no less of a key role.

Alternatives to Money Creation by the Central Bank and Commercial Banks

The current monetary system in the euro area is characterized by money creation by the central bank and commercial banks. Alternative setups that have been investigated or applied elsewhere have tilted this balance either more towards the central bank or to commercial banks as money creators. The two corner solutions to this spectrum, as illustrated in the figure, are worth highlighting: The first one would give the central bank the sole responsibility for issuing money. This solution is known as "mono-banking." In this case, there would be no commercial bank money; all businesses and individuals would essentially hold their money at the central bank. The second corner solution would give commercial banks the role of the sole issuer of money. This solution is referred to as "free banking" and was applied in the United States in the nineteenth century,[3] before the Federal Reserve System was established (BIS 2003).[4]

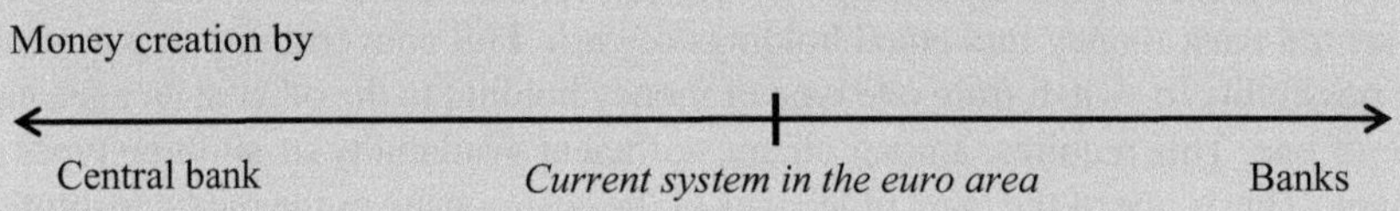

1.2 The Financial System

The core function of the financial system lies in redistributing financial resources and risks across individuals and institutions in the economy.

[2]Only the euro has the status of legal tender in the euro area. This is set out in Art. 128 of the Treaty on the Functioning of the European Union as regards euro banknotes and in Regulation EC/974/98 as regards euro coins.

[3]The free banking era in the United States started in 1836, when the charter of the Second Bank of the United States expired. It was transformed into a system of state-chartered banks during the American civil war. This system ended in 1913 with the creation of the Federal Reserve System.

[4]If the money definition is broadened from the three types of money described in this book, additional alternatives to money creation by the central bank and commercial banks exist. For instance, physical tokens, privately issued notes, electronic money or digital currencies are potential substitutes for the three main types of money.

- For instance, Marie uses the financial system by obtaining a loan from her bank to purchase her apartment. Instead of waiting until she has saved enough, she was able to borrow the funds from the bank to acquire the apartment at a much earlier stage in her life. When taking out the loan, she promised the bank to repay the loan over the following years with some interest. Loans are an example of the distribution of financial resources via the financial system.
- The property insurance Marie took out for the apartment is another example of a financial service. Without insurance, she would bear the entire risk of damages to her apartment herself, for instance from bursting water pipes and related flooding. By taking out insurance, she could shift this risk to the insurance company (or to be precise, the insurance company will bear the costs associated with the materialization of the risk). In return, Marie has to pay regular premiums to the insurance company. Insurance contracts are an example of the transfer of risks via the financial system.

The redistribution of financial resources and risks in the financial system can be direct or indirect. These alternatives are known as direct and indirect finance, given that only the latter involves financial intermediaries, such as banks or insurance companies. What they have in common is that they connect those with a surplus of funds (lenders, depositors, investors) to those who need funds (borrowers, businesses). Take Marie's mortgage loan as an example of indirect finance. Marie borrowed the funds from the bank, which serves as a financial intermediary.[5] Alternatively, Marie could have chosen to borrow the funds from her parents. This would have constituted direct finance, given that she would not need any intermediary for this transaction. Another alternative would have been for her to rely on her own savings to finance the apartment. In that case, known as self-financing, she would not need to borrow funds from another party. However, as mentioned above, it would take her many more years to have sufficient savings to purchase an apartment of similar value. Using the financial system to borrow the funds allowed her to bring forward the purchase to an earlier stage of her life.

1.2.1 Financial Institutions

We will start the overview of the key components of the financial system in the euro area with financial institutions, followed by markets and infrastructures. We will discuss the four main types of financial institutions in the euro area:

[5] As discussed in Box 1.2, the loan provided by the bank to Marie is not funded by existing deposits but creates a corresponding new deposit at the time of lending. Nevertheless, the bank fulfills an intermediary function by offering both lending and depositing services.

Fig. 1.7 Total assets of financial institutions in the euro area. Source: ECB (2017e)

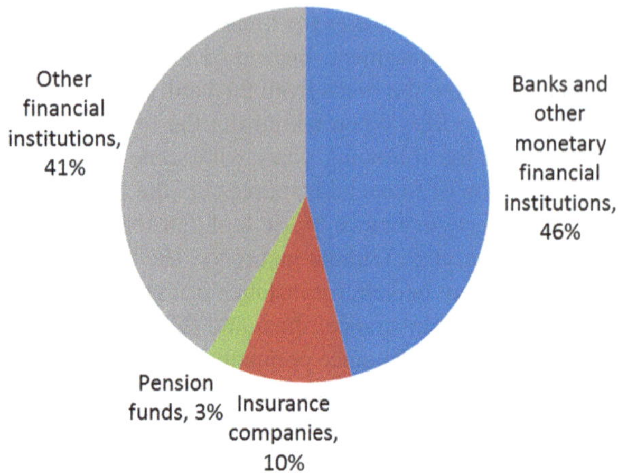

1. **Banks**
2. **Insurance companies**
3. **Real money investors:** These are nonbank financial institutions that primarily invest their own funds rather than borrowed funds.
4. **Shadow banks:** These are entities that perform credit intermediation without being fully licensed banks.

All these institutions serve as intermediaries in the financial system. Before we discuss their main characteristics and differences, it is worth making some observations on their overall size and relevance for the euro area.

- *The financial sector in the euro area holds total assets of approximately 75 trillion euros or around seven times euro area GDP in 2016.* A large part of it (46% as of end-2016) is held by banks and other monetary financial institutions, as illustrated in Fig. 1.7.[6] About 10% are held by insurance companies, 3% by pension funds, and 41% by other financial institutions, which includes other real money investors and shadow banks.
- *In absolute amounts, the financial sector is largest in Germany, France, Italy, and Spain.* Given that three quarters of the euro area population live in the four countries, this is hardly surprising. As a percentage of GDP, the financial sector is largest in Luxembourg, Malta, Ireland, the Netherlands, and Cyprus.
- *The size of the financial sector has increased since the onset of the global financial crisis due to the strong growth of the other financial institutions segment.* At the same time, the size of the banking sector remained broadly stable after having shown rapid growth in the years prior to 2008 (ECB 2017e).

[6]Other monetary financial institutions include for instance money market funds. These institutions only account for a small fraction of the stated share of 46% of total assets.

Banks

Banks are the primary financial institutions in the euro area. Practically all adults living in the euro area are bank customers and use their services on a very regular if not daily basis. Banks are also the most relevant financial intermediaries from the perspective of monetary policy and from the perspective of financial stability, as we will explain in the next chapters of this book. Let us first reflect on the economic function of banks and point out some key characteristics of the euro area banking sector. So what do banks do?

- *Firstly, banks intermediate funds in the economy.* Banks borrow from individuals and businesses with surplus funds and lend to individuals and businesses with a shortage of funds. For instance, Marie borrowed funds from her bank to purchase her apartment.
- *Secondly, banks transform the intermediated funds as regards their scale, maturity, and availability.* Transformation of scale means that the individual deposits and the individual loans granted need not have similar amounts. A bank may collect many small deposits of less than 1000 euros each and grant a loan of 100,000 euros (see in a stylized fashion in Fig. 1.8). Another important transformation is associated with the maturity of the intermediated funds. Bank deposits tend to be short term, while loans are offered at higher maturities. In accounting terms, the average maturity of the bank's assets exceeds the average maturity of its liabilities. The degree of maturity transformation varies across banks. Using again the example of Marie, we can observe that her loan (an asset of her bank) has a maturity of 15 years, while her deposits (liabilities of the bank) are primarily in the form of her current account, i.e., readily available funds. The third important transformation relates to the availability of the funds that are intermediated through banks. In short, this aspect indicates that if Marie wants to deposit 1000 euros in her bank account, she can expect her bank to always accept the new deposit, even if the bank does not see interesting lending opportunities. Likewise, Marie can expect the bank to pay out her deposits, irrespective of the loan redemptions by other customers to her bank.
- *Thirdly, banks take risks in the process of credit intermediation and transformation, which they need to actively manage.* Common risk types for banks are credit risk, market risk, interest rate risk, liquidity risk, and operational risk. Banks can

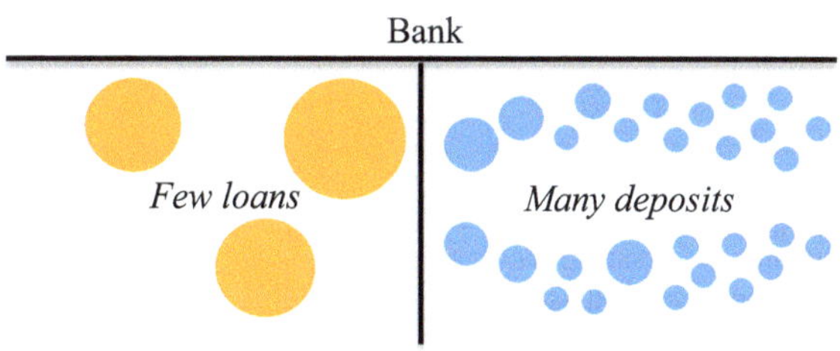

Fig. 1.8 Transformation of scale

also be significantly exposed to other risk types depending on their business model. At the most basic level, some borrowers may not be able to repay their loans and thus default on their obligations, leading to a materialization of credit risk. Alternatively, securities the bank holds may lose in market value (market risk) or the bank may face difficulties in obtaining sufficient funding (funding liquidity risk). Banks need to measure these and other risks they are exposed to and manage them on a constant basis. Risks can for instance be managed by hedging the interest rate position,[7] adjusting the asset and liability structure, or changing the pricing of loans and deposits.

- *Fourthly, banks earn a positive interest margin in the process of credit intermediation and may thus build a buffer to cover unexpected losses.* In the intermediation process, banks typically charge their borrowers a higher interest rate than the interest rate they pay their depositors. In other words, banks earn a positive interest margin, arising from the difference between lending and deposit rates. In recent years net interest margins by euro area banks have typically been in the range of 0.5–2%.[8] From a system-wide perspective, earning sufficient net interest income is important for the ability of banks to create internal buffers to cover unexpected losses, i.e, losses that have not been priced in when granting the respective loans.

The asset and liability sides of the bank balance sheet reflect their function as financial intermediaries. The liability side entails deposits, wholesale funding, and other liabilities (i.e., the source of funds) while the asset side comprises loans, securities, and other assets (i.e., the use of funds). The bank's capital is the residual between the value of its assets and liabilities. This is a key aspect to bear in mind in the discussion of capital adequacy in Chap. 4. Capital is not held on specific accounts but derives from the value of all other items on the balance sheet.

Figure 1.9 illustrates a stylized bank balance sheet with the mentioned items. Assets and liabilities are typically sorted by their respective liquidity and maturity. The most liquid assets (central bank money and cash reserves) are listed at the top, followed by securities, loans, and other assets, with the least liquid assets (such as investments with no active market) at the bottom. On the liability side, the short-term liabilities are at the top, followed by borrowings with longer maturity, and eventually capital at the bottom. Per definition capital does not have any maturity.

Understanding the banking system also requires knowledge how banks can fail. The two principal ways how a bank can fail are illiquidity and insolvency. We will briefly describe the two concepts in the following, as they are central to the

[7]Hedging the interest rate position means taking measures to reduce interest rate risk. For instance, a bank that has granted floating-rate loans and has taken fixed-rate deposits can enter into an interest rate swap (discussed later in this chapter). In the swap, the bank pays the variable rate and receives the fixed rate. After entering into the swap, the bank is not affected by changes in the interest rate anymore.

[8]The average net interest margin of euro area banks was 1.2% in the first half of 2016 (ECB 2016b).

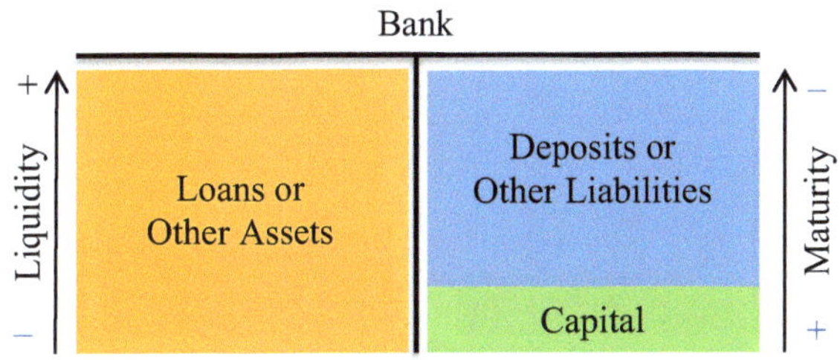

Fig. 1.9 Bank balance sheet

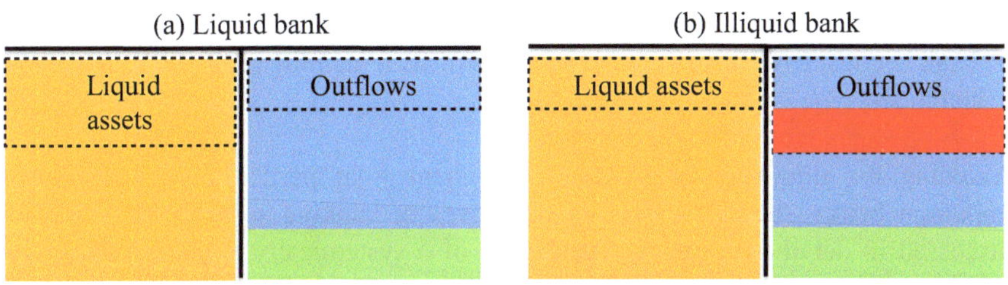

Fig. 1.10 Bank liquidity and illiquidity

understanding of monetary policy, banking supervision, and financial stability in the next chapters. Let us start with illiquidity.

- *Illiquidity:* Fig. 1.10 shows the stylized balance sheets of a liquid bank (left-hand side) and an illiquid bank (right-hand side). In the first case, the bank holds liquid assets that are sufficient to meet expected cash outflows. In practice, it means that the bank may have to make payments of 1mn euros on the next day and currently has liquid assets of 2mn euros. This is more than enough to cover the outflows and the bank is considered liquid. In the second case, the bank holds liquid assets that are insufficient to meet expected cash outflows. For instance, it may have to make payments of 2mn euros and has only reserves of 1mn euros. This is obviously not enough and the bank will fail to meet its obligations in full. Hence, the bank is considered illiquid, which is the first example of a bank default.
- *Insolvency:* Another possibility for a bank default is the bank's insolvency. The solvency of a bank is related to its capital position as illustrated in Fig. 1.11. In the first case, the bank has sufficient capital to cover unexpected losses.[9] For instance, some large borrowers of the bank may default simultaneously, which decreases the value of the banks' loan book and thus diminishes its capital position. Nevertheless, the capital position still remains positive after the losses are recorded. In the second case, the bank has insufficient capital to cover unexpected losses. The economy may witness a strong downturn with an increase in unemployment and many businesses shutting down. This situation triggers very large

[9]Expected and unexpected losses will be discussed in Chap. 4.

Fig. 1.11 Bank solvency and insolvency

losses for the bank, which wipe out more than its entire capital. In this case, the bank is considered insolvent, as the value of its remaining assets falls short of its liabilities.

Avoiding the illiquidity or insolvency of banks—in particular of systemically important banks—is one of the key objectives of banking supervision. It will be discussed in detail in Chap. 4. The failure of a systemically important bank also exerts significant negative externalities to the rest of the financial system and the broader economy. In particular, it may weaken the confidence in the banking system and impose large losses on depositors and financial institutions that provided funds to the bank. Preventing the failure of systemically important banks is, therefore, also a key objective of financial stability policy, as we will discuss in Chap. 5.

In addition to their relevance as financial intermediaries, several specific arrangements set banks apart from other financial intermediaries and nonfinancial corporations. These arrangements are the result of past policy choices that underpin the financial system in its current form. They relate to four broad issues: (1) the role of banks in money creation, (2) the operationalization of monetary policy, (3) the existence of financial safety nets, and (4) the special relationship of banks and the State. Let us briefly go through these specific arrangements that are crucial to understand subsequent chapters of this book.

- *Role in money creation:* This specificity of banks was already discussed in the overview of the monetary system. To recap, some liabilities of banks are used as commercial bank money, i.e., as a means of payment in the economy. In addition, banks play a decisive role in the circulation of cash in the economy through their branch and ATM networks. Banks assume both roles on a system-wide basis in the euro area, with oversight by the central bank. As discussed in subsequent chapters, the involvement of central banks is significantly more stringent with respect to the cash function than regarding the creation of commercial bank money. The latter is predominantly in the domain of commercial banks in the current setup of the euro area monetary system, with limited interference by central banks.

- *Operationalization of monetary policy:* A second unique characteristic of banks compared to other financial intermediaries is that they perform regular refinancing operations with the central bank, through which they have access to central bank money. These operations serve as the main avenue through which monetary policy is implemented in the euro area. The way this is essentially done is by adjusting the scope and terms of the operations, thus transmitting the chosen monetary policy stance to the banking sector. Banks then pass the changes on to the broader economy through their regular operations. The role of banks in the transmission of monetary policy will be discussed in Chap. 2.
- *Financial safety nets:* Banks further benefit from two special arrangements, which are known as financial safety nets and offered solely to banks. The first safety net is the so-called lender of last resort function of central banks vis-à-vis banks. This function essentially allows central banks to provide liquidity to banks in emergency situations. The provided funds are known as emergency liquidity assistance (ELA) in the euro area. The specific rules for granting ELA and the relation of ELA to regular monetary policy operations will be discussed in Chap. 2. The second safety net is deposit insurance. In all member states, bank deposits up to 100,000 euros held by an individual depositor per bank is covered under a so-called deposit guarantee scheme (DGS). This means that depositors are promised to be reimbursed for up to this amount of their deposits in case the bank becomes illiquid or insolvent. The existence of the DGS enhances the trust the public has in the safety of their bank deposits. In a sense, the safety net supports the role of banks as creators of commercial bank money. As the deposit guarantee scheme is a policy instrument to support financial stability, it will be further discussed in Chap. 5.
- *Relationship with the State:* In addition to these special arrangements, banks in the euro area are characterized by close financial and political relationships to the State in which they are located. This relationship has several dimensions.

  – At the level of *financial linkages*, banks play an important role in the issuance and distribution of sovereign debt, for instance by taking the role of a primary dealer for government bonds. Banks are also active participants in auctions of Treasury bills and hold government bond on their own books, for instance as a liquidity buffer or to meet regulatory requirements. This is particularly the case for sovereign debt instruments in the country in which the respective bank is located, yet the extent of such "home bias" varies by bank in different parts of the euro area. Additional financial linkages relate to equity shares that are directly or indirectly held by the State in some banks. For instance, the State may be a co-owner of banks as a result of bailouts during the financial crisis or due to close historical ties.
  – Apart from direct financial linkages, the relationship between banks and the State is also characterized by implicit liabilities for public finances. These are particularly related to the potential failure of banks, in particular of banks that are considered too big to fail (TBTF). For instance, a non-negligible number of

euro area banks were bailed out during the financial crisis since 2008 on the justification that their failure would have sent shock waves to the financial system and made an already difficult economic situation even worse. We will get back to the TBTF issue in Chap. 5.

– Finally, there is also a *political dimension* to the close relationship between banks and the State. To some extent, this proximity is related to the function of banks as providers of credit to the economy. Due to the predominance of indirect finance through banks, the level and type of investments in the economy largely depend on lending activities by banks.

Based on these introductory comments, we can take note of several key characteristics of the banking sector in the euro area.

- *Firstly, the euro area banking sector is very large.* The total assets of euro area banks amounted to 24.2 trillion euros as of end-2016 (ECB 2017e, data on a consolidated basis), which corresponds to more than 2.2 times GDP. At the country level, the largest banking sectors are those of France and Germany with total assets slightly above 7 billion euros, followed with some distance by Spain (3.6 trillion euros) and Italy (2.7 trillion euros) (ECB 2017e).
- *Secondly, the sector is tiered and dominated by large banks in each country.* 120 euro area banking groups hold more than three quarters of total banking sector assets. These banks are directly supervised by the ECB as part of the single supervisory mechanism (SSM), as Chap. 4 will explain in more detail. Some of these large banking groups are global players such as Deutsche Bank, BNP Paribas, or Santander. For convenience, we will refer to them as first-tier banks. Other large euro area banks are important players in their own member states or a number of member states. They are often universal banks and have close ties to the domestic political establishment, as do their first-tier counterparts. We will refer to these banks as second-tier banks in the remainder of the book.[10] In addition, numerous smaller banks operate in the euro area, which we will call third-tier banks. These small and medium-sized banks either have a local or regional focus in their operations or are specialized in certain market segments such as private wealth management or public finance. In some member states, in particular Germany and Austria, many third-tier banks are closely associated with second-tier banks within decentralized savings and cooperative sectors. The prevalence of third-tier banks in a few member states also explains the high number of approximately 5000 banks that operate in the euro area as a whole (ECB 2017e). Figure 1.12 illustrates a stylized version of the interbank network in the euro area, comprising the three tiers (as nodes) and their financial interlinkages (as lines).

[10]The classification of banks into three tiers is used for illustrative purposes only. It captures some characteristics of the euro area banking sector, in particular its distribution by size and level/type of international activities. Banks could also be classified differently by applying other criteria.

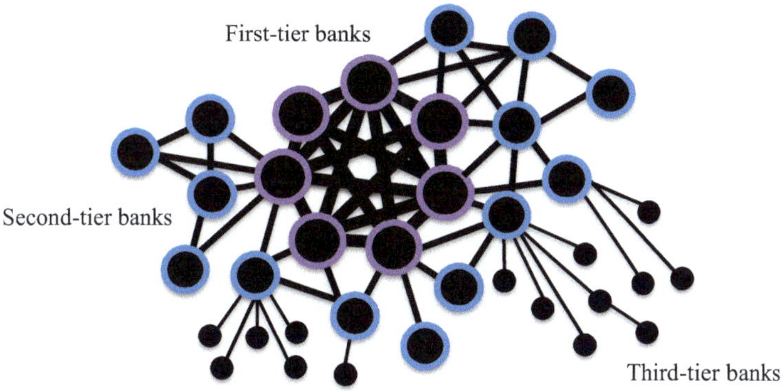

Fig. 1.12 Stylized interbank network in the euro area

- *Thirdly, the euro area banking sector witnessed significant growth and transformation from the early 1990s to the onset of the global financial crisis in 2007.* The main trends of this period were more pronounced international activities, both within and outside the euro area, high credit growth in some market segments, and expanding operations beyond core business areas on the promise of higher returns. Ever since 2008, the banking sector has gone through a major crisis that effectively reversed these trends and at the same time revealed significant vulnerabilities of individual banks and the banking sector as a whole. We will discuss these developments and the policy response in more detail in subsequent chapters. For now, let us turn to other financial intermediaries in the euro area, which have also grown in importance in recent years.

Insurance Companies

Insurance companies promise compensation to their customers should certain events occur, in return for regular payments. For instance, Marie took out property insurance for her apartment. This means that she makes regular premium payments to the insurance company. In case of a flooding in her apartment, the insurance company promises to make a payment to Marie. The payment allows her to cover the costs to restore the apartment without having to rely on her savings. The insurance company uses the regular premiums it receives from Marie and other customers to invest in securities and other assets. The balance sheet of an insurance company thus shows on the liability side its obligations to policyholders (so-called technical reserves) and on the asset side the investments of the insurance premiums (usually predominantly securities, see Fig. 1.13). The level of maturity transformation is significantly lower than in banks, given that insurance companies do not issue commercial bank money or other short-term deposits. Instead, both sides of insurance balance sheets are typically characterized by a large portion of medium- to long-term financial instruments. This is in particular the case in the life insurance segment where insurance policies are rather long term.

Fig. 1.13 Insurance balance sheet

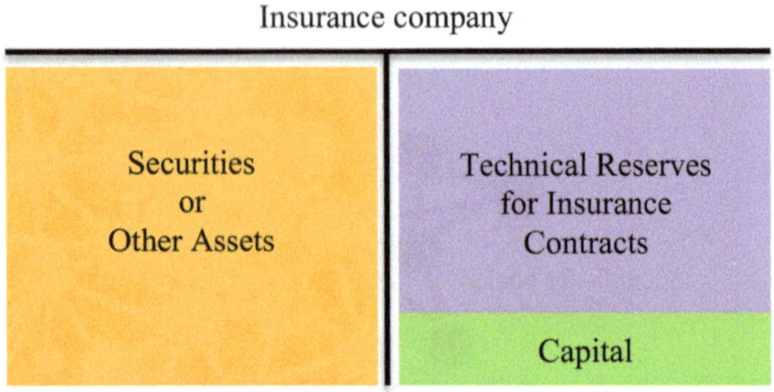

The failure of an insurance company is typically less damaging to the financial system and broader economy than the failure of a bank. As illustrated in Fig. 1.13, the liabilities of insurance companies mostly take the form of insurance obligations, which can be less easily withdrawn than commercial bank money and other deposits from banks. Hence, the liquidity risk inherent in the business model of an insurance company is typically much lower than that of a bank. Nevertheless, insurance companies may become insolvent if they incur large losses on their investments. Should an insurance company be brought down by massive losses, it would fail to honor the promises it has given to its insurance policy holders. This would obviously hit those that took out insurance. For instance, Marie's life insurance policy would suddenly become worthless, should her insurance company collapse. Furthermore, she would have to find a new property insurance company without being able to claim her paid premiums. As regretful as the situation may be at the micro-level, at the system level the direct financial effects of the default of a large insurance company are different and likely less damaging than those caused by the default of a large bank. We will get back to this point when discussing financial stability policy in Chap. 5.

The development of the insurance sector in the euro area is quite heterogeneous. Total assets of insurance companies in the euro area amounted to 7.6 trillion euros or approximately 70% of GDP as of end-2016. Unlike banks, insurance companies continued to grow steadily ever since the onset of the global financial crisis. On a country level, the insurance sector is particularly developed in France and Germany, with other important insurance markets being located in Italy, Belgium, and Luxembourg. The latter country is also a base for reinsurance activities. The two main insurance segments—life insurance and nonlife insurance, such as property, car, or casualty insurance—are more or less balanced in the euro area as a whole but they vary significantly across countries. While life insurance dominates the insurance markets of France or Belgium, nonlife insurance accounts for a larger share of the German market.

Real Money Investors

The third category of financial intermediaries comprises various nonbank financial institutions with relatively low leverage. This category includes mutual funds, defined-contribution pension funds, private equity funds, hedge funds, asset management companies, and others. For overview purposes, we put all these institutions in one group and refer to them collectively as real money investors. The term indicates a key characteristic these institutions share, which is the fact that they primarily invest their own funds rather than borrowed funds. In other words, their balance sheets include much less liabilities or other obligations than those of banks (which are the most leveraged type of financial institution due to taking deposits) and insurance companies (which have insurance obligations as liabilities). As a consequence, the financial leverage of real money investors, which is measured as total assets over total equity, is significantly lower than that of banks and insurance companies. Apart from this common characteristic, the real money investors are quite heterogeneous. The main types of real money investors are the following:

- **Mutual funds** pool money from many individuals and purchase securities which are typically focused on a specific asset class and region (e.g., emerging market equities). An example is the mutual fund in which Marie invested some of her savings. The income earned as well as any capital gains are distributed by the mutual fund among the investors that have provided the capital. For the management of their investments, mutual funds charge investors various fees. A significant part of mutual funds located in the euro area have a globally diversified investor base and hold a large share of assets outside the euro area.
- **Defined-contribution pension funds** invest in various asset classes based on regular contributions made by employers or individuals that save for their retirement. The funds are accumulated during the person's professional life based on private contractual arrangements. Upon reaching the retirement age, a monthly pension is paid out by the pension fund to the individual in addition to any public pension received. The investment risk of this type of pension fund is typically borne by the beneficiary and not the fund or a sponsor. If the investments perform worse (or better) than expected, the monthly pension payments will be lower (or higher, respectively). In the euro area, pension funds are particularly large institutions in the Netherlands with total assets of 1.4 trillion euros (end-2016). Other important markets are Ireland, Germany, and Italy, while in some other countries such as France they are virtually nonexistent. The heterogeneity across the euro area primarily reflects differences in the reliance on public or private pension schemes. Overall, the total assets of euro area pension funds were 2.3 trillion euros as of end-2016, which includes both defined-contribution and defined-benefit funds.[11]

[11]Defined-benefit funds promise a certain pension to beneficiaries. The investment risk is therefore borne by the pension fund, unlike in the case of defined-contribution funds, where the beneficiary bears the investment risk. In this respect, defined-contribution funds are more similar to other real money investors, such as mutual funds, than defined-benefit funds, which need to engage in asset-liability management due to the promises made.

- **Private equity funds** raise capital from institutional investors or wealthy individuals and invest them in equity of private companies. Target companies are often established companies facing difficulties in their respective market segment or companies with unused growth potential. Private equity funds typically get actively involved in the management and/or restructuring of these companies. A related group of equity funds are **venture capital funds**, which specialize in the financing of start-ups and businesses in early stages of their operations. Overall, the size of private equity and venture capital funds in the euro area is dwarfed by banks and other financial institutions. As a percentage of GDP, their activities are most significant in the Netherlands and France.
- **Asset managers** receive funds from other institutional investors, nonfinancial businesses, and wealthy individuals and manage them on their behalf. Some of the largest financial institutions in the world are asset managers, such as Blackrock with $5.1 trillion assets under management by end-2016.
- Other real money investors include hedge funds, endowments, foundations, individuals, and sovereign wealth funds. While some of these investor types are important players on the global financial markets, they play a minor role in the euro area financial sector.

Shadow Banks

In addition to banks, insurance companies, and real money investors, a number of other entities operate in the financial system and perform similar functions as banks. These entities are labeled shadow banks. The term indicates two key characteristics: Firstly, they perform bank-like functions in selected segments outside the regular banking sector. Secondly, public knowledge about their activities is rather limited. In other words, these entities operate in the shadow of other and more regulated financial institutions. Which types of institutions exactly fall in the perimeter of shadow banks varies in the literature, yet most common definitions involve an element of credit intermediation outside the regular banking sector.

- **Money market funds** are a typical example of shadow banks. They take deposits and invest them in short-term liquid debt instruments, while being subject to light regulation. Money market funds in the euro area are mainly located in Ireland, France, and Luxembourg. Many of these funds have a nonresident investor base and also hold non-euro area debt instruments.
- Other examples of shadow banks are investment funds that are involved in credit intermediation and financial vehicle corporations (FVCs), which are engaged in securitization activities and particularly prevalent in the Netherlands and Ireland. In addition, various types of special purpose vehicles (SPVs) are common in the euro area financial system as well, often linked to regular banks but designed in a way that avoids consolidation into their balance sheets.
- Lastly, there are numerous other financial institutions in some member states—in particular in the Netherlands and Luxembourg—that are no regular type of financial institutions in official statistics and also included in the shadow banking category.

1.2.2 Financial Markets

Financial markets are places where financial instruments are bought and sold. Financial instruments cover equity, debt, and derivatives. Bonds or stocks, for instance, fall within this category, whereas real assets such as houses or cars do not. The main financial markets in the euro area are:

1. **Money market**—for short-term debt instruments
2. **FX market**—for currencies
3. **Fixed income market**—for medium- to long-term debt instruments
4. **Equity market**—for stocks
5. **Derivatives market**—for a range of instruments that allow the transfer of specific risks, such as interest rate swaps or oil futures.

Money Market

Banks and other financial institutions use the money market to borrow and lend commercial bank money at short maturities of up to 1 year. Ordinary individuals such as Marie are typically not involved in this market. Nevertheless, the money market assumes a very important role for the functioning of the financial system and for the conduct of monetary policy. Figure 1.14 shows the development of two key money market indicators for the euro area (EONIA and 6-month Euribor), which will be discussed in the following.

Money market instruments can be secured or unsecured.

- *Unsecured money market instruments* include interbank loans or deposits that are created when a bank lends surplus liquidity to another bank that has liquidity needs. More standardized forms of unsecured instruments are tradable and thus more liquid from the lender perspective, given that the lending institution may sell its claim to another institution before repayment. Tradable money market instruments are certificates of deposit (CDs), which are mostly used by banks,

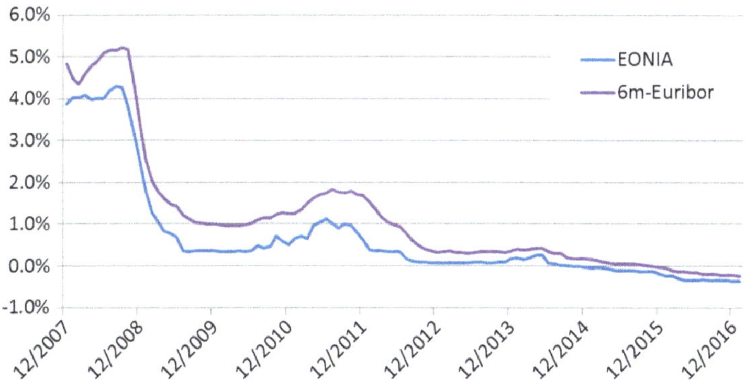

Fig. 1.14 Selected money market indicators. Source: ECB (2017a)

commercial paper, which is primarily issued by large nonfinancial corporations, and Treasury bills, which are issued by the State. All these instruments are short term (i.e., with maturities of 1 day up to 1 year) and unsecured (i.e., only based on the creditworthiness of the borrower and no additional safeguards).
- *Secured money market instruments* use another asset as collateral for the short-term borrowing transaction, which lowers the counterparty risk. For instance, a bank may pledge securities to receive liquidity for 1 week. After the week, the money is returned and the pledge is removed. Should the bank default during the week, the lender can use the securities to cover his losses. Such secured transactions on the money market are known as repurchase operations or repos. Their main advantage lies in allowing financial institutions to borrow short term at low cost, given that their counterparties take a lower risk due to the pledged collateral.

The daily turnover of the euro area money market was approximately 1.1 trillion euros in Q2 2015 (ECB 2015). Its key importance for the smooth functioning of the banking system was prominently illustrated in the money market freeze following the collapse of Lehman Brothers in September 2008. At that time, the activity on money markets fell substantially amid widespread mistrust among banks, which greatly exacerbated the risks to global financial stability. We will discuss this memorable episode in Chap. 3.

Box 1.3 Euro Area Reference Rates

Money market interest rates serve as reference rates for many financial contracts. For instance, Marie's mortgage loan may have a variable interest rate of Euribor (as the reference rate) plus 2 percentage points. While a large number of reference rates are used in financial instruments in the euro area, the most common are Euribor and Libor.

Euribor (Euro Interbank Offered Rate) serves as a key reference rate for money market transactions in the euro area. Its purpose is to reflect the average rate at which large banks currently lend to each other in euro on an unsecured basis. Euribor is reported for maturities from 1 week to 1 year, of which the 3m-Euribor and 6m-Euribor are the most widely used rates. The figure below plots all Euribor rates as of 4 August 2017. The resulting function is called the swap curve. The name stems from their use in interest rate derivatives, which we will discuss further below. At the short end, the swap curve shows another important market rate, the so-called EONIA (Euro Overnight Interest Average). This rate indicates the weighted average rate at which 43 major banks in the euro area lend to other "prime banks" overnight, i.e., until the next business day.

(continued)

Box 1.3 (continued)

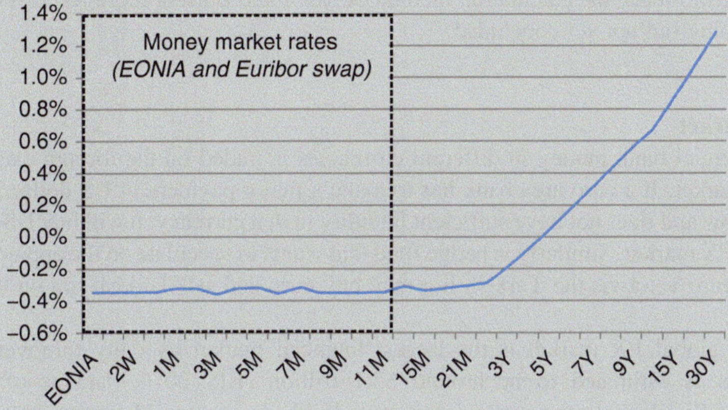

Source: Reuters

Libor (London Interbank Offered Rate) is the equivalent to Euribor for the US dollar and other global currencies. It represents the average interest rate at which major banks would currently lend to each other in the respective currency on an unsecured basis. The rate is termed Libor as it is determined by bankers in the London interbank market.[12] To provide an example, the 3m-USD-Libor expresses the rate at which a major bank would lend USD to another major bank with a maturity of 3 months and no collateral. It is also worth noting that reference rates such as Libor or Euribor are typically quoted as per annum rates.

A major deficiency of Euribor and Libor is that they are based on daily surveys rather than actual money market transactions. Euribor is published on a daily basis by the European Banking Federation. It is determined based on a daily survey among 43 major banks which are asked to indicate the rate at which interbank deposits are offered within the euro area among "prime banks." Euribor is then computed as an arithmetic average of the bank responses, excluding the 15% highest and lowest responses. This calculation method is obviously prone to manipulation as banks may provide biased indications and collude to game the average rate, which, to recall, serves as a reference rate for many other transactions. Allegations that Libor and Euribor had been rigged by a number of large banks became public in 2012. Several regulatory and judicial investigations followed, as well as substantial settlement fees paid by some large banks such as Deutsche Bank or UBS. By 2016,

(continued)

[12]Libor rates are published by Intercontinental Exchange (ICE), a US-based financial infrastructure provider. Until 2014, they were published by the British Bankers Association.

Box 1.3 (continued)
efforts to make the calculation method of Libor and Euribor more robust were ongoing but not yet concluded.

FX Market

Commercial bank money in different currencies is traded on the foreign exchange (FX) market. If a euro area bank has to make a major payment in US dollar 2 days from now and does not have sufficient liquidity in that currency, it will buy US dollar on the FX market. Similarly, a hedge fund that wants to speculate on the appreciation of the euro vis-à-vis the Turkish lira may buy euro and sell Turkish lira on the FX market.

The global FX market is the largest financial market by daily turnover. The turnover is estimated to be around $5.1 trillion (BIS 2016, data as of April 2016).[13] Similarly to the money market, individuals such as Marie are usually no direct participants in this market (with the exception of a minor retail niche that is irrelevant from a system perspective).

The FX market is probably the most integrated market in the world. The market has expanded strongly since the end of the Bretton-Woods System, which led to the widespread use of floating exchange rates by major economies. The size of the FX market was further boosted by financial liberalization and increasing world trade in the 1990s and 2000s. In line with the high turnover on the FX market and the strong market presence of global banks serving as dealers, several market conventions have emerged that are globally respected.

- *Firstly, currencies are referred to by their three-letter ISO country code, also known as the SWIFT code*. Typically, the first two digits are the country code and the third one the currency name. For instance, USD denotes the US dollar, GBP the British pound, JPY the Japanese yen, and HUF the Hungarian forint. EUR is the exception that proves the rule. Some important exchange rates from a euro area perspective are illustrated in Fig. 1.15.
- *Secondly, there are certain conventions for quoting currency pairs*. The underlying currency is always quoted first and the accounting currency second (e.g., EUR-HUF). The FX rate indicates how many units of the accounting currency equal one unit of the underlying currency. For instance, the EUR-HUF exchange rate of 315 indicates that 315 Hungarian forint equal 1 euro. In the FX market,

[13]The average daily turnover on the global FX market, which is measured every 3 years by the Bank for International Settlements (BIS), includes spot transactions of $1.7 trillion (these are short-term cash transactions), FX swaps of $2.4 trillion (see overview of the derivatives market further below), and other FX derivatives. These data are as of April 2016.

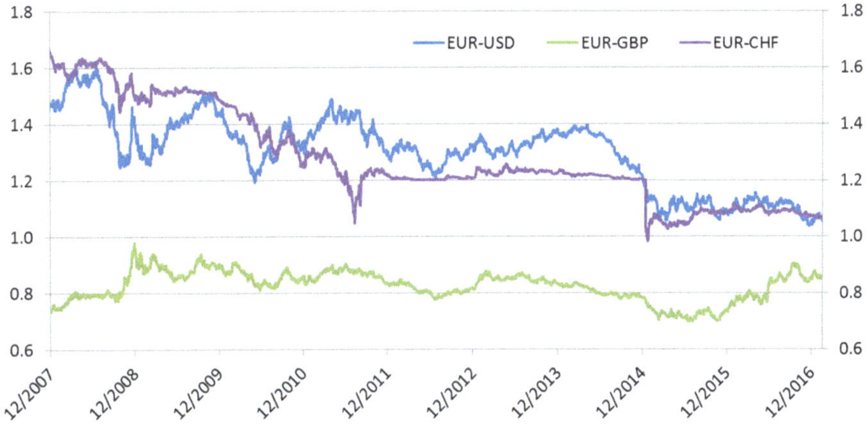

Fig. 1.15 Selected FX rates. Source: ECB (2017b)

conventions have developed in which way the currency pairs are commonly quoted.[14]

- *Thirdly, two rates are quoted for each currency pair, the so-called bid and ask prices.* The euro area bank that wants to buy US dollar has to pay the ask price in the transaction. This means it has to pay a higher euro amount than it would get in case it were to sell the equal amount of US dollar to the market. The difference between bid and ask prices indicates the liquidity of the currency pair. The more transactions there are for the exchange rate, the lower the bid-ask-spread (and the lower the profits for the dealer).

Fixed Income Market

Debt instruments with maturities of more than 1 year are issued and traded on the fixed income market. They are of key importance for the medium to long-term financing of governments, financial institutions, and businesses. The investor pool is typically large, ranging from banks, insurance companies, and real money investors to individuals, businesses, governments, and central banks. Prior to 2008, the fixed income market had been widely perceived as a haven of stability, in particular the markets for sovereign bonds of advanced economies and other securities with high credit ratings. This perception has changed in recent years, which has policy implications that we will discuss in subsequent chapters.

[14]These conventions are based on a ranking of major currencies that starts with EUR, GBP, AUD, NZD, and USD. Hence, all currency pairs to the EUR are quoted with EUR as the underlying currency (e.g., EUR-USD, EUR-GBP, or EUR-JPY). For the USD, most currency pairs are quoted with the USD as the underlying currency (e.g., USD-JPY) with the exception of pairs such as EUR-USD and GBP-USD.

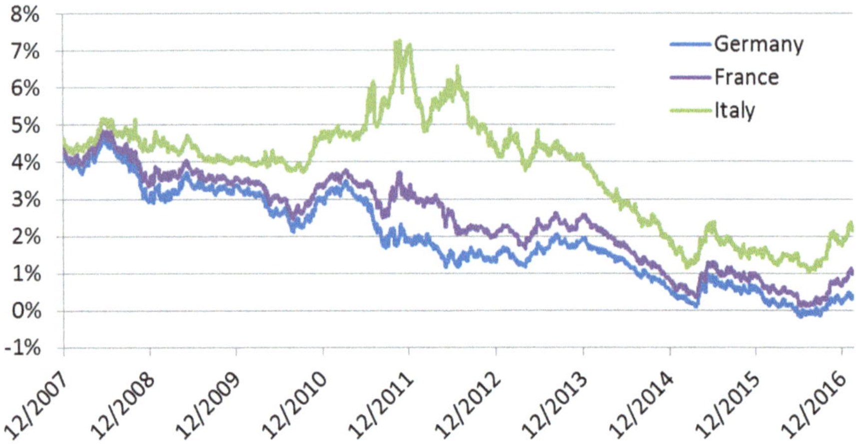

Fig. 1.16 Selected 10-year government bond yields. Source: Investing.com

The fixed income market in the euro area can be organized along several dimensions:

- By *type of issuer* into sovereign bonds (as shown in Fig. 1.16), corporate bonds, bank bonds (such as medium-term notes), and debt instruments issued by other financial institutions. Another category of fixed income issuances, which needs to be mentioned due to their prominent role during the financial crisis, is comprised of securitizations. They are essentially asset-backed securities (ABS) that are issued by special-purpose vehicles (SPVs). For instance, a bank may transfer a corporate loan portfolio to an SPV, which pays for the transfer by issuing ABS. The securities are typically issued in various tranches that have different risk and return characteristics. The issuance of European securitizations experienced robust growth prior to 2008, yet at significantly lower levels than in the United States. Activity significantly decreased during the crisis and has remained at levels similar to the early 2000s in recent years.
- By *secured or unsecured* transactions, similar to money market instruments. An example for a secured instrument is a covered bond, which may be issued by a bank and provides the investor with a distinct advantage compared to unsecured bonds: In case of issuer default, it triggers the carve-out of selected assets (the so-called cover pool) from the bank's balance sheet. These assets are transferred to another entity and used to repay the covered bond. This feature promises a higher recovery rate for holders of covered bonds compared to unsecured bondholders.
- By insolvency rank into *junior or senior* instruments. The former are typically more risky as they are designed to absorb losses prior to senior bonds (yet only after the equity stake, which per definition does not have to be repaid, unlike fixed income instruments).

- By *external credit ratings*, which are provided by Moody's, S&P, Fitch, and other credit rating agencies. Ratings usually range from AAA (best) to D (worst, default rating), with BBB-and above constituting investment grade. Instruments with ratings below this threshold are referred to as junk bonds.
- By *other contractual terms* such as maturity, coupon (floating or fixed rate), or structure (e.g., with interest rate caps).
- By distinguishing transactions in the *primary market*, where bonds are issued and thus provide financing to the issuer, and the *secondary market*, where existing bonds are traded and thus provide market liquidity. Some primary markets are rather restrictive such as sovereign bond markets in which banks typically serve as primary dealers.

Equity Market

Stock exchanges are the most prominent part of financial markets in terms of media coverage. Every day there are media reports about the recent performance of individual stocks (such as a large German carmaker or an Italian electricity company) and equity market indexes (such as DAX or CAC-40). The DAX and CAC-40 indexes indicate the performance of listed companies on the German and French stock exchanges, respectively. Another major equity index in the euro area is Euro Stoxx 50, which shows the performance of the 50 largest and most liquid stocks in the euro area, with subindexes for various industries such as banks (see Fig. 1.17). Most equity trading takes place on electronic platforms rather than physical stock exchanges, even though the latter are still shown visualized in equity market reports on TV news. In the euro area, the largest stock exchanges in terms of market capitalization are NYSE Euronext and Deutsche Boerse.

Trading takes place on exchanges and over-the-counter. Similarly to the fixed income market, we can distinguish the primary market (where stocks are issued and

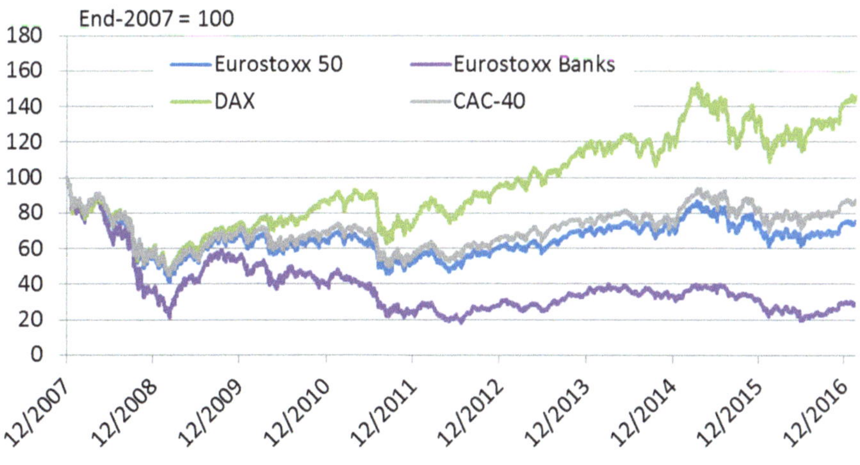

Fig. 1.17 Equity market indicators. Source: Euronext, Stoxx, Yahoo Finance

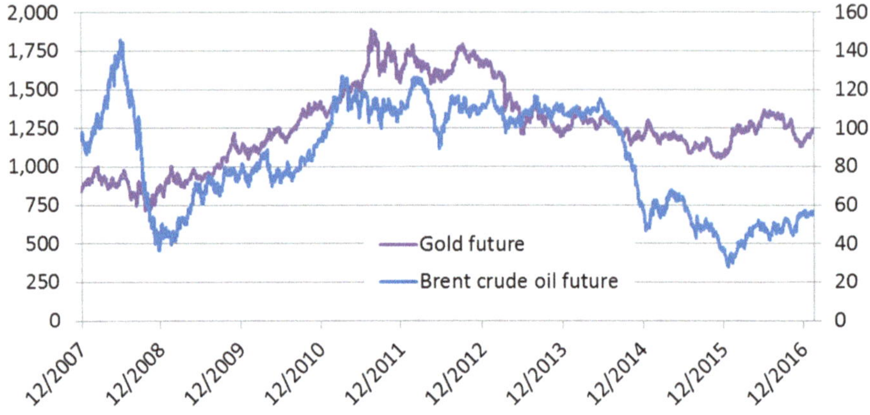

Fig. 1.18 Derivative market indicators. Source: Quandl

the first investors subscribe) and the secondary market (where existing stocks are bought and sold). Listed shares are also traded outside of exchanges, which is then referred to as equity trading on the over-the-counter (OTC) market. In addition, unlisted shares are also part of the equity market, as they may be bought and sold outside of exchanges. Many small and medium-sized enterprises in the euro area are for instance private companies, i.e., their shares are not traded on stock exchanges but for instance held by the founding family, other private investors, private equity funds, or other financial institutions.

Derivatives Market

The final section of the financial market allows participants to transfer specific risks. Derivatives are instruments that relate to an underlying asset, such as a certain company share, and derive their value from the asset's price (or alternatively from a market rate, such as an interest rate or an FX rate). Two examples are shown in Fig. 1.18 (gold future and Brent crude oil future). They can be traded on exchanges or over-the-counter, i.e., outside of exchanges. The derivatives market has shown rapid growth and transformation in the years prior to the global financial crisis. The crisis led to a significant fall in activity, in particular in the over-the-counter segment. In the euro area, large banks dominate the market and assume the role of dealers in key derivative instruments, such as interest-rate swaps or credit-default swaps (CDS).[15]

Derivatives can be used to manage existing risks or to take new risks.

[15]The buyer of a CDS (e.g., CDS on Argentina) purchases credit risk protection on an underlying asset (Argentinian government bonds in this example). If the underlying asset defaults, he will be compensated for the loss. In return, he needs to make regular payments to the seller of the CDS, similarly to insurance payments. In case the underlying asset does not default, the seller of the CDS benefits from regular payments that he receives from the CDS buyer.

- Using derivatives to manage existing risks is known as hedging. An example is an airline that would like to be protected against higher oil prices and thus buys a call option on oil.[16] Similarly, a bank may reduce its interest rate risk by entering into an interest rate swap. In both cases, risks are transferred to another entity at relatively low cost, similar to what insurance contracts do, as discussed earlier.
- Using derivatives to take new risks is sometimes referred to as speculation. For instance, a wealthy individual may want to bet on higher oil prices or falling share prices. Derivatives are well-suited instruments for such purposes for two reasons: Firstly, they can be tailored to the needs of the client (e.g., betting on falling share prices of a specific segment such as Australian mining companies). This is done through the use of financial engineering, a task that is primarily done by banks and essentially refers to the combination or modification of various derivatives. Secondly, derivatives may leverage client returns, i.e., provide the prospect of large positive (or negative) returns. In other words, the payoff for the client can be significantly higher than its original investment and depend on the movement of the underlying asset prices (e.g., oil price), potentially resulting in large profits or losses.

Derivatives can be classified by instrument, underlying asset, or structure:

- The main *instruments* are forwards, futures, swaps, and options:
  - A *forward* is an obligation to buy or sell an asset for a certain price at a specified future date (e.g., to sell 1000 shares of Deutsche Bank on 30 November 2017 for 20 euros per share).
  - A *future* is a standardized form of a forward that is traded on an exchange (e.g., future on German government bonds with maturity July 2018).
  - A *swap* is essentially an exchange of two future cash flows. For instance, two banks may enter into an interest rate swap on 100 million euros for a period of 2 years that swaps a floating interest rate, such as Euribor, for a fixed interest rate of 0.03%. This means that bank A pays 3 million euros in each year to bank B. In turn, bank B makes variable payments to bank A at specified dates, which depend on the development of Euribor.
  - An *option* gives the holder the right to buy or sell an asset for a certain price at a specified future date. If the option is exercised, which depends on the movement of the underlying asset price, the seller of the option has the obligation to sell (buy) the asset to (from) the option holder. In other words, the option holder can actively decide to sell (or buy) the specified asset at the agreed price, while the option seller assumes the passive role of the corresponding counterparty. If the option gives the option holder the right to buy, it is referred to as a call option. An option that gives the holder the right to sell is known as a put option (e.g., put option on Eurostoxx-50).

[16]Call options are explained further below in this section.

- The *underlying assets* are those traded on the already discussed financial markets (money market, FX market, fixed income market, and equity market) as well as the commodity market. Commodity derivatives are typically linked to the market prices of oil, precious metals, or agricultural products (e.g., gold and Brent crude oil futures, as shown in Fig. 1.18). The market for commodity derivatives broadened and deepened significantly since the late 1990s.
- The *structure* of derivatives ranges from plain-vanilla instruments, which are simple "off-the-shelf" derivatives, to highly structured instruments, which are the product of financial engineering.

1.2.3 Financial Infrastructure

Financial institutions and markets would not be able to operate without a functioning infrastructure. The third component of the financial system could be described as its pipes and is probably its most technical and least understood part. Its functioning is taken for granted and rarely receives public attention, yet it is essential for the execution of payments and other financial transactions. Similar to pipes in a building, its relevance becomes clearly visible when parts of it break down or individual participants are cut out. The main elements of the financial infrastructure are the payment system as well as the clearing and settlement system for securities and derivatives.

The payment system allows individuals, businesses, and financial institutions to transfer funds among each other. The funds can be commercial bank money or CBM in the case of interbank payments. Different payment systems are used for large-value transactions and retail payments:

The large-value payment system is used by banks for their own operations and for payments of their customers. It performs large payments that are typically time critical and lower in number than retail payments. Most large-value payments in the euro area are conducted through a system known as TARGET2 that is operated by the central banks of the euro area. It allows CBM payments across euro area banks that are settled within just a few minutes and without any netting. The average volume of transactions that is channeled through TARGET2 each day amounts to 1.8 trillion euros (2015 data) and the average transaction size is 5.3 million euros (ECB 2016a). It is worth adding that TARGET2 is not only used for interbank and customer payments but also for monetary policy operations (see Chap. 2) and payments related to other financial infrastructures.

The retail payment system is used for transactions by individuals and businesses that are typically low in value, less time critical, and high in number. To get back to our example, Marie uses the retail payment system by paying her monthly electricity bills, receiving her salary, or paying by card in a shop. Most retail payments fall in one of three categories that are of broadly similar relevance in the euro area:

- Firstly, *credit transfers* are electronic payments that are for instance initiated through online banking.

- Secondly, *direct debit* are recurrent payments that are initiated by the payment recipient with pre-authorization by the payer, for instance for settling utility bills.
- Thirdly, retail payments can be made by *debit or credit cards*, which requires financial infrastructure to process them as well.

In all three cases, a payment instruction is sent to a financial institution (in most cases a bank) that executes it using its own infrastructure or services of third parties, typically by netting the payment orders.

In the euro area, the retail payment system is rather fragmented across countries but has seen a significant harmonization in practices ever since 2014 with the launch of SEPA, the single euro payments area. The key objective of SEPA is to allow EU residents to make retail payments to any other individual or business in the EU[17] in a reliable, safe, and fast way, i.e., with settlement on the next business day. With the introduction of SEPA, bank account numbers were transformed into IBAN that follow a common structure and thus allow their unique identification.[18] Figure 1.19 shows the development of retail payment transactions in the EU in the period 2000–2013 by number of transactions per capita and year. In particular, it shows the strong growth in credit and debit card payments during this period.

In addition to payment services, financial infrastructure is needed for the clearing and settlement of securities and derivatives. For instance, an insurance company may only be able to purchase an Italian government bond in the secondary market if it uses several infrastructure service providers for trading, clearing, settlement, and related services.

- *Trading:* The insurance company needs to find a counterparty that is willing to sell the government bond, for instance on a regulated exchange or a multilateral trading facility.
- *Clearing:* Once the insurance company has identified the selected counterparty, the obligations of the two parties need to be determined prior to settlement. While this is a straightforward task in case of the government bond purchase, which would be typically done through the security settlement system, clearing can become more complex if, for instance, two banks enter into a derivative contract and agree to netting with other transactions through a clearing house. Furthermore, some standardized derivatives are cleared through central counterparties (CCPs) that act as intermediaries to all transactions on the market. In the example of the two banks, the CCP would simultaneously enter into opposite positions with the buyer and seller of the respective derivative, thus eliminating the counterparty risk between the two banks.

[17]SEPA also covers some non-EU countries (Iceland, Norway, Switzerland, Liechtenstein, Monaco, and San Marino).

[18]An IBAN (International Bank Account Number) always consists of a country code (DE), two check digits, the bank and/or branch code, as well as the account number.

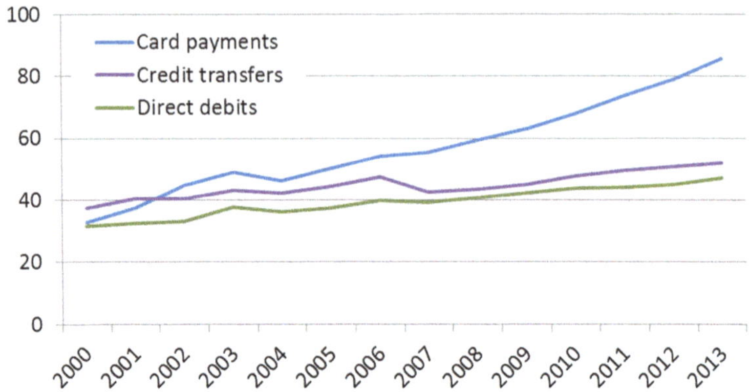

Fig. 1.19 Retail payment transactions in the EU (number per capita and year). Source: ECB (2017c)

- *Settlement:* Financial infrastructure further needs to take care that the transaction is settled as agreed. In the case of the government bond purchase, the insurance company needs to make the payment and the security settlement system will upon receipt of the payment confirmation transfer the bond to the insurance company. Settlement systems in the euro area are operated by various central securities depositories (CSDs) and two international CSDs (Euroclear and Clearstream). From 2016 onwards, the Target 2 Securities project of the Eurosystem gradually creates a pan-European platform for security settlement with payment in CBM.
- *Other services* related to trade execution include financial messaging services (for instance, the widely used service SWIFT) or trade repositories that store post-trade data for use by public authorities and selected market participants.

Central banks have both operator and oversight functions regarding financial infrastructure in the euro area due to their importance for the economic and financial system. As mentioned above, central banks operate several key infrastructures such as TARGET2, while private firms offer a broad range of services in all segments. The main reason for the operative involvement of central banks in large-value payment systems lies in their crucial role for the conduct of monetary policy and the limitation of systemic risks. Furthermore, it supports the trust of the general public in the safety of the currency. The reliable and safe functioning of the payment system is of vital importance for economic activity in general and for the millions of financial transactions that are performed in the euro area every day. The oversight function on financial infrastructure will be discussed in the context of financial stability in Chap. 5.

Putting All Components Together

A key observation in our *tour d'horizon* of the monetary and financial system has been the prominent role of banks. As the treatment of banks will be one of main threads in the following chapters on monetary policy, banking supervision, and financial stability, let us briefly recall some relevant aspects we identified so far:

- The *monetary system* assigns banks the power to create commercial bank money, to provide cash to individuals and businesses, and to transmit the central bank's monetary policy stance through operations with central banks in CBM, the third type of money to which only banks have access.
- The *payment system* gives banks an important role as provider of payment services to individuals and businesses, by offering bank accounts, electronic transfers, and card payments.
- The *financial system* is dominated by banks, which account for almost half of its total assets. Banks are the main deposit-taking institutions in the euro area. Their operations are supported by the existence of a deposit guarantee scheme and the availability of emergency liquidity support by the central bank. The structure of the sector can be described as tiered with a dominant position of large institutions. Banks further tend to have a special relationship to the State in the form of financial and political linkages.
- Banks are key players in various *financial markets*, such as the money market, the FX market, parts of the fixed income market, and derivative markets. Banks are further involved in the determination of key reference rates that are used in many financial instruments.
- The banking system witnessed some *critical failures* over the past decade, which we will discuss in more detail in Chap. 3. After strong growth and transformation of banks in the precrisis period, the global financial crisis demonstrated the negative externalities that can be triggered by the failure of systemically important banks. Several large and medium-sized banks in the euro area were bailed out by the State to prevent their failure and related effects, sometimes at substantial cost to public finances.

Another key observation is that the system is based on fiat money in a broad sense. As discussed, all three types of money are essentially created out of nothing and rely on public trust to maintain their function over time. They need to be available as a means of payment in sufficient quantity and broadly maintain their purchasing power. Given that something as fragile as public trust provides the foundation of the system implies that the issuers of money—central banks and banks—have the responsibility to act prudently in deploying their money creating powers. We will get back to this point in subsequent chapters.

Let us now move to the three policy areas through which the central bank can influence the functioning of the monetary and financial system. In the next chapter, we will first discuss the central bank responsibility for monetary policy, starting with a brief introduction to the Eurosystem and the ECB as the key player for monetary policy.

References

Bank for International Settlements (BIS). (2003). *The role of central bank money in payment systems*. Accessed from https://www.bis.org/cpmi/publ/d55.pdf

BIS. (2016). *Triennial Central Bank survey of foreign exchange and derivatives market activity*. Accessed from http://www.bis.org/publ/rpfx16.htm

European Central Bank (ECB). (2015). *Results of the Euro Money Market Survey 2015*. Accessed from https://www.ecb.europa.eu/press/pr/date/2015/html/pr150930.en.html

ECB. (2016a). *TARGET Annual Report 2015*. Accessed from https://www.ecb.europa.eu/pub/pdf/other/targetar2015.en.pdf

ECB. (2016b). *Annual Report 2015. Consolidated balance sheet of the Eurosystem as at 31 December 2015*. Accessed February 16, 2017, from https://www.ecb.europa.eu/pub/pdf/other/eurosystembalancesheet2015.en.pdf?4cc7ded4ebf63c42d3ee71de168611b4

ECB. (2016c, May 4). Press release. Accessed from https://www.ecb.europa.eu/press/pr/date/2016/html/pr160504.en.html

ECB. (2017a). *Statistical data warehouse*. Accessed February 16, 2017, from http://sdw.ecb.europa.eu/

ECB. (2017b). Euro Foreign Exchange reference rates. Accessed February 16, 2017, from https://www.ecb.europa.eu/stats/exchange/eurofxref/html/index.en.html

ECB. (2017c). *Types of payment*. Accessed February 16, 2017, from https://www.ecb.europa.eu/paym/retpaym/undpaym/paymtyp/html/index.en.html

ECB. (2017d). Consolidated balance sheet of the Eurosystem as at 31 December 2016. Accessed August 16, 2017, from https://www.ecb.europa.eu/pub/pdf/other/eurosystembalancesheet2016.en.pdf?6e118392f8774c739e6ef64f0513aadf

ECB. (2017e). *Report on financial structures*. Accessed November 14, 2017, from https://www.ecb.europa.eu/pub/pdf/other/reportonfinancialstructures201710.en.pdf

Euronext. Accessed March 30, 2017, from https://www.euronext.com

Investing.com. Accessed March 30, 2017, from https://www.investing.com/

Quandl. Accessed March 30, 2017, from https://www.quandl.com

Stoxx. Accessed March 30, 2017, from https://www.stoxx.com/

Yahoo Finance. Accessed March 30, 2017, from http://finance.yahoo.com/

Further Reading

European Central Bank (ECB). (2010). *The payment system – payments, securities, derivatives, and the role of the Eurosystem*. Accessed from https://www.ecb.europa.eu/pub/pdf/other/paymentsystem201009en.pdf

Haldane, A., & Piergiorgio, A. (2009, September). *Banking on the State*. Speech at the Federal Reserve Bank of Chicago Conference on 'The International Financial Crisis: Have the Rules of Finance Changed?', Chicago. Accessed from http://www.bis.org/review/r091111e.pdf

2 Monetary Policy

Monetary policy is a shared responsibility by the ECB and national central banks in the euro area. This chapter explains how it is conducted in practice and how it affects the financial system as well as the broader economy. The chapter is structured as follows: First, we discuss the objectives that are pursued by monetary policy and the institutions that are involved. Second, we investigate which policy instruments are used, including both standard and nonstandard measures. Lastly, we put euro area monetary policy in a global context and discuss the responsibility of central banks for foreign exchange policy vis-à-vis non-euro area countries in Europe and other parts of the world.

2.1 Policy Objectives and Institutional Setting

Monetary policy is conducted for the whole euro area, which comprises 19 EU member states. The countries are Austria, Belgium, Cyprus, Estonia, Finland, France, Germany, Greece, Ireland, Italy, Latvia, Lithuania, Luxembourg, Malta, the Netherlands, Portugal, Slovakia, Slovenia, and Spain (see Fig. 2.1). The euro was introduced as the common currency of 11 EU member states in 1999, starting with euro-denominated CBM and commercial bank money. In 2002, euro banknotes and coins were put in circulation.

The Eurosystem consists of the European Central Bank (ECB) and the national central banks (NCBs) of the euro area. While the latter were responsible for monetary policy in the respective national currencies (such as German mark or Italian lira) prior to 1999, the ECB was established with the introduction of the euro. The ECB is jointly owned by all the NCBs and located in Frankfurt am Main. The Governing Council, its highest decision-making body, is responsible for monetary policy decisions and their implementation in the euro area. The Governing Council is composed of the six members of the ECB's Executive Board, including its President (Mario Draghi at the time of writing) as chair, and the 19 governors of the NCBs of the euro area. The governors of the NCBs have 15 voting rights that are

M. Fandl, *Monetary and Financial Policy in the Euro Area*, Springer Texts in Business and Economics, https://doi.org/10.1007/978-3-319-72643-4_2

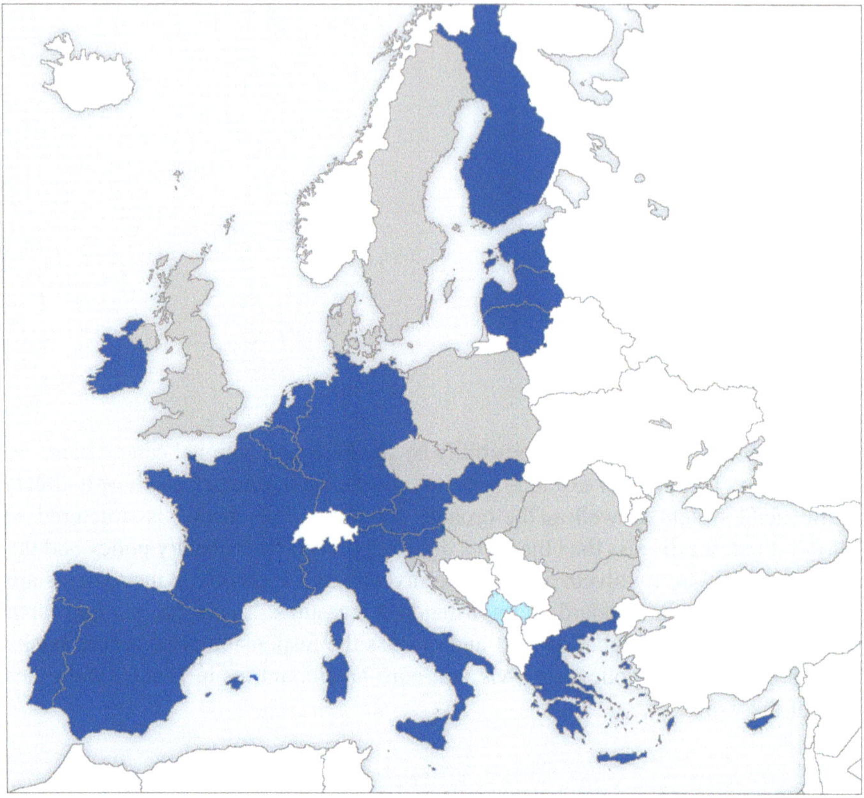

Fig. 2.1 Map of the euro area. Source: Author's representation. Legend: Dark blue (euro area member states), gray (EU member states outside the euro area)

assigned on a rotating basis. Monetary policy meetings of the Governing Council usually take place every 6 weeks.

The ECB is granted full independence in its decisions on monetary policy. Its independence is anchored in Article 130 of the Treaty and considered a cornerstone of a prudent and time-consistent monetary policy. Independence implies that neither the ECB nor the NCBs shall seek or take instructions from governments, banks, EU institutions, or other bodies in its actions. The provision is intended to minimize political involvement in monetary policy and therefore prevent it from being driven by electoral cycles or other political considerations, such as financing the budgets of member states. To foster the independence of the ECB, the members of the Executive Board have long terms of 8 years, without the possibility of being reappointed. The ECB is also financially independent and strictly prohibited from granting loans or other financing to governments and other public authorities in the euro area (prohibition of monetary financing, Article 123).

The mandate of the Eurosystem sets price stability as its primary objective. The mandate is spelled out in the Treaty on the European Union.[1] Article 127 of the Treaty states that

> the primary objective (...) shall be to maintain price stability. Without prejudice to the objective of price stability the ESCB shall support the general economic policies in the Community with a view to contributing to the objectives of the Community.

The objectives of the Community are laid down in Article 3 and include among others "*balanced economic growth*" and "*aiming at full employment.*" This part of the mandate implies that in situations where price stability is maintained but the economy experiences a strong downturn, the ECB needs to contribute to the policy objective of output stabilization, for instance by pursuing accommodative monetary policy to counteract the economic slowdown.

Why has price stability been assigned as the primary objective of the Eurosystem? To answer this question, let us get back to our example of Marie. Imagine that Marie lives in an economy in which the average inflation rate is not 1% but 10%. What would be the effect of such high inflation on Marie's situation?

- First of all, Marie's salary would be unlikely to grow at a similar rate of 10% per year. In other words, the prices of the goods and services she consumes will rise faster than her salary. Over time she will be worse off as her real income decreases. In economic terms, we can say that salaries and wages are less flexible than prices. Inflation of 10% thus implies a greater loss in Marie's purchasing power than inflation of 1%.
- With high inflation, it is difficult for Marie to distinguish between changes in the overall price level and changes of prices of individual goods and services. For instance, with average inflation of 10%, it is difficult to assess whether having dinner in a restaurant has become relatively more expensive compared to the price of other goods. Low and stable inflation, on the contrary, supports such comparisons, which is particularly important for businesses. At the system-wide level, there is evidence that price stability supports the productive use of financial resources in the economy.
- The mortgage loan that Marie took out to purchase her apartment would likely be more expensive in an environment of high inflation. This is due to the fact that long-term interest rates include an inflation risk premium to compensate holders of debt instruments for the loss in purchasing power associated with inflation. By containing inflation, central banks limit inflation risk premiums and contribute to low nominal interest rates.
- If Marie sells her apartment after some time, she would likely face a higher tax burden in an economy with average inflation of 10% compared to 1%. This is due

[1]The mandate refers to the ESCB, the European System of Central Banks, which includes all central banks of EU member states. This reference was included in the Treaty under the presumption that all EU member states would eventually join the monetary union.

to the fact that tax systems are typically not indexed to inflation. Higher inflation increases the real burden on taxpayers in case of high inflation. In the specific example, Marie may have to pay taxes on the capital gain, i.e., the difference between the sale price and the purchase price of her apartment. Capital gains are likely to be higher in a high-inflation environment, as 1 euro in a few years has a much lower purchasing power than 1 euro today. This creates a tax burden on Marie in real terms, which could be minimized in an environment of low inflation.

- Imagine that Marie's neighbors are a successful lawyer and a retired lady who lives on a small pension and lifetime savings. High inflation impacts the three of them in quite different ways. Wealthy individuals, such as the lawyer, have more leeway in protecting their assets from high inflation. For instance, they are able to re-allocate their investment portfolios by buying real estate or shares. These investments tend to provide protection against inflation. By contrast, poor individuals are hit more severely, as they need to consume a larger part of their income despite the higher price level. In addition, they typically hold their savings in rather liquid products, such as savings accounts, which offer little protection against inflation. Elderly people, such as the retired lady, also tend to be hit more by high inflation than young people. This is due to the fact that they are much less likely to work but rely on their savings, which tend to be rather liquid, in order to support their daily expenses.[2,3] In short, maintaining price stability avoids the described social consequences of high inflation, which would be more severe for the retired lady than for the successful lawyer in our example.
- Lastly, maintaining price stability is also related to preserving the function of money. Money is ultimately a social convention that relies on public trust. The central bank is the monopoly issuer of cash and CBM and promises that money will broadly maintain its function as a store of value over time. Persistent high inflation would undermine the credibility of this promise. Hence, it is important for central banks to broadly preserve the purchasing power of money.

The Eurosystem applies a quantitative definition of price stability with a medium-term orientation. The Governing Council interprets price stability as the objective to "*maintain the euro area inflation rate at levels below, but close to 2% over the medium term*" (ECB Press Release 8 May 2003).[4] This definition provides a clear yardstick to which the European citizens can hold the ECB accountable. Let us take a closer look at the elements of this quantitative definition of price stability:

- The *euro area inflation rate* is specified as the year-on-year increase in the Harmonized Index of Consumer Prices (HICP) for the euro area. Eurostat, the

---

[2]This was for instance the case in Germany in the early 1920s.

[3]Elderly people with significant wealth are for the reasons described less affected by high inflation, unless inflation gets out of control.

[4]Previously, the ECB had defined price stability as euro area inflation "below 2%" (ECB Press Release 13 October 1998), i.e., without the addition "close to" 2%.

statistical agency of the European Union, publishes this measure on a monthly basis for individual countries and the euro area as a whole. The HICP index is based on a representative basket of consumer goods and services in each member state, which is adjusted from time to time to reflect changes in consumer behavior. The objective of HICP is to measure the average level of consumer prices (i.e., not asset prices and not changes of relative prices either). Due to differences in consumption behavior, the composition of the representative baskets of consumer goods varies across the euro area, yet the computation method is harmonized. Eurostat also provides details on the main drivers of price level changes (e.g., increased food prices or falling energy prices) when publishing HICP data.

- The target level of *below, but close to 2%* raises the question why this level was chosen. Several arguments underpin this policy decision: Firstly, a higher target level would cause the undesired effects of high inflation that we just described. Secondly, a lower target level may risk inflation to become negative, which many economists believe to pose risks to economic activity and/or constrain the central bank's ability to influence the price level. Thirdly, the target rate refers to inflation in the euro area as whole, i.e., the weighted average inflation rate of all euro area member states. Inflation will always be higher than the average in some parts of the euro area and lower in others. Hence, a lower target rate than close to 2% may raise the likelihood of persistent deflation in some countries. Lastly, a target level is better suited than a target range (e.g., 1–3%) to anchor public expectations about future inflation rates. How well the anchoring of inflation expectations works in practice depends on the credibility of monetary policy to achieve the target level in the medium term.
- The *medium-term orientation* allows the ECB to let inflation fluctuate in the short term. Short-term changes in the price level may for instance be caused by a sudden change in energy prices. Such price changes are practically impossible to avoid in a market-based economy. In the medium term, the ECB is, however, committed to return inflation to its target level through appropriate policy action. This aspect of the price stability definition contributes to a steady hand in monetary policy decisions.

Price stability according to the quantitative ECB definition has been reached in the early years of the euro area. Figure 2.2 shows the year-on-year changes in HICP inflation as well as a market-based indicator of inflation expectations for the euro area. We can identify three main phases from 1999 to 2016:

- From 1999 to 2008, euro area inflation averaged around 2%, roughly in line with the policy objective of "below, but close to 2%," before becoming more volatile thereafter. This first phase is commonly referred to as the 'Great Moderation', which started in the early 1990s and was characterized by low inflation in many advanced economies. A relatively stable level of consumer prices during this phase was the result of many factors, including more global competition, increased world trade, and strong economic growth in emerging markets. The Great Moderation ended with the eruption of the global financial crisis in 2008.

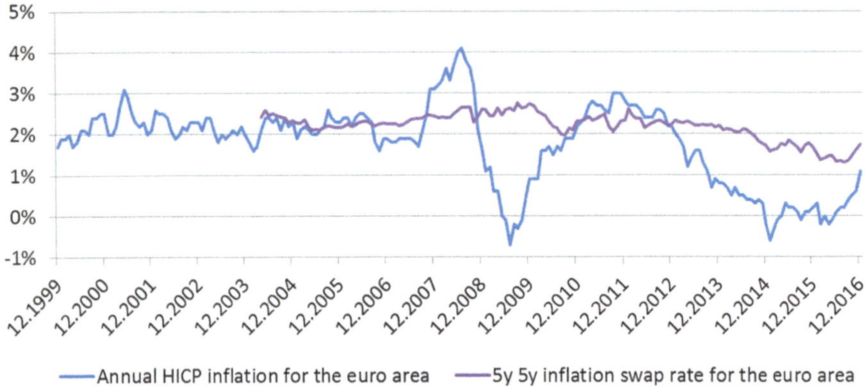

Fig. 2.2 Euro area inflation and inflation expectations 1999–2016. Source: ECB (2017b)

- From 2008 to 2013, inflation showed increased volatility, yet inflation expectations remained firmly anchored at close to 2% (see Fig. 2.2). Inflation in the euro area increased in 2008, driven by a jump in commodity prices, fell sharply in the 'Great Recession' of 2009, and again exceeded the target level of the ECB in 2011 and 2012. Nevertheless, inflation expectations remained at a similar level as in the pre-crisis period. Inflation expectations by market participants can be derived from surveys, derivatives, or fixed-income instruments.[5]
- From late 2013 to the time of writing (early 2017), both the inflation rate and inflation expectations declined significantly. Lower inflation was mainly the result of a sharp decline in commodity prices, low economic growth in the euro area, and a slowdown in some key emerging markets. This development prompted the Governing Council to introduce the Extended Asset Purchase Program in early 2015. We will get back to this program, which is colloquially known as quantitative easing, later in this chapter.

The ECB cannot influence the price level directly but needs to rely on the transmission of its policy decisions to the economy. The euro area is a market-based economy and as such prices are largely set by private businesses. Hence, there is a discrepancy between the ECB's monetary policy instruments and its final objective of price stability. They are only indirectly connected through the so-called transmission mechanism of monetary policy. The transmission mechanism is a web of interactions with various economic variables, such as the money and credit supply, investment, output, and the exchange rate. As illustrated in Fig. 2.3, its starts with

[5]Inflation expectations can be derived from surveys (e.g., the quarterly ECB survey of professional forecasters), inflation swaps (i.e., derivatives that swap inflation against a fixed interest rate), or by comparing the yield of an inflation-indexed bond to the yield of a nominal bond by the same issuer.

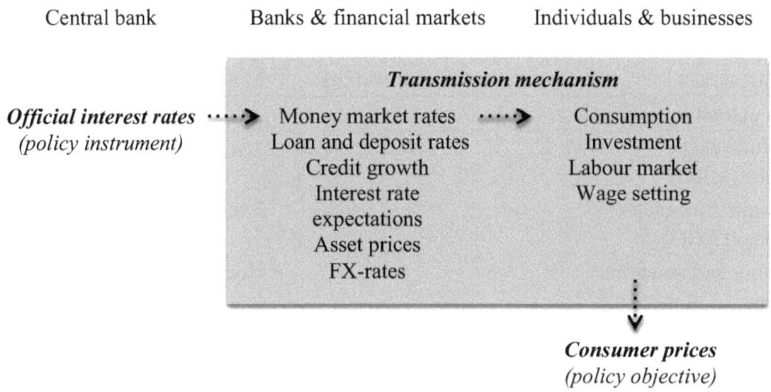

Fig. 2.3 Monetary policy transmission mechanism

official interest rates as the main instrument and ends at changes of consumer prices as the ultimate objective. The monetary policy stance is first transmitted to banks and financial markets, influencing money market rates, loan and deposit rates, asset prices, etc. With some time lag, they also lead to changes of other economic indicators, such as consumption and investment, and eventually have a bearing on consumer prices. Transmission also works through the FX-rate, which affects the prices of imported goods. Empirical studies show that the overall transmission of official interest rate changes into price level changes takes approximately 1–2 years. This finding implies that monetary policy decisions need be forward-looking and preemptive. It also provides an additional argument why a focus on short-term inflation developments would not be adequate for conducting monetary policy.

Monetary policy decisions of the Governing Council are published in a press release on the day of the respective meetings. The press release is followed by a press conference with the ECB President, who provides explanations for the decisions and responds to questions by journalists. On 9 March 2017, for instance, the Governing Council decided in its monetary policy meeting that "the interest rate on the main refinancing operations and the interest rates on the marginal lending facility and the deposit facility will remain unchanged at 0.00%, 0.25% and −0.40% respectively." In the following section, we will explain these three official interest rates and the underlying central bank operations.

2.2 Policy Instruments

Standard Monetary Policy Instruments

In order to achieve its primary objective, the Eurosystem uses a set of monetary policy instruments and procedures. This set forms the operational framework to implement the single monetary policy. The regular instruments used by the Eurosystem in the implementation of monetary policy, which are referred to as

Table 2.1 Standard monetary policy instruments

Policy instrument	Liquidity providing	Liquidity absorbing	Maturity	Frequency
1. Open market operations				
Main refinancing operations (MRO)	√		1 week	Weekly
Long-term refinancing operations (LTRO)	√		3 months	Monthly
Fine-tuning and structural operations	√	√	Non-standardized	
2. Standing facilities				
Marginal lending facility	√		Overnight	At the discretion of counterparties
Deposit facility		√	Overnight	
3. Minimum reserve requirements				

standard monetary policy instruments in this textbook, fall into three categories (see Table 2.1)[6]:

1. **Open market operations**,[7]
2. **Standing facilities**, and
3. **Minimum reserve requirements**.

Central banks supply to the banking system the amount of liquidity consistent with a desired level of short-term interest rates. This is achieved through open market operations and requires analysis and forecasting of the liquidity situation of banks located in the euro area. The central bank can conduct both liquidity-providing and liquidity-absorbing transactions with commercial banks. In liquidity-providing operations, the central bank provides CBM to the banking system, while in liquidity-absorbing operations the level of CBM in the banking sector is reduced (see Fig. 2.4).

Open-market operations include the following instruments:

- *Main refinancing operations (MRO):* These operations are performed weekly, with a maturity of 1 week. They can be conducted as a so-called fixed-rate tender or as a variable-rate tender.[8] The applicable interest rate is the main refinancing

[6]The ECB guideline on the implementation of the Eurosystem monetary policy framework (so-called general documentation) is available at https://www.ecb.europa.eu/ecb/legal/1002/1014/html/index-tabs.en.html

[7]All references to open market operations in this textbook refer to standard monetary policy operations and exclude outright asset purchases, which are considered nonstandard measures and discussed separately.

[8]A fixed rate tender with full allotment is executed in the following manner: In the first step, banks submit bids regarding the amount of CBM they would like to obtain, provided they have sufficient collateral. In the second step, central banks allocate CBM based on the received bids. Banks need to

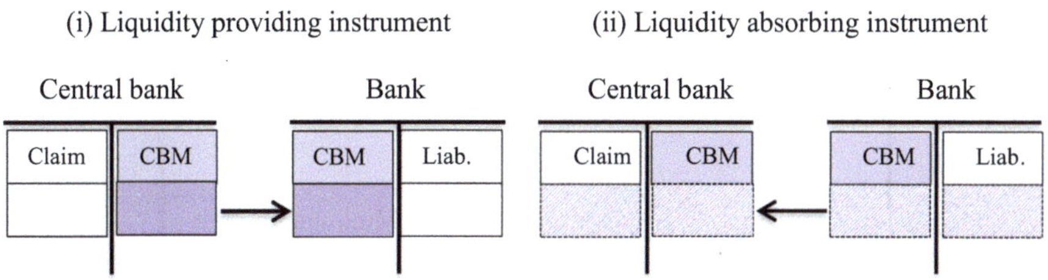

Fig. 2.4 Central bank liquidity provision

rate, which is also known as the policy rate of the ECB. MROs serve to steer short-term interest rates, to manage the liquidity situation, and to signal the monetary policy stance in the euro area.

- *Long-term refinancing operations (LTROs):* These operations are performed monthly, with a maturity of 3 months. LTROs are normally executed via variable rate procedure. LTROs provide additional, longer-term refinancing to the banking sector.
- *Fine-tuning operations* and *structural operations*: These transactions are not performed on a regular basis.

Two standing facilities are available to banks:

- The first is the *marginal lending facility*, which provides liquidity overnight, i.e., until the next business day.
- The second is the *deposit facility*, which absorbs liquidity overnight.

The interest rate charged by the ECB for using the marginal lending facility is always higher than the main refinancing rate, while the interest rate paid on the deposit facility is always lower. The rationale is that the central bank as the monopoly supplier of CBM charges a higher interest rate for providing CBM than for accepting it. The higher interest rate that is charged for using the marginal lending facility provides an incentive to banks to primarily use MROs and LTROs for their regular liquidity needs.

All banks that are counterparties of the Eurosystem need to comply with its reserve requirement. This means that they are obliged to hold a minimum amount of CBM on their account at the central bank. Since January 2012, the reserve requirement stands at 1% of the reserve base (reduced from 2% that was effective since January 1999).[9] The reserve base is essentially a specified part of the liability

pay a fixed rate (i.e., the main refinancing rate at the time of the operation) as interest to the Eurosystem. Full allotment means that all bids are fully satisfied, i.e., all banks that participate in the tender receive the CBM liquidity they have requested, as long as they have sufficient collateral. ECB tenders are usually completed within 24 h from their announcement.

[9]The reserve requirement is calculated as the reserve base times the reserve requirement, less a lump-sum allowance per bank.

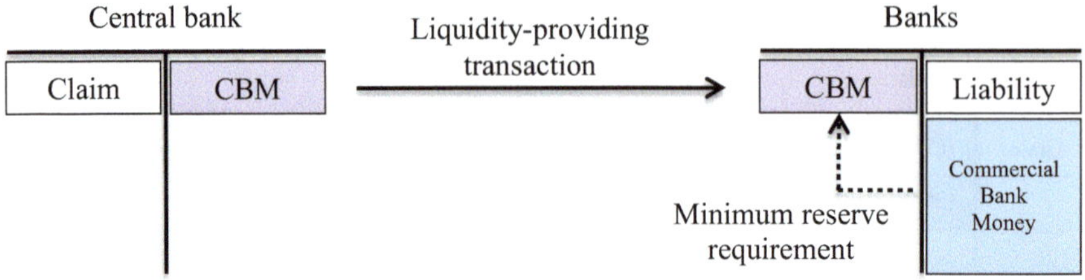

Fig. 2.5 Standard monetary policy operations

side of banks' balance sheet and includes commercial bank money and some other deposits and issued securities. Figure 2.5 provides a stylized illustration: Banks need to a hold a certain amount of CBM, which they may have received through a liquidity-providing transaction by the central bank, on their account at the central bank.

The minimum reserve needs to be maintained in the form of CBM, i.e., on the bank's account at the central bank. Compliance with the reserve requirement is calculated on the basis of a 6-week average for each bank, with remuneration of minimum reserves at the main refinancing rate. If a bank does not meet the reserve requirement, it has to pay a penalty.[10]

Alternative Reserve Requirements

The current reserve requirement is an example of fractional reserve banking at a rather low level. The term indicates that banks only need to hold a fraction of issued commercial bank money (in a broad sense) in the form of CBM. Alternative setups that have been investigated or applied elsewhere have chosen different reserve requirements. At the lowest level, the reserve requirement is zero, i.e., the demand for CBM is minimized. At the highest level, the reserve requirement is 100%. In this constellation, all commercial bank money that is created by private banks needs to be fully deposited at the central bank. This policy option, which is known as full reserve banking, was advocated in the Chicago Plan in the 1930s. As no country has ever applied the system, we have no historical experience about its functioning in practice.

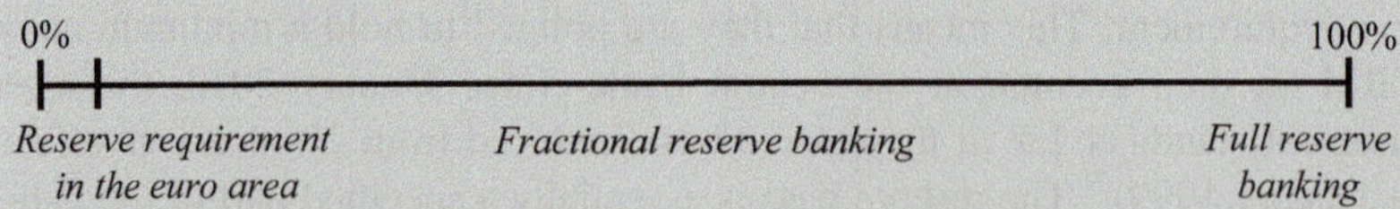

The reserve requirement can also be differentiated by type, maturity, and currency of commercial bank money and other liabilities. For instance, central

(continued)

[10]The penalty is the reserve shortfall times the rate of the marginal lending facility plus 2.5%.

banks may set different reserve requirements by type and maturity of commercial bank money (in a broad sense), other customer deposits, issued securities, or other liabilities. Many central banks in emerging markets with high degrees of deposit dollarization or euroization also differentiate reserve requirements by currency (e.g., setting a higher requirement for foreign-currency deposits in order to provide an incentive to keep deposits in local currency).

Some central banks use reserve requirements as the main instrument to perform monetary policy and thus change them frequently. The most prominent example for such use of reserve requirements is the People's Bank of China. Lowering reserve requirements allows it to provide additional liquidity to the banking system, while leaving policy rates unchanged. For instance, in April 2015, it reduced the reserve requirement ratio from 19.5% to 18.5%, while the main policy rate remained at 5.35%.

The three official interest rates set by the ECB create an interest rate corridor that plays a crucial role in the money market. The upper and lower bounds of the corridor are defined by the interest rates on the marginal lending facility and deposit facility, while the main refinancing rate is always inside the corridor. Figure 2.6 illustrates the development of the interest rate corridor for the period 2004–2015. The figure also shows the development of a key short-term interest rate of the money market in the euro area, known as EONIA (Euro Overnight Index Average, see discussion in Chap. 1). EONIA is the weighted average rate at which major banks in the euro area lend to other "prime banks" overnight. As the figure indicates, EONIA was at all times within the interest rate corridor set by the ECB and until late 2008 close to the main refinancing rate. EONIA always exceeds the ECB deposit rate, given that banks would have no incentive to lend to another bank overnight at a lower rate than what they would receive when holding the funds at the central bank. From the perspective of monetary policy, it is worth noting that the average rate at which banks exchange short-term liquidity in the money market is evidently influenced by the three official interest rates set by the ECB. This is the first step of the previously mentioned monetary policy transmission mechanism.

Figure 2.6 also illustrates the accommodative monetary policy stance by the ECB from late 2008 to date. The main refinancing rate was reduced from 4.25% in September 2008 to 1% in early 2009 and further to reach 0% in 2016. EONIA hovered around 0% since 2012. In addition, the interest rate corridor was narrowed from ±1% as of September 2008 to +0.25%/−0.40% as of end-2016. The figure also shows that the rate of the deposit facility turned negative in 2014. Overall, the development of official interest rates reflects the accommodative monetary policy stance that the ECB pursued ever since late 2008.

Let us now turn to the specifics of the stated credit operations between banks and the central bank. These transactions take the form of central bank repos (repurchase operations), which are essentially a type of secured loan between the central bank

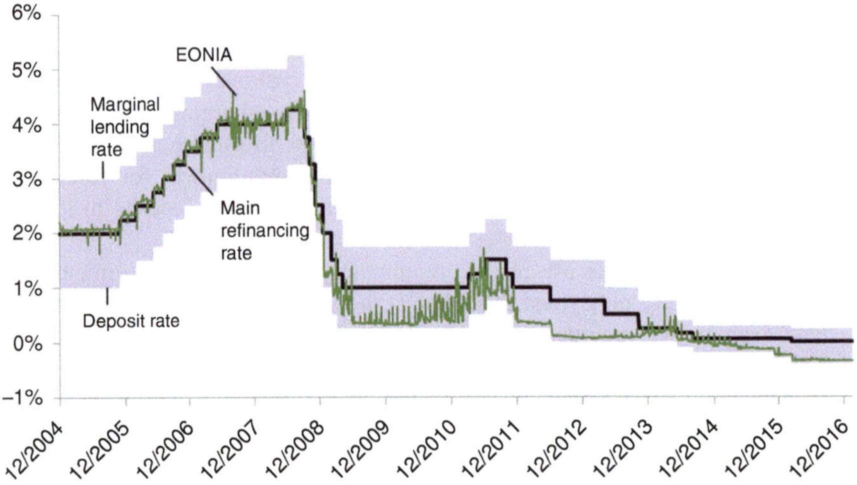

Fig. 2.6 Interest rate corridor. Source: ECB (2017b)

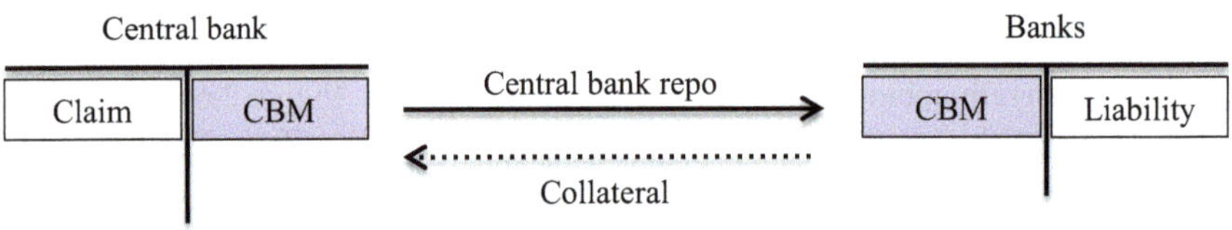

Fig. 2.7 Central bank repo

and a commercial bank. As illustrated in Fig. 2.7, the central bank provides liquidity in CBM to the respective bank, while the bank pledges certain assets as collateral. On the bank balance sheet, the transaction creates an asset (new CBM holding) and a corresponding liability (vis-à-vis the central bank). In case the bank cannot repay the central bank upon maturity of the repo (e.g., after 1 week for main refinancing operations), the central bank can liquidate the collateral and thus be compensated through this avenue. In the standard case in which the bank can repay the central bank, the collateral pledge is lifted and CBM is repaid to the central bank, i.e., the corresponding CBM leaves the system. In the following, we will briefly describe the eligibility requirements for banks and collateral for these operations.

A bank has to meet four criteria to be an eligible counterparty for monetary policy operations: First, it must be subject to the Eurosystem's minimum reserve requirement. Second, the bank has to be financially sound. At the minimum, financial soundness requires the bank to comply with the regulatory capital requirements that we will discuss in Chap. 4. Third, the bank must be subject to at least one form of harmonized Union/EEA supervision by competent authorities or a standard comparable to supervision by competent authorities. Fourth, the bank must fulfill certain operational requirements. Overall, about 1700 banks were recorded as eligible counterparties in the Eurosystem as of end-2013. However, only a smaller part acted as regular bidders in MROs.[11]

The Eurosystem applies the principle that all credit operations need to be based on adequate collateral. Adequate collateral means that the central bank is protected against losses from its operations. To achieve this objective, the Eurosystem applies several rules:

- *The Eurosystem only accepts collateral that meets certain criteria that are set by the Governing Council.*[12] For instance, marketable assets must be denominated in euro[13] and have a credit rating of at least BBB−.[14] Marketable assets that are eligible as collateral are specified on the ECB website.
- *Haircuts are applied on the pledged assets to take their riskiness into account.* For instance, for the same maturity, a low-rated corporate bond receives a higher haircut than a German government bond. A bank has to post more of the former as collateral in order to obtain an equal amount of CBM.
- *Furthermore, the Eurosystem performs frequent revaluations of the pledged collateral.* Should its market price experience a strong decline, it will request additional collateral.[15]

The composition of collateral mobilized by counterparties witnessed significant changes during the crisis. As illustrated in Fig. 2.8, the collateral pledged by banks for monetary policy operations includes a broad range of fixed-income instruments (government bonds, corporate bonds, covered bonds, asset-backed securities, etc.), and nonmarketable assets (mostly loans). The figure also shows the change in the collateral pool during the crisis years, with a notable increase in the use of nonmarketable assets from 2008 to 2012.[16]

Credit operations are performed by national central banks in the euro area. The ECB delegates this task to the individual NCBs, which implement the operations for banks in their respective jurisdictions. For instance, a German bank will obtain CBM

[11]ECB Annual Report 2013, p. 87.

[12]The respective legal documentation is available on the ECB website (so-called General Framework and Temporary Framework).

[13]Denominated in euro or in the former currency of a euro area member state.

[14]The Eurosystem applies a harmonized rating scale of so-called credit quality steps. The minimum rating requirement is credit quality step 3, which is equivalent to external credit ratings of BBB+ to BBB−.

[15]Counterparties in Eurosystem operations usually hold more collateral than needed for refinancing operations. Margin calls would only occur in case of under collateralization. Furthermore, they would not only depend on the market price but also on the credit quality.

[16]Collateral predominately takes the form of fixed income instruments, as shown in figure. These instruments can be issued by central governments, regional governments, banks, corporates, or special-purposes vehicles (as in the case of asset-backed securities). They are typically marketable, which means that they can be sold on a market. In addition to marketable securities, the Eurosystem also accepts other assets, such as credit claims, that are nonmarketable but fulfil certain criteria, for instance as regards their credit risk.

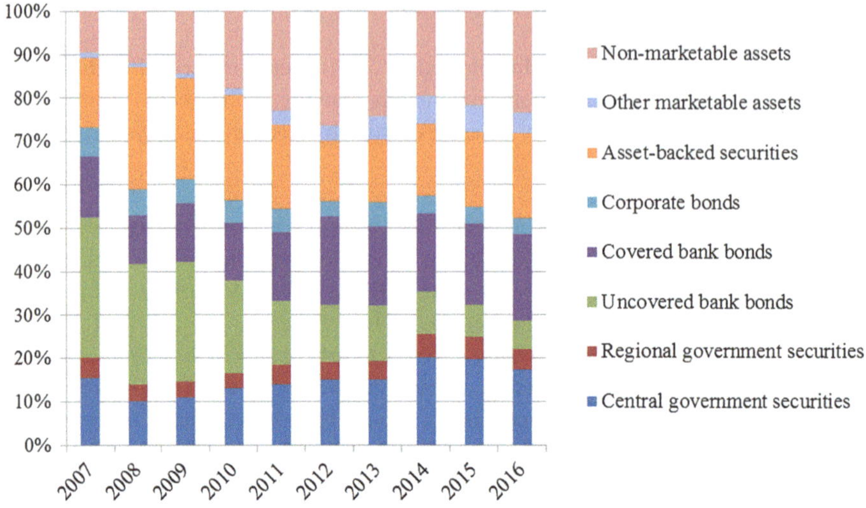

Fig. 2.8 Composition of used collateral. Source: ECB (2017c)

liquidity through operations with the Bundesbank and a Portuguese bank will obtain CBM liquidity from the Bank of Portugal. This decentralization of monetary policy operations does not have major consequences for participating banks,[17] as the Eurosystem treats all euro area banks that qualify as eligible counterparties equally, irrespective of their size or location.

The use of monetary policy instruments is shown in the Eurosystem balance sheet. An extract of the balance sheet is presented in Fig. 2.9, which shows the volume of liquidity-providing and liquidity-absorbing operations over time (see Annex E for a simplified presentation of the overall Eurosystem balance sheet).

- *Above the line, the figure indicates liquidity-providing operations through MROs, LTROs, the marginal lending facility, and other operations.* Their aggregate volume increased during the crisis. In addition, the figure shows nonstandard measures such as 3-year LTROs and asset purchases from 2009 to 2016. We will discuss these nonstandard measures in the next section.
- *Below the line, the figure shows liquidity-absorbing transactions, including the use of the deposit facility.* The deposit facility was little used before the financial crisis and became heavily employed ever since 2008, in particular during the second half of 2011 and 2012. The increased use of the deposit facility reflects strains in the interbank market, as market participants would distribute liquidity surpluses across the system in normal times. We will get back to these crisis developments in subsequent chapters.

[17]The discussion does not take risk-sharing arrangements within the Eurosystem into account. Due to their complexity, they have to remain outside the scope of this introductory textbook.

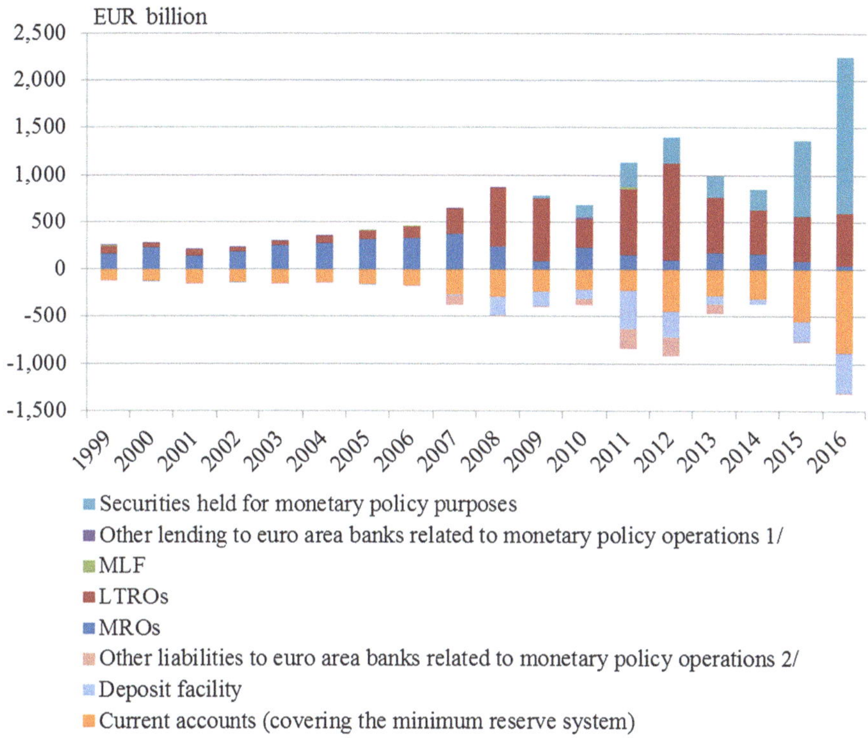

Fig. 2.9 Eurosystem balance sheet: Liquidity-providing and liquidity-absorbing operations. Source: ECB (2017g). Note: 1/ Includes fine-tuning reverse operations, structural reverse operations, and credit related to margin calls. 2/ Includes fine-tuning reverse operations, fixed-term deposits, and deposits related to margin calls

Nonstandard Monetary Policy Measures

Nonstandard monetary policy operations have been applied extensively ever since 2007, when the, European banking sector entered into crisis mode. The crisis led to an impairment of the monetary policy transmission mechanism (see Fig. 2.3) and limited the room for further loosening, given that the policy rates were reaching the so-called zero lower bound (see Fig. 2.6). Nonstandard measures were meant to complement the reductions in the policy rate in the presence of these conditions.[18] Figure 2.10 provides an overview of the main standard and nonstandard policy instruments in the euro area.

The Eurosystem started to use nonstandard measures from the onset of the global financial crisis. The collapse of Lehman Brothers in September 2008 triggered a bold

[18]Some publications refer to nonstandard measures by other terms such as "non-regular monetary policy operations."

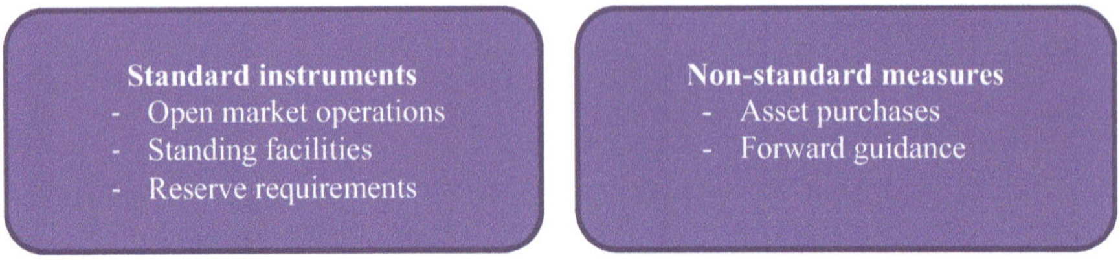

Fig. 2.10 Key instruments for monetary policy implementation

monetary policy response by central banks in major advanced economies, including the ECB. In addition to the standard monetary policy measures described above (i.e., lower official interest rates, more CBM liquidity provided), the response included measures that had not been applied previously, including various asset purchase programs. In the following, we present these measures in the order of their first application, from the onset of the global financial crisis in 2007 up to early 2017.

- *LTROs with higher maturities* than in the regular 3-month LTROs were applied from August 2007 onwards. LTROs with a maturity of 6 months, 1 year, and 3 years were offered to banks at several points during the crisis years. As shown in Fig. 2.9, they were very sizeable operations, in particular the 3-year LTROs that were launched in end-2011 and early-2012, totaling about 1 trillion euros.
- *Fixed-rate full allotment* was introduced in October 2008. Previously, the ECB applied the variable-rate tender procedure.[19] The move towards fixed-rate full allotment in October 2008 facilitated credit operations during the global financial crisis by providing CBM to all eligible counterparties with sufficient collateral.
- The *definition of eligible collateral* was significantly extended since October 2008. With the background of stressed financial markets and strained liquidity positions by many euro area banks, the ECB started to accept lower-quality assets as collateral with appropriate haircuts. This gradual extension of the single collateral list is also reflected in the development of the collateral composition (see Fig. 2.8), including the increased share of nonmarketable assets.
- *FX liquidity facilities in USD and CHF* were offered to euro area banks from 2008 to 2012, in particular at times of significant market turmoil. They were designed to provide USD and CHF liquidity to banks via the Eurosystem instead of other participants in the FX markets, which would be the banks' counterparties in normal times. The reason for taking this policy measure was the lack of trust within the banking system and the associated funding challenges.

[19]Under the variable-rate tender, the Eurosystem first announced a minimum bid rate. Banks then submitted bids for a desired amount of CBM and the interest rate they were willing to pay. Submitting multiple bids for various amounts was also possible. Upon receiving the bids, the Eurosystem allotted a predefined amount of CBM, starting with the banks with the highest bids and applying their respective interest rates. This feature implied that some banks did not receive the full amount of CBM they had submitted its bids for.

- The *Covered Bond Purchase Program* was announced in May 2009 as the first asset purchase program by the Eurosystem.[20] Under this program, the Eurosystem could purchase euro-denominated covered bonds from euro area banks. Three covered bond purchase programs were put in place so far. In October 2014, the Eurosystem started to buy covered bonds under a third covered bond purchase program (CBPP3). This program is still in place as of early 2017 as a part of the Extended Asset Purchase Program (EAPP).
- The *Securities Markets Program (SMP)* was introduced in May 2010 at the time when the first Greek Program was signed. It allowed the Eurosystem to purchase government bonds and other securities of crisis countries to "ensure depth and liquidity in those market segments which are dysfunctional" (ECB Press Release 10 May 2010). Following the decision to initiate the Outright Monetary Transactions (OMT) program (see next bullet point), the SMP was terminated. The existing securities in the SMP portfolio will be held to maturity. At its peak, the SMP portfolio amounted to 210 billion euros. To prevent an impact of the purchases on total CBM liquidity in the banking system, the Eurosystem sterilized the SMP-related funds that were provided to banks by performing weekly liquidity-absorbing operations. These operations were discontinued in June 2014.
- The *Outright Monetary Transactions (OMT) program* was announced in August 2012.[21] It allows the Eurosystem to purchase government bonds of euro area crisis countries under an EFSF/ESM Program as long as the country is fully compliant with its conditionality. Purchases under OMT are also sterilized by liquidity-absorbing operations. Importantly, the OMT program has not been applied in practice yet. Its announcement in the summer of 2012 was, however, an important factor to restore market confidence during the euro area sovereign debt crisis.
- *Forward guidance* was first applied by the Governing Council in July 2013. Unlike other nonstandard measures, this measure is nonfinancial and aimed at influencing market expectations of the future path of short-term interest rates. Following the Governing Council meeting of July 2013, the ECB communicated that it expected key ECB interest rates to remain at present or lower levels for an extended period of time. This expectation was based on an overall subdued outlook for inflation extending into the medium term.
- The ECB announced in October 2013 that the swap arrangements with the Federal Reserve, the Bank of Japan, the Bank of England, the Bank of Canada, and the Swiss National Bank are converted into *standing arrangements* until further notice.
- A *4-year Targeted LTRO (TLTRO)* was announced in June 2014. This instrument shares some similarities with other LTROs but has a maturity of 4 years and links the total amount provided to the banks' lending behavior. After an initial

[20]The purchases started in July 2009.

[21]Technical features of the OMT program were released in September 2012.

allotment of 4-year TLTROs, banks could only obtain more funds under this facility if they provided new loans in excess of certain benchmarks. In early 2016, the ECB announced that it would launch a new series of TLTROs from June 2016 onwards.

- The *ABS Purchase Program (ABSPP)* was launched in November 2014 and allows the Eurosystem to purchase asset-backed securities (ABS) from euro area banks. The ABSPP stimulates the issuance of new securities by banks, thereby allowing them to diversify their funding sources for both existing claims and new lending. It is still in use as of early 2017, in the meanwhile as a pillar of the EAPP.
- The most widely noted nonstandard measure was the ECB's launch of the *Expanded Asset Purchase Program (EAPP)* in January 2015. Some observers have referred to this measure as quantitative easing. Given its relevance from a monetary policy perspective, we discuss its objective and functioning in some detail in Box 2.1.

Box 2.1 Extended Asset Purchase Program (EAPP)

Upon its announcement, the EAPP consisted of monthly asset purchases by the Eurosystem of 60 billion euros "*until at least September 2016 and in any case until the Governing Council sees a sustained adjustment in the path of inflation that is consistent with its aim of achieving inflation rates below, but close to, 2% over the medium term*" (ECB Press Release 22 January 2015). In 2016 and 2017, the Governing Council decided to adjust the pace of monthly asset purchases and the timeline of the program in the following main steps:

- In March 2016, the target volume of monthly asset purchases was revised upward to 80 billion euros, while the timeline was extended to at least March 2017.
- In December 2016, the target volume of monthly asset purchases was reduced to 60 billion euros from April 2017 onwards. The timeline was extended until at least end-2017.
- In October 2017, the Governing Council decided to continue net asset purchases at a monthly pace of 30 billion euros from January to September 2018, "*or beyond, if necessary, and in any case until the Governing Council sees a sustained adjustment in the path of inflation consistent with its inflation aim.*" (ECB Press Release 26 October 2017)

The main objective of EAPP is to raise the euro area inflation rate back to its target level of below, but close to 2% (see Fig. 2.2). Asset purchases increase the volume of CBM in the system and are intended to reduce long-term interest rates, which should stimulate lending conditions, economic activity, and consumer prices.

(continued)

Box 2.1 (continued)

The EAPP covers purchases under four programs:

- The *Covered Bond Purchase Program (CBPP3)*, using the program discussed above
- The *ABS Purchase Program (ABSPP)*, using the program discussed
- The *Public Sector Purchase Program (PSPP)*, which was started in March 2015 and constituted a step-change in asset purchases by the Eurosystem
- The *Corporate Sector Purchase Program (CSPP)*, which was announced in March 2016

The PSPP allows purchases of government bonds and other public sector securities in the secondary market. The Eurosystem does not conduct purchases in the primary market, regardless of the type of security. This was decided by the Governing Council in view of the prohibition of monetary financing, which is anchored in Article 123 of the Treaty on the Functioning of the European Union. Before the PSPP announcement in January 2015, the Eurosystem refrained from purchases of public sector securities, unlike other central banks such as the US Federal Reserve, the Bank of Japan, or the Bank of England. In the following, we will explain the key characteristics of PSPP, starting with eligible counterparties and assets:

- *PSPP asset purchases are carried out jointly by the ECB and the NCBs.* 80% of the purchases are conducted by NCBs on their own account and risk, while 20% are risk shared within the Eurosystem. The capital share of NCBs in the ECB determines the volume of their respective purchases. Banque de France for instance buys much more assets under this program than the Central Bank of Malta. The limited risk-sharing mechanism, which deviates from the standard practice of full risk sharing in monetary policy operations, reflects the coexistence of 19 national fiscal policies in the euro area countries.
- *Sellers are eligible counterparties* for monetary policy operations and other counterparties that the NCBs trade with as part of their own investment activities in euro-denominated securities.
- *Eligible assets* are fixed income instruments issued by euro area central and regional governments, public sector agencies, international organizations, or multilateral development banks. The Eurosystem explained that it intended to allocate 90% of the total purchases to government bonds and recognized agencies and 10% to securities issued by international

(continued)

Box 2.1 (continued)

organizations and multilateral development banks.[22] The instruments must have an investment-grade rating and a remaining maturity between 2 and 30 years.[23] Additional eligibility criteria were defined for countries under EU/IMF Programs. Furthermore, limits apply to the total volume of securities purchased by specific instrument or issuer (both generally set at 33%).[24]

- To limit the impact of purchases of securities on market liquidity and collateral availability, the Eurosystem offers banks the *possibility to borrow the purchased securities for a certain period of time (securities lending).*

In March 2016, the ECB announced the Corporate Sector Purchase Program (CSPP) as the fourth program under the EAPP. It allows the Eurosystem to purchase corporate bonds by companies established in the euro area which need to be rated investment grade by at least one recognized rating agency.[25] First purchases under the CSPP started in June 2016.

The figure shows the evolution of EAPP holdings of the Eurosystem.

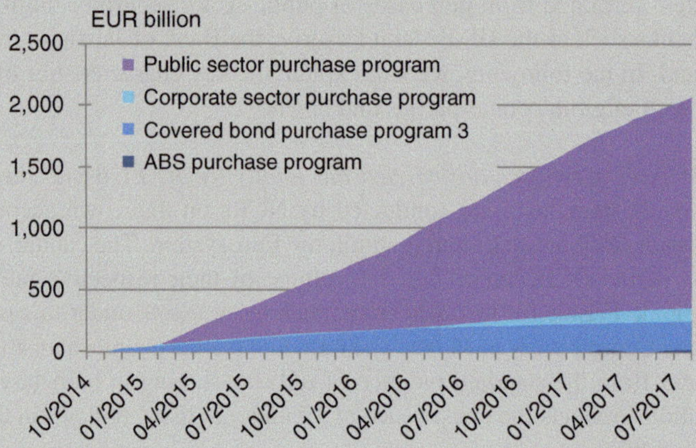

Source: ECB (2017d)

[22]From March 2015 until March 2016, these figures were 88% and 12%, respectively.

[23]A difference between PSPP and SMP lies in the fact that purchased government bonds under PSPP have the same rank as other senior creditors, while under SMP the Eurosystem has a preferred creditor status.

[24]The limit per instrument (the so-called issue share limit) for EU supranational bonds is 50% and 25% for those securities where the Eurosystem might otherwise have a blocking minority for the purposes of collective action clauses. The limit per issuer (the so-called issuer limit) for EU supranational issuers is 50%.

[25]The rating agency needs to be eligible under the Eurosystem's credit assessment framework.

Emergency Liquidity Assistance

The Eurosystem has an additional tool to provide CBM liquidity to banks outside of monetary policy operations, known as Emergency Liquidity Assistance (ELA). ELA is typically designed to address idiosyncratic liquidity shortages of individual credit institutions. We already mentioned it in Chap. 1 as part of the financial safety net that is available to the banking system. ELA transactions differ from monetary policy transactions in several key aspects:

- Firstly, ELA is intended to be solely used *for a limited period of time and for banks that are solvent but face temporary liquidity problems*. Such situations are likely to occur during crisis situations. The solvency of the bank needs to be assessed by the relevant supervisory authority (see Chap. 4).
- Secondly, central banks charge banks a *penalty rate* for obtaining ELA, i.e., an interest rate that exceeds the main refinancing rate.[26]
- Thirdly, the *collateral definition* is different from standard monetary policy operations. NCBs typically accept lower-quality assets as ELA collateral as well and counterbalance the lower quality by applying higher haircuts than those used for assets in the single collateral list.

ELA can be provided to banks by their respective NCB, yet the ECB Governing Council has the possibility to object. A key characteristic of ELA is that it is not considered part of the single monetary policy of the Eurosystem but a task that is performed by NCBs as a national task and thus on their own account. All risks and costs related to ELA are thus borne by the respective NCB. The process of granting ELA is as follows[27]:

- *A bank that faces a temporary liquidity problem provides an ELA request to its NCB.* Typically, the bank will apply for ELA if it has insufficient collateral for monetary policy operations or if it has lost its eligibility as counterparty for monetary policy operations (e.g., because of concerns regarding its financial soundness).
- *The NCB checks whether the criteria for granting ELA are fulfilled and the relevant supervisory authority assesses the bank's solvency.* If all the criteria are met, the NCB provides the relevant information (counterparty, amount, maturity, collateral, haircuts applied, etc.) to the ECB.
- *The Governing Council reviews the request by the NCB and, if the overall volume of the ELA envisaged exceeds 2 billion euros, may object to granting ELA with a two-third majority.* The Governing Council will for instance consider the overall size of granted ELA and its terms (which may create moral hazard by banks if

[26]For instance, Eurobank, a large Greek bank, indicated in an investor presentation of October 2015 that it paid an effective interest rate of 1.55% on ELA, while the ECB's main refinancing rate stood at 0.05% (https://www.eurobank.gr/Uploads/pdf/Eurobank_Presentation_October2015.pdf).

[27]The ELA procedure is described in the following document: https://www.ecb.europa.eu/pub/pdf/other/201402_elaprocedures.en.pdf?10cc0e926699a1984161dc21722ca841

they are too generous). In addition to new applications, the Governing Council also reviews the total ELA provided by the individual NCBs on a regular basis and may decide to object or not object to a ceiling for the total amount of ELA calibrated by the respective NCB.

- *If the Governing Council does not object, the NCB is allowed to provide the requested ELA to the bank.* Thereafter, the provided ELA and its collateral are closely monitored by the respective NCB and the ECB.

The Eurosystem only discloses limited information on the provided ELA. For most of the crisis years, no information was provided regarding the amounts involved or ceilings applied.[28] The disclosure policy changed in 2015, when the Governing Council decided to grant NCBs the option to communicate the ELA ceiling in their country, if they deemed such communication useful. A key factor that influences the disclosure policy by central banks on ELA lies in the sensitivity of information about ELA provided to individual banks, as demonstrated by the case of the UK-based bank Northern Rock in 2007. At that time, the bank faced liquidity problems and requested ELA from the Bank of England. The ELA request leaked to the media, which triggered a run by depositors on the bank. The Northern Rock case has become a common reference to illustrate the sensitivity of ELA-related information. It also served as a reminder that bank runs can still occur in advanced economies such as the UK.

Box 2.2 Why Do Banks Need Central Bank Money?

Suppose you are the liquidity manager of a medium-sized bank in the euro area. Why would you be interested in engaging in central bank operations to obtain central bank money (CBM), instead of meeting all funding needs through customer deposits or transactions with market participants (such as issuing bonds)? To answer the question, we need to take a closer look at the way banks manage their liquidity.

Banks need to manage their liquidity position on a daily basis in order to maintain a sufficient liquidity buffer to meet liquidity outflows (e.g., to repay an interbank loan or to meet customer cash needs). If a bank were unable to meet its liquidity outflows, it would become illiquid and fail, even though it may be solvent and profitable. To avoid this situation, the bank needs to hold a certain amount of liquid assets (in the broad sense) and money (in the narrow sense), which is the most liquid asset due to its function as a means of payment. Most banks hold all three types of money that we discussed in Chap. 1: (1) CBM (at the bank's account at the central bank), (2) commercial bank money (at accounts of other banks), and (3) cash (in vaults and ATMs). The three types of money are used for different purposes: Cash is held to meet

(continued)

[28]The balance sheet of a central bank also includes ELA transactions, though not in a single balance sheet item.

Box 2.2 (continued)
customer needs (such as cash withdrawals at ATMs). Banks also need to hold commercial bank money to pay taxes or salaries of their staff. Interbank payments can be made both in CBM and commercial bank money, as discussed in Chap. 1. This begs the question why banks need CBM at all.

There are several reasons why banks hold CBM in addition to commercial bank money and cash.

- *Banks need to fulfill the reserve requirements set by their central bank.* As discussed earlier, a part of their commercial bank money (and some other liabilities) needs to be held in the form of CBM at the central bank.
- *Banks use CBM to make interbank payments in euro.* Euro area banks primarily use TARGET2 to make payments among themselves in CBM. In principle such interbank payments could also be made in commercial bank money, as it is common practice by many third-tier banks in the euro area that are no counterparties with the Eurosystem. However, every interbank payment in EUR is ultimately reflected in a CBM payment at the central bank. Using commercial bank money just means using another (first- or second-tier) bank as intermediary to aggregate and settle payments.
- *CBM is an attractive funding source for banks, in particular for banks with limited market access.* For instance, many first- and second-tier banks in crisis countries have increased their reliance on central bank funding due to restricted market access, accommodative monetary policy, and recourse to ELA.
- *Most banks hold excess reserves above the reserve requirement for precautionary purposes.* If needed, the excess reserves can be quickly converted into other types of money, such as cash.

2.3 Policy Process

The monetary policy process in the euro area is illustrated in Fig. 2.11. It essentially has three phases: Economic and monetary analysis, policy decisions, and policy operations.

Economic and Monetary Analysis

The analysis of risks to price stability provides the basis for monetary policy decisions. It is conducted by the ECB and all NCBs of euro area countries on a regular basis. The members of the Governing Council are briefed about the findings and discuss them during monetary policy meetings of the Governing Council. To strengthen the cooperation among NCBs before the meetings and prepare joint policy recommendations, the ECB and NCBs have set up the **Monetary Policy**

Fig. 2.11 Monetary policy process in the euro area

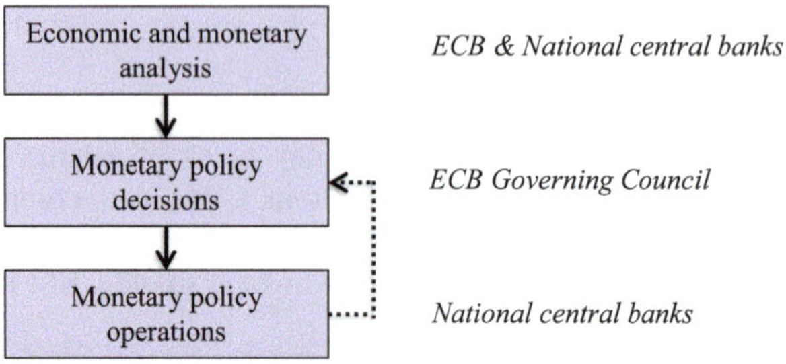

Committee (MPC) as a platform that includes senior officials responsible for monetary policy analysis. The MPC may for instance develop a nonstandard measure to address a part of the transmission mechanism that is not working properly.

The ECB follows a two-pillar approach in its analysis for monetary policy purposes. The two pillars are economic and monetary analysis.

- *Economic analysis* focuses on real economic variables. Recent data for the euro area and individual member states serve as the obvious starting point, e.g., on HICP inflation, the main drivers of inflation, GDP growth, consumption, unemployment, and other indicators. The analysis of observed developments would, however, not be sufficient for monetary policy, as policy measures only affect the price level with a time lag. The ECB, therefore, performs forecasts of the stated variables, which are published on a quarterly basis in the Economic Bulletin on the ECB website.[29] In addition to observed and forecasted indicators, economic analysis takes developments in other policy areas into consideration, in particular fiscal policy (e.g., impact of a VAT increase on inflation), as well as changes in the external environment (e.g., emerging market slowdown or falling commodity prices).
- *Monetary analysis* focuses on financial variables. Analysts for instance investigate the development of monetary aggregates (see Box 2.3), which many empirical studies show to be correlated with inflation in the long term. Monetary analysis further studies developments in the money market, in particular the short-term interest rates (EONIA, Euribor) as the first step of the transmission mechanism. As discussed above, the proper functioning of the money market is a precondition for conducting monetary policy. Furthermore, the analysis also covers the fixed-income market, in particular the structure of the yield curve and long-term interest rates, as well as bank credit (e.g., volume and terms of new bank lending) and other assets markets.

[29]ECB staff forecasts are included in the March and September issues of the Economic Bulletin, while the joint forecasts of the Eurosystem are presented in June and December. Other institutions such as the International Monetary Fund or the European Commission also publish forecasts for euro area countries in regular intervals.

Box 2.3 Monetary Aggregates in the Euro Area

Three monetary aggregates are used for monetary analysis. They refer to narrow (M1), intermediate (M2), and broad (M3) definitions of money. As M1 is included in M2 and M2 is included in M3, the three aggregates share a similarity with Russian matryoshka dolls that can be placed inside another. The figure shows the volumes of the three monetary aggregates M1, M2, and M3 in the euro area as of end-2016.

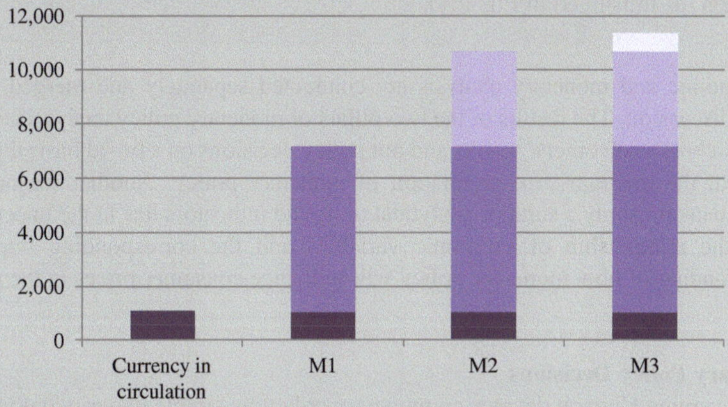

Source: ECB (2017e)

How do the three monetary aggregates relate to the three types of money in the euro area (cash, commercial bank money, and CBM)?

- *Cash* (sometimes referred to as currency in circulation) is the narrowest definition of money. It provides the basis for all three monetary aggregates. In other words, it is an even smaller matryoshka doll than M1.
- *M1* includes cash and a narrow definition of commercial bank money (overnight deposits).
- *M2* includes M1 and additional elements of commercial bank money, which are not immediately available but still highly liquid. These are term deposits with maturities up to 2 years and sight deposits that are redeemable with a notice period up to 3 months.
- *M3* includes M2 and some marketable instruments (such as repos) that are issued by banks and money market funds. The instruments need to be highly liquid and characterized by limited price variation in order to serve as substitutes for commercial bank money.

As the monetary aggregates look at the money supply from the perspective of the nonbank system, they exclude CBM from their definition. As mentioned

(continued)

Box 2.3 (continued)
in Chap. 1, only banks can hold CBM, while individuals, businesses, and nonbank institutions can only hold commercial bank money and cash (as illustrated earlier on in Fig. 1.6). There is only an indirect link between the monetary aggregates and the amount of CBM in the system, given that banks have to hold CBM to meet reserve requirements and the minimum reserves to be held are linked to the volume of commercial bank money in the system (as illustrated in Fig. 2.3).

Economic and monetary analysis are conducted separately and merged in the policy discussion. The results of the two pillars of monetary policy analysis are used to cross-check each others' results and put policy decisions on a broad basis that is in line with the medium-term orientation of monetary policy. Another reason why central bankers apply a suite of analytical tools and indicators lies in the uncertainty about the relationship of economic variables and the corresponding imperfect understanding of how monetary policy will influence consumer prices in the period ahead.

Monetary Policy Decisions

The Governing Council decides on monetary policy by simple majority, taking into account the findings of economic and monetary analysis. The Governing Council holds monetary policy meetings every 6 weeks or more often if needed. These meetings typically start with a presentation of the results of economic and monetary analysis, followed by a discussion among the members. After the discussion, the Governing Council takes decisions in every monetary policy meeting, applying the already mentioned rotation principle and a simple majority rule. In practice, the ECB intends to reach a broad consensus among the members of the Governing Council, i.e., preferably decisions to be taken by unanimity or a large majority.

The monetary policy decisions are communicated to the public directly after each meeting. As already mentioned, monetary policy meetings of the Governing Council are followed by a press release and a press conference with the ECB President. The press conference always starts with a press statement by the President, in which the findings of the economic and monetary analysis that underpin the policy decision are presented. In addition, the ECB publishes the detailed analysis in the form of the Economic Bulletin as well as the minutes of monetary policy meetings on its website.

While monetary policy decisions are taken in full independence, the ECB needs to be accountable for its decisions to the general public. Accountability refers to the responsibility to explain the motives for taking certain decisions and to provide convincing responses to questions. The ECB is accountable to the citizens of the euro area and their representatives, e.g., the members of the European Parliament (the only directly elected representatives at the EU level, see Annex A). The ECB Presidents appears in front of the Economic and Monetary Affairs (ECON)

Committee of the European Parliament four times a year to explain the current monetary policy stance and answer to questions. Members of the European Parliament can also submit written questions to the ECB, which are published together with the response on the ECB website.

Monetary Policy Operations

Monetary policy operations are performed by national central banks in the euro area, as described above. The Eurosystem executes the decisions of the Governing Council (e.g., to decrease the interest rate on the deposit facility) in a coordinated and decentralized manner. Regular activities include the weekly tenders for MROs, monthly tenders for LTROs, the assessment of counterparty eligibility and collateral quality, and the conduct of asset purchases under EAPP. All national central banks report their activities to the ECB in order to have a common Eurosystem view on the state of monetary policy operations.

Feedback from monetary policy operations is provided to the Governing Council as input to their decisions. For instance, the operations side may observe that banks are running out of eligible collateral or are unable to obtain FX liquidity in the market. Such information is obviously relevant for policymakers. To foster information exchange and cooperation among senior officials in the Eurosystem that are involved in this field, a dedicated committee, known as the Market Operations Committee (MOC), is established, similarly to the Monetary Policy Committee (MPC) in the field of monetary policy analysis. Lastly, it is worth mentioning that the main statistics of monetary policy operations (e.g., asset purchases or use of the deposit facility) are also published on the ECB website for the Eurosystem as a whole.

Alternative Monetary Policy Strategies

The current monetary policy strategy in the euro area is characterized by a focus on medium-term price stability based on economic and monetary analysis. Alternative setups that have been investigated or applied elsewhere have chosen different targets.

- One alternative option is "*inflation targeting*," which is similar to the current strategy, yet pays less attention to monetary developments. This option has become popular among several advanced economies and emerging markets in the 1990s and 2000s. As of end-2016, it is for instance applied by the Czech Republic, Sweden, or Canada.
- Another option is "*monetary targeting*," which aims at influencing the development of monetary aggregates, i.e., pays less attention to consumer price inflation.
- A third option is "*FX rate targeting*," under which monetary policy is conducted with a primary focus on the development of the FX rate. Many

(continued)

European countries pursued this option prior to the creation of the common currency (see Box 2.4). As of end-2016, it is for instance applied by Denmark or Bulgaria, as we will discuss in the next section.

- A fourth option is to make monetary policy *more rules-based*. For instance, the Taylor Rule was developed in the 1990s as a guide for setting official interest rates. It attracted significant interest by central bankers and academics in the early 2000s. The Taylor Rule is a simple formula that takes into account the current output and price level of an economy, compares them to certain reference levels, and produces a recommended official interest rate.

2.4 International Dimension

The monetary policy of the ECB has an effect on the FX rate of the euro to other currencies. To which extent a central bank intervenes in the FX market to affect the exchange rate is known as exchange rate policy (FX policy). In the case of the euro, the ECB takes FX developments of the euro vis-à-vis currencies of major trading partners into account in their monetary policy but does not intervene in the FX market on a regular basis. In other words, the ECB follows an FX policy, which is known as a floating FX regime, and lets the euro fluctuate vis-à-vis other currencies. According to the Treaties, the choice of FX regime is made jointly by the ECB and the ECOFIN, the ministers of finance in the European Union (see Annex A).[30] In this section, we will first introduce the various FX regimes in place in Europe and other parts of the world and then describe the policy interaction of the ECB with other central banks in this policy area that is closely intertwined with monetary policy.

The Euro and Other European Currencies

The nine EU countries that are not part of the euro area vary among each other as regards their FX policies vis-à-vis the euro. Some countries let their currency float to the euro (e.g., the United Kingdom), while others intervene occasionally (e.g., Sweden) or regularly (e.g., Hungary) to prevent strong FX rate movements. Other countries manage their FX rate within a small band (Denmark) or have a currency board regime that pegs their currency at a fixed rate to the euro (e.g., Bulgaria). Figure 2.12 provides an overview of the FX regimes that are in place across Europe. The map also shows that two non-EU countries (Montenegro and Kosovo[31]) use the euro without being members of the euro area (highlighted in light blue in Fig. 2.14).

[30]De facto, exchange rate arrangements of the euro are a joint responsibility of the ECB and the Eurogroup (ECB 2011, p. 14).

[31]At the time of writing, Kosovo is not recognized as a country by five EU member states.

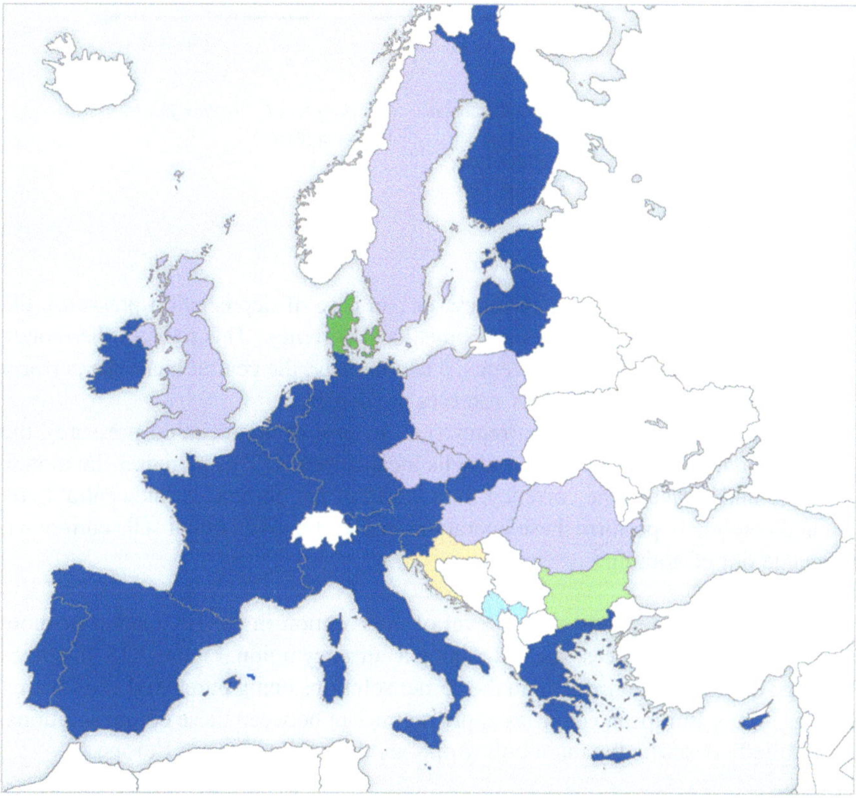

Fig. 2.12 FX regimes in Europe. Source: Author's representation. Legend: Dark blue (euro area member states), light blue (countries that have unilaterally adopted the euro), dark green (countries in ERM2), light green (currency board framework), light amber (tightly managed float), and light purple (pure or managed float)

Before discussing these FX regimes, we need to clarify how central banks can intervene in the FX market.

Central banks can intervene in the FX market through reserve operations. All central banks in Europe hold and manage the official reserves of their country (see Annex E). The reserves are shown on the asset side of the central bank balance sheet and include gold as well as liquid high-quality instruments such as government bonds of advanced economies. A significant part of these instruments is denominated in foreign currencies, thus the name FX reserves. Now suppose a situation in which the country's currency strongly depreciates (or appreciates) vis-à-vis the euro. Some central banks may want to avoid this development and counteract it by performing reserve operations:

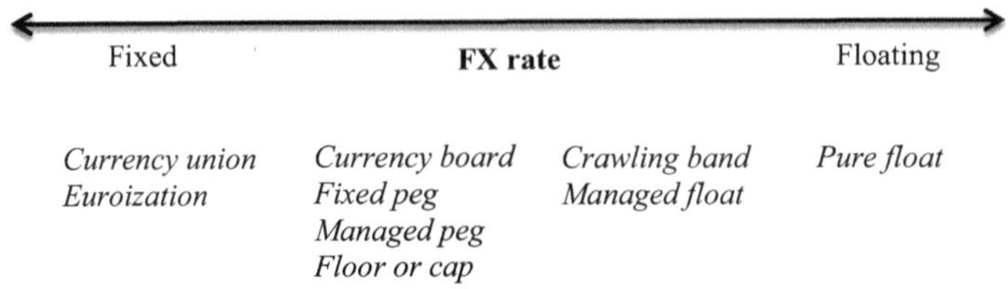

Fig. 2.13 FX regimes

- If the aim is to support the currency (i.e., in case of depreciation pressure), the central bank sells FX reserves and buys local currency. This reduces the money supply and strengthens the currency. Theoretically, the central bank can perform these operations until all its FX reserves are depleted.
- If the aim is to weaken the currency (i.e., in case of appreciation pressure), the central bank buys FX reserves and sells local currency. This increases the money supply and weakens the currency. In a world of fiat currencies, the central bank can theoretically perform these operations endlessly, given that it sells currency it created out of nothing.

The FX regime depends on the level of intervention in the FX market or more fundamental policy choices, such as joining a currency union. Figure 2.13 illustrates the range of possible regimes, with the corner solutions being pure fixed and floating regimes. Many European countries apply regimes in between these corner solutions. Let us briefly describe the main policy options that are in place in Europe.[32]

- A *currency union* is created if a group of countries give up their national currencies and introduce a common currency. The euro area is an example of a currency union. Eleven countries agreed on 31 December 1998 on an irrevocable fixing of their national currencies to the euro (e.g., 1.96 German mark into 1 euro), which was introduced in the form of commercial bank money and CBM on the next day.
- *Euroization* describes the decision of a country to give up its previous currency and introduce the euro. This can happen with agreement of the ECB (e.g., San Marino, Monaco and Vatican) or unilaterally (e.g., Montenegro, Kosovo). In the latter case, the countries have to obtain euro-denominated commercial bank money and cash in the market for use in their economies, while their banks are barred from obtaining euro-denominated CBM.
- A *currency board* is an FX regime in which the currency is fixed to the euro at a certain FX rate and the central bank promises holders of the currency to exchange their money holdings into an equivalent amount of the anchor currency. In order to maintain the fixed FX rate, the respective central bank needs to be able and

[32]The ECB publishes a "Convergence report" for EU member states that have not adopted the euro yet on an annual basis (e.g., ECB 2016). Among others, the report describes the exchange rate regime in place between the respective countries and the euro area.

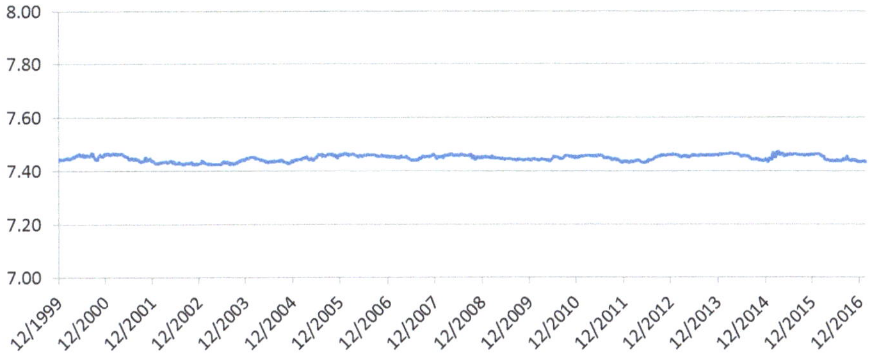

Fig. 2.14 EUR-DKK exchange rate. Source: ECB (2017f)

willing to intervene in the FX market to maintain the rate at all times. Estonia and Lithuania used to have currency boards prior to joining the euro area. Bulgaria and Bosnia/Herzegovina also have currency boards to the euro at a rate of 1.96.[33] A similar FX regime to a currency board is a *fixed peg* that fixes the FX rate to an anchor currency (e.g., the euro) at a certain level.

- A *managed peg* allows a currency to fluctuate to the euro within a certain band, typically around a target FX rate. The Danish krone is an example of a managed peg within a rather tight band of $\pm 2.25\%$ vis-à-vis the euro (see Fig. 2.14). As of early 2016, Denmark was the only EU country in the so-called Exchange Rate Mechanism 2 (ERM2). Any country that wants to join the euro area needs to be in ERM2 for two consecutive years. Another European country that has a tightly managed exchange rate to the euro (yet, outside ERM2 and applying a broader band) is the Croatian kuna.
- Introducing a *floor (cap)* on the FX rate signals to the market that the central bank is ready to intervene in order to prevent its currency from appreciating (depreciating) beyond a certain threshold. For instance, the Swiss central bank introduced a floor on the EUR CHF exchange rate of 1.20 during the euro area sovereign debt crisis in 2011. The floor was removed in early 2015 (shortly before the ECB announcement of the EAPP), resulting in a strong appreciation of the Swiss franc. The Czech koruna is another example of a currency with a floor to the euro.
- If a high-inflation country pegs its currency to the euro, its currency will experience constant depreciation pressure, making it difficult to maintain the peg

[33]Bulgaria used to have a fixed peg to the German mark at a rate of 1:1. When Germany joined the euro, the fixed peg of Bulgarian leva to the euro was set at 1.96, i.e. the conversion rate of German mark to the euro.

through intervention. Some countries therefore decide to gradually adjust the band in which they let their currencies fluctuate, thus allowing a controlled depreciation. Such type of FX regime is known as a *crawling band*.

- A *managed float* is one of the most common types of FX regimes in emerging markets. It describes a floating FX rate, which is managed by occasional interventions by the central bank—in particular, in cases when the currency strongly depreciates. Within the European Union, the Hungarian forint is an example of a managed float.
- A *pure float* denotes an FX regime that lets the FX rate to be determined solely by market forces, without any intervention by the central bank. The British pound is an example of a pure float vis-à-vis the euro.

Non-euro area EU countries that want to join the euro need to comply with certain convergence criteria, also known as the Maastricht criteria. The criteria are summarized in Table 2.2. They refer to sound monetary policy (low inflation rate), sound fiscal policy (limits on budget deficits and public indebtedness), moderate long-term interest rates, and a stable FX rate (at least 2 years within the ERM2 with max. 15% fluctuation). The ECB publishes a convergence report every 2 years, showing the compliance of non-euro area EU countries with these criteria. To start the accession procedure, a country needs to submit an application and prove that it meets the convergence criteria. The ultimate decision on accepting a country into the euro area lies with the EU Council (see Annex A).

The ECB and the governors of all EU central banks meet at least quarterly. The forum is called the General Council of the ECB. It does not take decisions on monetary policy but discusses policy-relevant issues such as the convergence report or major developments on FX markets.

Table 2.2 Convergence criteria for joining the euro area

Issue	Indicator	Criterion
Sound monetary policy	HICP inflation	Not higher than the inflation rate of the three EU member states with the lowest inflation plus 1.5%
Sound fiscal policy	Budget deficit as a percentage of GDP	Not higher than 3%
	Government debt as a percentage of GDP	Not higher than 60%
Moderate long-term interest rate	10-year government bond yield	Not higher than 10-year government bond yield in the three EU member states with the lowest inflation plus 2%
Stable FX rate	Membership in the Exchange Rate Mechanism 2 (ERM2)	At least for 2 years and within a band of ±15%

Box 2.4 A Short History of European Monetary Integration

Western Europe became part of the Bretton-Woods System after the end of the Second World War. The postwar international monetary system was named after the location of its founding conference (Bretton Woods, New Hampshire) and was characterized by a regime of fixed exchange rates between all participating currencies and the US dollar. The International Monetary Fund (IMF) was created as a new institution to support the system of fixed exchange rates. Many economists share the view that the Bretton-Woods System played an important role in supporting the reconstruction of Western European economies in the postwar period.

The Bretton-Woods System came to an end in the early 1970s, driven by diverging developments across participating economies. Amid several reasons that led to the demise of the system, the United States ran significant current account deficits during the early 1970s, while other economies such as Germany were under constant appreciation pressure amid persistent current account surpluses. When the system was eventually discontinued, floating FX rates became the international norm. Nevertheless, several European countries agreed on a system of managed FX rates within tight bands in order to prevent large fluctuations of FX rates among each other. The system was called the European Monetary System (EMS) and came into existence in 1979. The German mark served as the de-facto anchor currency in the EMS.

The Delors Report, published in 1988, provided a blueprint for the creation of an economic and monetary union. The report laid out a roadmap towards a European monetary union in three phases, the last one being the introduction of the euro. The years following the publication of the report saw significant steps in European integration, which culminated in the Maastricht Treaty of 1992. The Treaty created the European Union and the euro as its single currency.

The European Monetary System came under significant pressure on FX markets shortly after the Maastricht Treaty was signed. This episode entered history books as the EMS crisis of 1992. At that time, Germany pursued a restrictive monetary policy to maintain price stability in the context of German reunification. Given the anchor role of the German mark in EMS, other European economies had to implement similar monetary policies as Germany in order to keep the exchange rate in the agreed tight bands, leading to a downturn of their economies. In this environment, several participants on the FX markets launched speculative attacks against weaker European currencies in the EMS in the expectation that they would eventually abandon the strong link to the German mark and depreciate. The speculators succeeded in several cases, such as Italy (depreciation of the Italian lira) or the United Kingdom (withdrawing its EMS participation). The exchange rate crisis ended when the EMS was modified to include significantly wider FX bands towards the

(continued)

Box 2.4 (continued)
German mark of ±15%. The wider bands allowed more flexibility of participating countries in their monetary policy and remained in place until the introduction of the euro in 1999. The Maastricht Treaty was eventually adopted by all member states of the European Community, yet two countries (United Kingdom and Denmark) opted out of becoming members of the euro area as well.[34]

In the run-up to monetary union, the potential lack of discipline in national fiscal policies was considered to be the major risk factor to the single currency. To mitigate the risk, the Maastricht Treaty laid down strict limits on budget deficits and public debt, as discussed in the context of the convergence criteria above. If a country violated these limits, it could not join the euro area and would be subject to penalties. In addition, a 'no bailout clause' was included in the Treaty to prevent a country from relying on others in crisis situations. The Maastricht criteria and the compliance of EU member states became a central theme in European economic policy in the second half of the 1990s. Eventually, the decision on the founding members of the euro area was made not only based on the original convergence criteria but also on political considerations.

The euro was introduced in 1999 with 11 founding member states. The European Monetary Institute, which was founded in 1994, became the European Central Bank (ECB) in 1998 and took over the responsibility for monetary policy decisions in the euro area. The introduction of the euro triggered a strong move towards financial integration, starting with money markets and increasing cross-border activities of banks. Also long-term interest rates in participating countries started to significantly converge in the early 2000s, which may suggest that market participants either considered financing difficulties of euro area countries very unlikely or did not consider the "no bailout clause" to be credible.

The euro area witnessed significant enlargement in its first decade. Greece joined in 2001, Slovenia in 2007, Cyprus and Malta in 2008, and Slovakia in 2009. At the same time, only minor steps were made towards deeper integration in other policy areas such as fiscal policy or labor policy. In addition, and with the benefit of hindsight, not much attention was paid to widening cross-country differences within the euro area (e.g., wages, prices, consumption, productivity, private indebtedness, real estate prices). The euro was widely perceived as a political and economic success, while emerging vulnerabilities in several countries remained unnoticed or unaddressed.

(continued)

[34]It is worth noting that only one EU country (Sweden) asked its population in a *dedicated* referendum whether it should join the euro.

Box 2.4 (continued)

The years from 2008 to date have been characterized by a series of crises. The global financial crisis hit the euro area with full force in the fall of 2008. It was followed by a bold monetary policy response by the ECB that prevented the financial system from collapsing, and a major economic downturn in 2009. The sovereign debt crisis erupted in Greece in 2010, followed by several other countries, bailouts in the form of EU/IMF Programs, and a major confidence crisis regarding the future of the euro area in 2011–2012. The period following these intense crisis years was characterized by prolonged recessions in some member states and the creation of the Banking Union, which put all euro area banks under a Single Supervisory Mechanism, led by the ECB. Chapter 3 will discuss the stated crisis episodes in more detail, as they are crucial to understand the challenges for monetary and financial policy in the euro area.

The Euro and Other Parts of the World

The floating FX regime of the ECB also applies to FX rates vis-à-vis other global currencies. The FX rates to other currencies, such as the US dollar or the Chinese renminbi, are determined by transactions on the FX market. Figure 2.15 shows the EUR-USD exchange rate as an example, which fluctuated with some episodes of appreciation and depreciation.

While the euro plays an important role among global currencies, international finance and trade remain dominated by the US dollar. A large share of world trade, international payments, and global financial assets under management is denominated in USD. The US dollar is also the primary choice for reserve managers around the world and accounts for roughly 63% of global FX reserves (see Fig. 2.16). In addition, the British newspaper The Economist (2015) estimates that roughly 60% of world GDP is produced in countries that either use the US dollar as legal tender, are highly dollarized, or have currencies that are effectively pegged to the US dollar.

The US dollar is a key currency for many emerging markets and developing countries. The financial systems of many developing countries are dollarized, in particular in Central and Latin America, Eastern Europe, Central Asia, and Africa. The extensive use of the US dollar has implications for the vulnerability of these countries in situations when their local currency strongly depreciates (e.g., making it more difficult for borrowers to service their USD-denominated loans). The euro, by contrast, is only rarely used in emerging markets outside of Europe, yet some developing countries have pegged their currencies to the euro (e.g., the West African Economic and Monetary Union or the Economic and Monetary Community of Central Africa).

The ECB is in steady contact with policymakers for monetary policy in other major economies through various platforms.

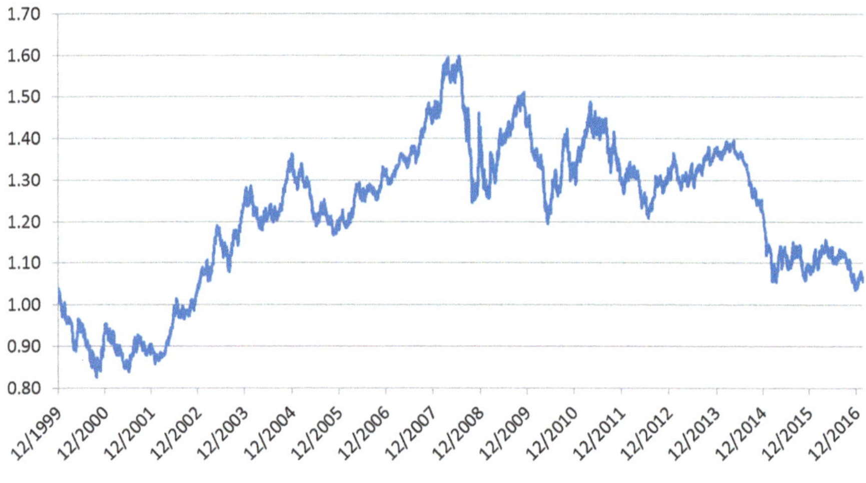

Fig. 2.15 EUR-USD exchange rate. Source: ECB (2017f)

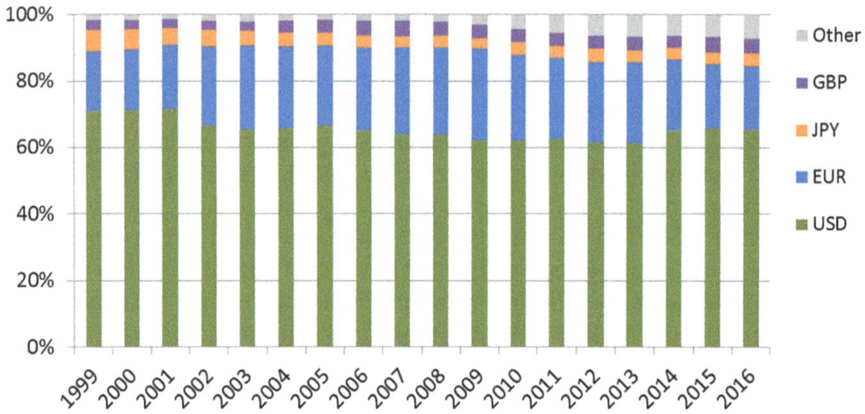

Fig. 2.16 Global FX reserves by currency. Source: IMF (2017). Note: Based on allocated reserves

- Bimonthly meetings with central bank governors of 30 major advanced and emerging markets take place at the Bank for International Settlements (BIS) in Basel.
- The ECB participates in the semi-annual meetings with central bank governors and treasury secretaries of most countries at the International Monetary Fund and World Bank in Washington DC (Spring Meetings in April and Annual Meetings in October).
- The ECB is involved in the meetings with central bank governors and ministers of finance of G-7 and G-20 countries. The G-7 is the forum of the seven largest

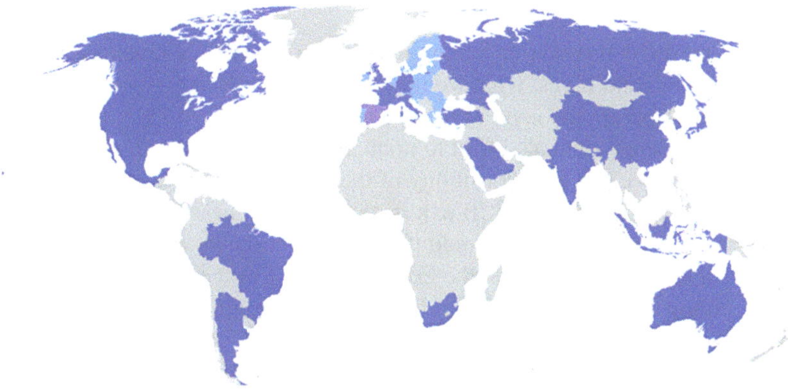

Fig. 2.17 G-20 countries. Source: Wikipedia (2017)

advanced economies (United States, Canada, the United Kingdom, Germany, France, and Italy). The G-20 includes the European Union and 19 major advanced and emerging economies (see Fig. 2.17), which together comprise approximately two-thirds of the world population and 85% of world GDP. The G-20 has risen in importance as a forum for economic policy coordination across countries during the global financial crisis.

- Selected central bank governors, including the Presidents of the Federal Reserve System and the ECB, ministers of finance, academics, and financial market participants, meet every August in Jackson Hole, Wyoming, upon invitation of the Federal Reserve Bank of Kansas. The annual Jackson Hole meeting serves as an opportunity to exchange views on monetary and financial policy as well as global economic developments.
- Lastly, the ECB also participates in various conferences on monetary policy and hosts the ECB Annual Forum on Central Banking in Sintra, Portugal.

Questions for Consideration

- Which analytical tools do we need to measure risks to price stability in the short and medium term?
- Can we think of better ways to measure inflation than the current method of calculating HICP?
- How dependent are central banks on the behavior of commercial banks to transmit the monetary policy stance to businesses and individuals?
- How can we measure the effectiveness of monetary policy instruments to contribute to price stability?

(continued)

- Should the ECB broaden or tighten the criteria for eligible counterparties and collateral, and if yes, what would be the likely effects?
- What is the appropriate level of reserve requirements?
- Should the Eurosystem also lend to nonbanks or governments?
- Should ELA become a responsibility of the ECB?
- When and how should the ECB exit its nonstandard measures?
- Under which circumstances should the ECB intervene in the FX market?
- How can the independence of the ECB and the NCBs be safeguarded?
- How transparent should central banks be regarding monetary policy operations and ELA?
- How can the understanding of monetary policy by the general public be improved?

References

European Central Bank (ECB). (2016). *Convergence report*. Accessed November 14, 2017, from https://www.ecb.europa.eu/pub/pdf/conrep/cr201606.en.pdf?a91977931874a7c6c63d80305b651394

ECB. (2017a). *Photo of the ECB Governing Council as at December 2016*. Accessed March 30, 2017, from https://www.ecb.europa.eu/ecb/orga/decisions/govc/html/index.en.html

ECB. (2017b). *Statistical data warehouse*. Accessed March 30, 2017, from http://sdw.ecb.europa.eu/

ECB. (2017c). *Eurosystem collateral data*. Accessed February 16, 2017, from https://www.ecb.europa.eu/paym/coll/Figures/html/index.en.html

ECB. (2017d). *Asset purchase programmes*. Accessed November 14, 2017, from https://www.ecb.europa.eu/mopo/implement/omt/html/index.en.html

ECB. (2017e). *Monetary developments in the euro area*. Accessed February 16, 2017, from https://www.ecb.europa.eu/press/pdf/md/md1612.pdf

ECB. (2017f). *Euro foreign exchange reference rates*. Accessed February 16, 2017, from https://www.ecb.europa.eu/stats/exchange/eurofxref/html/index.en.html

ECB. (2017g). *Eurosystem balance sheet: Assets and liabilities related to monetary policy operations from 1999 to 2016*. Accessed November 14, 2017, from https://www.ecb.europa.eu/pub/annual/balance/mpo/html/index.en.html

International Monetary Fund (IMF). (2017). *Currency composition of official foreign exchange reserves (COFER)*. Accessed February 16, 2017, from http://www.imf.org/en/Data

The Economist. (2015, October). *Special report on the dollar's role in the world economy*. Volume 417 Number 8958.

Wikipedia. (2017). *Map of the G-20 countries*. Accessed March 10, 2017, from https://de.wikipedia.org/wiki/Gruppe_der_zwanzig_wichtigsten_Industrie-_und_Schwellenl%C3%A4nder

Further Reading

European Central Bank (ECB). (2011). *The monetary policy of the ECB* (3rd ed., 2013). https://www.ecb.europa.eu/pub/pdf/other/monetarypolicy2011en.pdf

European Central Bank (ECB). (2015). *The role of the Central Bank balance sheet in monetary policy*. ECB Economic Bulletin 4/2015. https://www.ecb.europa.eu/pub/pdf/other/art01_eb201504.en.pdf

European Central Bank (ECB). (2017). *The international role of the euro*. https://www.ecb.europa.eu/pub/pdf/other/ecb.euro-international-role-201707.pdf?dbaa722edc894584fc5ca9db6d64364c

Praet, P. (2016, April). *The ECB's fight against low inflation: Reasons and consequences*. Speech at Luiss School of European Political Economy, Rome. https://www.ecb.europa.eu/press/key/date/2016/html/sp160404.en.html

3 The Financial Crisis in the Euro Area

Before entering into the discussion of banking supervision and financial stability, this chapter takes a step back and looks at the financial crisis in Europe since 2007. Recalling the main phases and policy responses during the crisis may help to understand the current state of euro area banks and the associated policy challenges. It is also useful to reflect on the precrisis period during which the euro area banking sector grew significantly in size and riskiness. While some reasons that led to the financial crisis were clearly outside the scope of bank supervisors, the crisis also revealed vulnerabilities of banks that were not sufficiently addressed by supervisory authorities in the early 2000s. The vulnerabilities became clearly apparent during the crisis, at a significant cost to euro area economies and public finances.

This chapter describes the development of the euro area banking sector from the precrisis period up to end-2016, with a focus on the crisis years. Since the sector covered around 5000 banks in 19 countries as of end-2016 with different business models and complexity, this overview abstracts from the heterogeneity within the sector and focuses on the main trends that affected the sector as a whole.

The financial crisis since 2007 can be separated into three main phases.

- *Phase 1: Global financial crisis and Great Recession (2007–2009).* The financial crisis started in the US subprime mortgage market and turned into a major liquidity and solvency crisis of US and European banks during 2008. After the collapse of Lehman Brothers in September 2008, the global financial system entered its most turbulent period in recent history, reflecting a major erosion of trust in the system. The financial crisis spilled over to other economic sectors, resulting in the Great Recession of most advanced economies (see Fig. 3.1). As regards the policy response, immediate systemic risks were addressed through expansionary monetary policy, as discussed in Chap. 2, and public support for ailing banks. Thereafter, policymakers focused on overhauling bank regulation and enhancing supervisory cooperation.
- *Phase 2: Sovereign debt crisis and renewed confidence crisis (2010–2012).* The financial crisis morphed into a sovereign debt crisis in early 2010. The crisis

M. Fandl, *Monetary and Financial Policy in the Euro Area*, Springer Texts in Business and Economics, https://doi.org/10.1007/978-3-319-72643-4_3

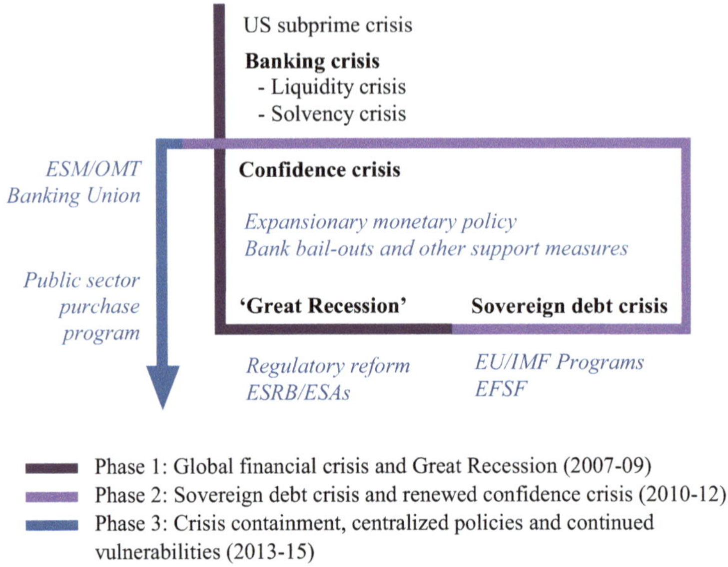

Fig. 3.1 Main phases and policy response of the crisis 2007–2015

originated in Greece and spread to several other euro area countries. Jointly, the national governments in the euro area prevented sovereign defaults mainly through public bailouts, while requiring substantial adjustments and policy reforms in the crisis countries in the context of EU/IMF Programs. By mid-2011, the crisis widened to larger euro area economies such as Spain, giving rise to another major confidence crisis. Widespread concerns about the long-term sustainability of the euro area dominated the following year and were only contained in mid-2012 by a move towards more centralized policies, such as the establishment of the ESM and the Banking Union. Also the ECB announcement of the Outright Monetary Transactions (OMT) program contributed to the gradual reduction of risk premiums on euro area government bonds.

- *Phase 3: Crisis containment, centralized policies, and continued vulnerabilities (2013–2015).* Confidence gradually returned to euro area sovereigns and banks from 2013 onwards. At the same time, vulnerabilities remained elevated, in particular related to crisis legacies in bank balance sheets and parts of the euro area economy. For instance, unemployment remained high amid prolonged recessions in several countries. As regards financial sector policy, Phase 3 was characterized by the establishment of the Banking Union and the SSM as its first pillar. Greece entered into another major crisis during 2015, which was followed by an agreement of euro area governments to a third EU Program.[1]

[1]The second Greek Program was agreed in early 2012.

Let us now turn to the main trends in the euro area banking sector, starting from the precrisis period.

Preface to the Crisis

The euro area was created during a historically favorable period. The 1990s and early 2000s were characterized by a wave of economic and financial globalization with sustained economic growth in key emerging markets, increased world trade, and surging cross-border capital flows. This environment created the Great Moderation with low inflation and low interest rates in advanced economies.

While monetary policy became a joint responsibility, banking supervision remained a national competence. In the newly created euro area, all supervisory tasks continued to be performed by central banks or national supervisory authorities in their respective jurisdictions. In several countries, the organization of supervisory tasks was inspired by the UK supervisory model, which assigned the responsibility for banking supervision to a dedicated financial supervisory authority outside the central bank.

The establishment of the euro area provided a boost to financial integration in Europe. Banks started to make euro-denominated interbank payments through the new TARGET system and within a short period of time an integrated money market developed. Many banks expanded their international operations through mergers, acquisitions, greenfield investments, and cross-border activities, both within and outside the euro area. For instance, German banks significantly increased their cross-border exposures by buying bonds of other euro area governments or banks. Italian and Austrian banks expanded their business operations to Central, Eastern, and Southeastern Europe through cross-border lending and foreign subsidiaries. Overall, the internationalization trend was most pronounced in the case of first- and second-tier banks.[2] One of the key motives for banks was the prospect of higher returns compared to the constrained profitability in their respective home markets.

The flipside of financial integration was strong credit growth in selected market segments, which fueled the buildup of imbalances. The availability of ample credit at low interest rates fostered consumption and real estate booms in several euro area countries, such as Ireland, Spain, or Cyprus. This development appeared favorable to banks and borrowers in the short term, but was a major contributing factor to the decline in asset quality during the crisis. Increased financial integration also resulted in a higher degree of interconnectedness within the banking sector through interbank markets and cross-border exposures. In other words, the lines in the bank network that were illustrated in Fig. 1.13 got thicker, while the nodes (indicating the total assets of individual banks) increased in size as well.

As banks became larger and more interconnected, they also became more fragile. Their vulnerability increased largely due to three trends:

[2]This chapter uses the classification of euro area banks into three tiers, which was introduced in Chap. 1.

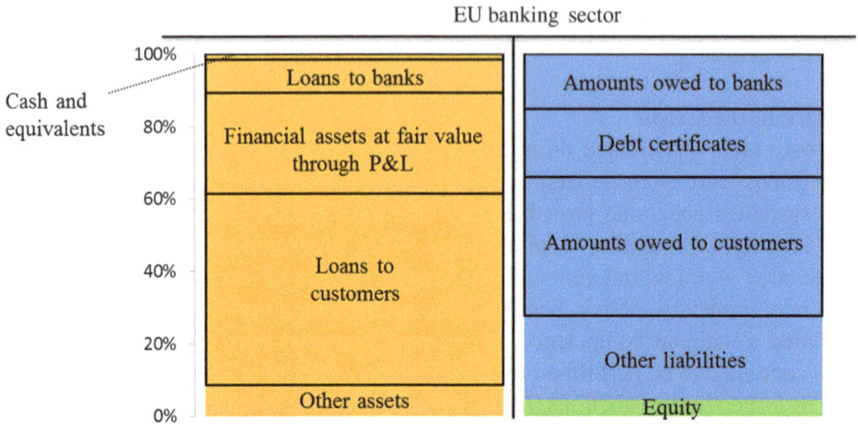

Fig. 3.2 Aggregate balance sheet of EU banks at end-2006. Source: ECB (2007)

- *Firstly, banks increased their leverage by incurring significant amounts of debt, while maintaining small capital buffers.* Higher leverage allowed banks to boost their return on equity. Target returns of 15–20% were common references in investor presentations during this period. Eventually, high leverage amplified the profits in the precrisis period as well as the losses when the crisis hit. In short, limited capital buffers meant that banks were not well prepared to absorb unexpected losses.
- *Secondly, banks increased their dependence on wholesale funding markets, taking advantage of the favorable market environment.* Similar developments could be observed in other advanced economies such as the United States or the United Kingdom. The reliance on wholesale funding made banks vulnerable to a sudden change in market conditions.
- *Thirdly, banks expanded their operations in nontraditional banking products, such as securitizations, derivatives, or foreign-currency loans.* While these products provided advantages in the form of higher profits in the short term, many banks did not fully grasp their risks or chose to ignore them. By and large, supervisors did not manage to prevent banks from engaging in these activities. Only when the crisis hit, banks and supervisors fully realized the riskiness of some of these products.

Overall, bank balance sheets showed roughly similar shares of intra-financial exposures and exposures to nonfinancial businesses or individuals in the precrisis period. Figure 3.2 shows the aggregate bank balance sheet of the EU banking sector as of end-2006.[3] Loans to customer accounted for only 53% of total assets, while loans to banks and financial assets measured at fair value—mostly vis-à-vis banks or

[3]Figure 3.2 shows the balance sheet composition of IFRS-reporting domestic banks in the EU as of end-2006.

other financial institutions—comprised 37% of total assets. A similar pattern can be observed on the liability side: The amounts owed to customers (38%) only slightly exceeded the amounts owed to banks and issued debt certificates (34%).

Phase 1: Global Financial Crisis and Great Recession (2007–2009)
The financial crisis started in the US housing market and spilled over to Europe in the summer of 2007. Increasing defaults were recorded in the US subprime mortgage market in early 2007. The risks of the respective mortgage loans did not stay on the books of the US-based institutions that had granted them but were transferred to a large pool of investors in the US, Europe, and other countries through securitizations. These transactions involved the transfer of mortgage loans to special purpose vehicles that refinanced the loans by issuing asset-backed securities in various tranches. When the underlying asset pools started to deteriorate, investors suffered losses on the values of the purchased securities and market liquidity evaporated as investors realized the heightened risks. In July 2007, the medium-sized German bank IKB was rescued due to large exposures to US subprime mortgage-backed securities. In August 2007, three investment funds by BNP Paribas, a French bank, faced difficulties in determining their net asset values and suspended payouts. This event triggered a strong reaction on money and wholesale funding markets in the euro area, sparking the first episode of the liquidity crisis. In November 2007, the United Kingdom experienced the first bank run in 140 years when Northern Rock ran into severe funding difficulties and was eventually nationalized.

Source: KAL (The Economist, October 2008)

The crisis fully erupted with the collapse of Lehman Brothers on 15 September 2008. The US investment bank had been one of the key players in the global derivatives and fixed income market. Market participants considered Lehman Brothers too-big-to-fail (TBTF) and expected the government to intervene, when the bank faced difficulties from its large exposure to the US subprime mortgage market. When the attempt to save the bank failed, its collapse sent shock waves to the global financial system, as market participants realized that banks which were so far considered TBTF could be allowed to fail, potentially bringing down parts of the financial system with them. The immediate reaction was a freeze on the interbank market for senior unsecured debt instruments and a drastic decline in money market transactions, which reflected the aversion by banks to lend surplus liquidity to other banks even for short maturities. Bank equities plunged during these weeks and bank credit default swap (CDS) spreads jumped to unrecorded levels.

Euro area banks were not only impacted on the funding side by the market events but also witnessed losses on their assets. The latter included outright losses on asset holdings (e.g., exposures to Lehman Brothers) and valuation losses due to holdings of illiquid risky investments, such as securitizations. Banks that were most hit during this phase were first-tier banks and second-tier banks with high wholesale funding reliance. The crisis deepened in October 2008 when economic and financial challenges became apparent in several countries surrounding the euro area. The three largest Icelandic banks defaulted and were nationalized, bringing the country to the brink of sovereign default. Hungary and several other countries in Central and Eastern Europe faced severe balance of payments difficulties and applied for EU/IMF Programs.[4]

The initial policy response to the global financial crisis was a combination of expansionary monetary policy and unprecedented public support for banks. The monetary policy response alleviated the liquidity strains in the euro area banking system but would not have been sufficient to prevent the likely failure of banks during this period. Against this background, governments stepped in and provided financial support to banks at a historically unprecedented scale. On 16 October 2008, the European Council (2008) announced that national governments in the EU were committed "that in all circumstances the necessary measures will be taken to preserve the stability of the financial system, to support the major financial institutions, to avoid bankruptcies, and to protect savers' deposits." Many observers understood this statement as a promise of national governments to do everything possible to prevent the failure of systemic banks in their countries. Shortly thereafter, many national parliaments adopted bank support packages, which enabled governments to provide capital injections, asset guarantees, or other measures to banks in their respective jurisdictions. From October 2008 onwards, national governments bailed out several euro area banks. Public support to the euro area banking sector eventually amounted to 160 billion euros in capital injections,

[4]Financial assistance by the EU was provided through balance of payments assistance programs.

735 billion euros in liability guarantees, and 129 billion euros in asset support from October 2008 to May 2010.[5]

After the collapse of systemic banks was prevented, the policy focus shifted to regulatory reform and enhancing supervision. The Basel Committee on Banking Supervision published the main elements of Basel III in late 2010. Around the same time, European policymakers changed the organizational arrangements for financial supervision in EU countries through the establishment of four new institutions: (1) the European Banking Authority (EBA) with a focus on banking supervision, (2) the European Insurance and Occupational Pension Fund Authority (EIOPA) with a focus on the supervision of insurance companies and pension funds, (3) the European Securities and Markets Authority (ESMA) with a focus on securities firms and markets, and (4) the European Systemic Risk Board (ESRB) with a focus on the financial system as a whole. All four institutions focused on enhancing supervisory cooperation and developing common standards in EU countries, while maintaining the national competence of the respective policy areas, including for banking supervision.

Phase 2: Sovereign Debt Crisis and Renewed Confidence Crisis (2010–2013)
The sovereign debt crisis started at the end of 2009 with concerns about the fiscal situation in Greece.[6] The country recorded a high budget deficit in 2009 that according to the Maastricht criteria needed to be reduced, while the economy was in a recession, which was amplified by precrisis imbalances. Moreover, the high level of public indebtedness raised market concerns about debt sustainability. These developments led to a strong increase in the yields of Greek government bonds. The first months of the sovereign debt crisis were characterized by emergency meetings of European policymakers and the slow realization that without external intervention Greece would default on its debt. This prospect raised major concerns as no mechanism was in place to deal with a potential sovereign default in the euro area.[7] At the time, many observers shared the view that a sovereign default of a euro area member state would have severe implications for other sovereigns and banks in Europe and the rest of the world. The crisis intensified until May 2010, when the euro area member states, jointly with the IMF, finally agreed with Greece on an EU/IMF Program with a total commitment of 110 billion euros. At the same time, the euro area governments committed to the establishment of the European Financial Stability Facility (EFSF) as a temporary new European institution to

[5]The total commitment provided by fiscal authorities amounted to 28% of euro area GDP (Stolz and Wedow 2010). These estimates do not account for repayments or proceeds to the public sector from the respective instruments.

[6]Sovereign refers to the central government, which is in charge of the federal budget and debt management. As with banks and other businesses, it is sometimes useful to take a balance sheet perspective on the sovereign. Outstanding government debt is shown on the liability side of the sovereign balance sheet.

[7]The Treaty only included the no-bail-out clause we discussed in Chap. 2.

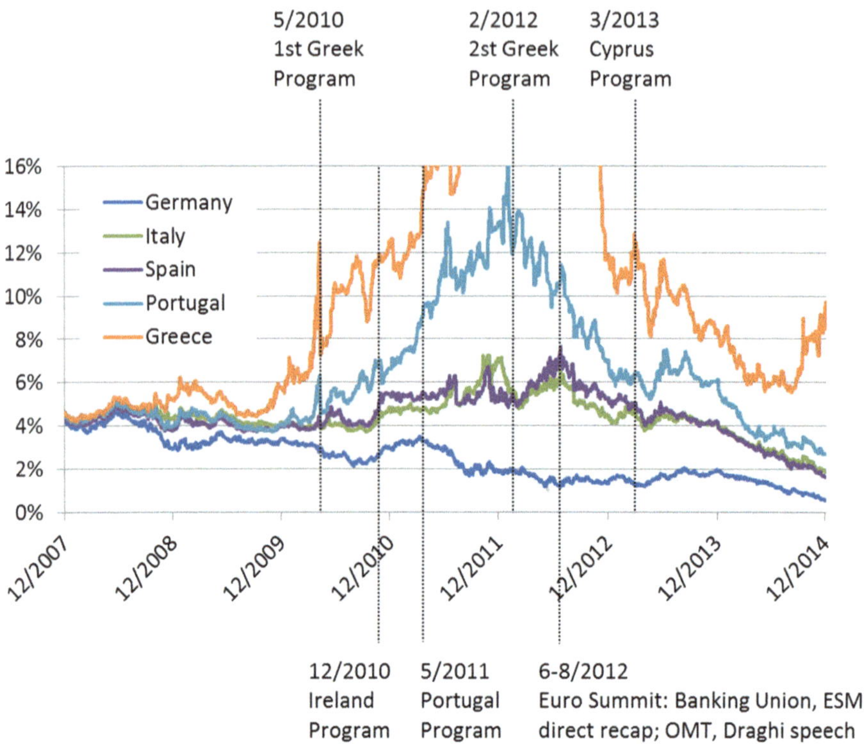

Fig. 3.3 Key dates of the sovereign debt crisis and 10-year government bond yields. Source: Investing.com, author's additions

channel loan disbursements in the Program context to Greece and other euro area countries that would require assistance as well.

After the agreement on the first Greek Program, sovereign bond yields continued to rise in a number of euro area countries, as shown in Fig. 3.3. This development partly reflected crisis conditions in the banking sector of these countries, which spilled over to the sovereign (see Box 3.2).

- *Ireland came under an EU/IMF Program in December 2010.* In the case of Ireland, the challenges to public finances stemmed more from explicit and implicit liabilities from the banking sector than from the country's fiscal performance. Several large Irish banks that were close to failure were nationalized at a significant cost to Irish taxpayers. In addition, the Irish government had provided extensive support to banks in October 2008 by issuing a blanket guarantee for all liabilities of Irish banks, which led to high payouts for the sovereign in the course of the crisis.

Source: KAL (The Economist, March 2013)

- *Portugal came under an EU/IMF Program in May 2011.* Shortly before the agreement, the EU Council decided to create the European Stability Mechanism (ESM) as a permanent new European institution that would take over the tasks of the EFSF and have a significantly higher committed capital by its member states (see Box 3.1). The key intention behind the ESM and the third bailout of a euro area country was to signal to market participants that euro area governments would not allow one of its fellow member states to fail. The hope was that these measures would finally limit the significantly widened bond yields in several countries.
- *The sovereign debt crisis escalated in July 2011, when the yields of some large euro area countries such as Spain and Italy started to increase* (see Fig. 3.3). This development gave rise to a confidence crisis regarding the future of the euro area. Spain entered into an ESM Program that was focused on bank recapitalization in July 2012. Around the same time, a move towards more centralized policies and risk sharing in the euro area managed to gradually restore the confidence of market participants.
- *In February 2012, euro area governments and the IMF agreed on a second Greek Program.* This Program did not only include higher bailout commitments by the official creditors but also a bail-in requirement for holders of Greek government bonds. The latter element, known as the private sector involvement (PSI), led to losses by euro area banks with significant holdings of these bonds—in particular Greek and Cypriot banks.

- *Cyprus came under an EU/IMF Program in March 2013 due to severe solvency issues in its banking sector and sovereign-bank linkages.* The Cypriot Program also included a bail-in of uninsured bank depositors and was accompanied by the application of capital controls. These policy tools for extraordinary circumstances will be discussed in Chap. 5.

Box 3.1 European Stability Mechanism (ESM)

The ESM was set up in 2012 as an intergovernmental institution that can provide financial assistance to euro area countries experiencing financial stress. It is held by the 19 euro area member states, which contribute to the capital of the ESM in proportion to their share in the total population and GDP of the euro area. The highest decision-making body is the ESM Board of Governors, which consists of the ministers of finance of the euro area countries. The institution is based in Luxembourg and its Managing Director was Klaus Regling at the time of writing.

The ESM has a maximum lending capacity of 500 billion euros. Its lending instruments are the following:

- *Loans to euro area member states in the context of ESM Programs:* Disbursement of these loans is conditional upon the implementation of reforms by the respective country in the context of a Program (see Chap. 4). The interest rate of the loans is related to the funding rate of the ESM. This instrument has been used in Cyprus and Greece since the establishment of the ESM.[8]
- *Loans for indirect bank recapitalizations:* This instrument can be used to cover capital shortfalls of systemically relevant banks if it is not possible to do so through private sector solutions, and the member state, in which the banks are domiciled, is not able to recapitalize the banks without adverse effects on its financial and fiscal sustainability. The recapitalization is indirect in the sense that loans are provided to the respective member state for this purpose. This instrument has been used for the recapitalization of Spanish banks in 2012.
- *Direct recapitalization of banks:* This instrument requires burden-sharing of existing liability holders of the respective bank through the application of the so-called bail-in instrument that will be described in Chaps. 3 and 4. The direct recapitalization instrument has not been used so far.
- *Other instruments to provide financial assistance:* They include precautionary credit lines as well as primary and secondary market purchases of sovereign debt instruments. These instruments have not been used so far.

(continued)

[8]The EFSF, the predecessor of the ESM, provided loans in the Programmes in Greece, Ireland, and Portugal. The ESM and the EFSF are separate entities but share staff and operations.

Box 3.1 (continued)

In the period 2010–2016, the ESM and its predecessor, the EFSF, disbursed a total of 254 billion euros to five countries (Greece, Ireland, Portugal, Spain, and Cyprus). The ESM raises funds in the financial markets through the issuance of short- and long-term debt instruments. The paid-in capital by the member states at the time of writing was approx. 81 billion euros.[9]

Box 3.2 Sovereign-Bank Risk Spillovers

All crisis countries during Phase 2 were characterized by risk spillovers between sovereigns and banks. In some countries, the sovereign debt crisis emerged in the public sector and adversely impacted banks and the broader economy (e.g., Greece). In other countries, the crisis emerged in the banking sector and adversely impacted public finances when governments supported domestic banks (e.g., Ireland, Spain). The figure below summarizes the main channels through which risks spilled over between the sovereign and banking sector (and vice versa). As they are important for the supervisory policy discussion in Chap. 4, let us go through the channels step by step.

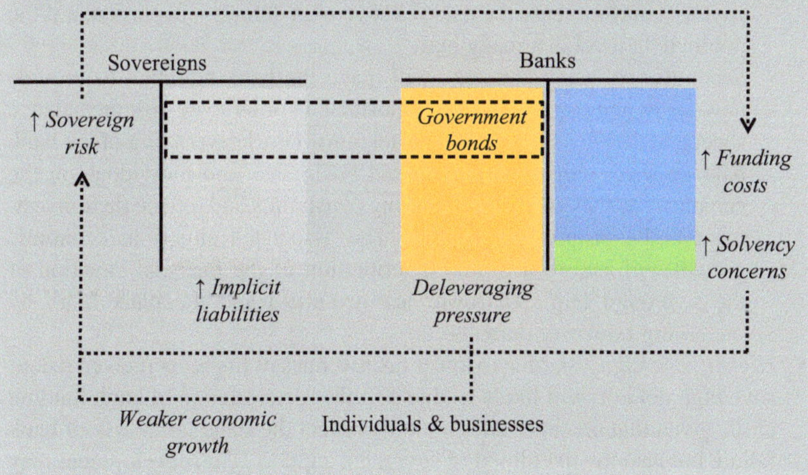

(continued)

[9]The total subscribed capital was 705 billion euros at the time of writing.

Box 3.2 (continued)

- For simplicity, let us treat all banks that are located in an individual euro area country as one systemic bank. The figure shows the balance sheets of this systemic bank and the respective sovereign. Now suppose that a strong economic and financial crisis hits the country, while the capital ratio of the bank is rather low. The bank's asset quality will deteriorate due to the crisis, raising concerns about the bank's solvency if its initial capital is rather low. This will lead to higher funding costs due to the increased risk of failure (shown on the right-hand side of the figure).
- *Higher banking sector risks* impact the sovereign through two main channels:
  - Firstly, they increase the implicit liability of bailing out the systemic bank (or more precisely the expected payout for the sovereign). Why the sovereign has such an implicit liability in the first place was already discussed in Chap. 1 in the context of the special arrangements between banks and sovereigns. In short, the sovereign may want to avoid the failure of a systemic bank, which per definition would have broad implications, and thus provide financial support to the bank. Getting back to the case at hand, the increase in the implicit liability will likely increase the funding costs of the sovereign, as the additional expected payment may increase the risk of a sovereign default—in particular if the public debt level is already high.
  - Secondly, solvency concerns will make the bank reluctant to provide new credit and eager to reduce exposures, in order to de-risk the balance sheet and thereby support the capital ratio. The deleveraging of the bank balance sheet will adversely impact businesses and individuals in the economy, as they may face financing constraints and reduce their investment and consumption activity. The associated slump in economic growth will lead to a further deterioration of the financial situation of the sovereign (e.g., by lower tax revenues) and the bank (e.g., by increasing borrower defaults).
- *Higher sovereign risk* (due to lower tax revenues or higher perceived risk of sovereign default) will likely lead to a further deterioration of bank funding costs, given that the latter does not only reflect the stand-alone risk of bank failure but also the likelihood of sovereign support. This development may give rise to the consequences already described above, thus completing the self-reinforcing adverse feedback loop. In other words, the stated crisis dynamics may create a vicious circle that increases bank and sovereign risk in lockstep and may result in their simultaneous default, unless the bank or the sovereign receives external assistance.

(continued)

Box 3.2 (continued)

- The stated risk spillovers are further *amplified by direct financial exposures in the form of government bonds.* Banks are large holders of government bonds in the euro area and sometimes also serve the role of primary dealers or market makers on government bond markets. In economic terms, higher sovereign risk directly translates into valuation losses on bank balance sheets that are proportional to the bank's holdings of the respective government bonds. In accounting terms, the treatment may be different, as lower bond prices are not always reflected in bank balance sheets with immediate effect.[10]

Banks in other euro area countries reacted to the sovereign debt crisis by reducing exposures to vulnerable countries. Exposure reductions were focused on sovereign and bank bonds in crisis countries and involved both outright sales and purchases of CDS protection. This trend contributed to the increase in risk premiums on the bond market, further fueling the adverse feedback loop described above. Some euro area banks also reduced their liquidity lines to foreign subsidiaries in these countries or exited the respective markets altogether. Banks engaged in these defensive activities not only to limit losses but also to shield themselves from potential market concerns due to heightened risk exposures to the respective sovereigns and banks.

At the same time, banks had to address other challenges. Many banks struggled with continued asset quality deterioration in other parts of their portfolios (i.e., not related to crisis countries) and shifted their focus on restoring capital positions and adjusting their business models to the new environment. For instance, many first- and second-tier banks reduced trading activities and selectively retrenched from international markets during this period. Banks that were nationalized during the crisis also had to engage in similar adjustments as part of their restructuring plans.

Phase 3: Crisis Containment, Centralized Policies, and Continued Vulnerabilities (2013–2015)

The sovereign debt crisis calmed down after a move towards centralized policies in 2012. As shown in Fig. 3.3, sovereign bond yields across the euro area started to decline in the second half of the year. In June 2012, the euro area governments decided to establish the Banking Union, which among others was intended to break the vicious circle of sovereign-bank risk spillovers in crisis countries (see Box 3.2). According to the agreement, this objective should be achieved by shifting supervisory competences from the national to the euro area level and complementing supervision by a joint system of resolving failing systemic banks to reduce the

[10] At times of heightened stress on bond markets, market participants tend to assess risks more based on the economic situation than on the accounting treatment.

implicit liabilities for the respective sovereigns. Joint supervision was meant to foster financial integration and ensure consistent strict supervision for all systemic banks in the euro area. The intention behind the Banking Union was to fundamentally change the way systemic banks would be supervised and resolved, thereby reducing the scope for unpleasant surprises by national governments.

While the situation on government bond markets stabilized, the euro area economy experienced a sluggish recovery that was held back by crisis legacies. Private debt levels were elevated in many subsectors after the precrisis boom and Phases 1 and 2 of the crisis, for instance many non-financial corporates in South European countries remained burdened by high debt. The volume of nonperforming loans continued to rise, yet at a slower pace than during the early crisis years. Also unemployment remained high in some parts of the euro area, exceeding levels of 25% in Greece or Spain, while several other euro area countries saw unemployment rates decline to levels around 5–7% (e.g., Germany or the Netherlands).

In the banking sector, the years 2013–2015 were characterized by the following main trends:

- *Banks struggled with the deterioration in asset quality, in particular stemming from nonperforming loans (NPLs) in market segments that had witnessed strong credit growth in the precrisis period.* At the same time, the levels of risk provisions were improved. New lending remained subdued for the euro area as a whole. Real estate markets showed heterogeneous behavior, with continued price declines in some countries and significant price increases in others (e.g., Germany).
- *Many banks strengthened their capital ratios ahead of the transition to Basel III and in response to revised expectations by bank supervisors and market participants.* The improvement in capital ratios was partly achieved by raising new capital and partly by reducing risk-weighted assets.
- *Profitability remained significantly lower than in the pre-crisis period.* In many banks, low or negative profitability during these years was the result of high risk provisioning, limited new business, and the ongoing process of balance sheet repair (e.g., writing off goodwill from precrisis acquisitions). Low profitability also constrained bank efforts to restore capital buffers from internal sources.

Source: KAL (The Economist, February 2015)

- *Many banks continued to adjust their business models, for instance by selling noncore subsidiaries or aligning their cost structure to lower profitability prospects.* This trend was particularly noticeable in the case of banks that had received public support and were subject to restructuring plans. Overall, the euro area banking system reduced its staff number by 12% or roughly 278,000 from 2008 to 2016.
- *Financial integration in the euro area broadly stabilized at a lower level than in the precrisis period.* While the fragmentation in the euro area money market that had been apparent during the sovereign debt crisis receded from 2012 to 2015, banks in some parts of the euro area still have not regained full access to the interbank market at the time of writing. In addition, euro area banks were on average less engaged in foreign operations through subsidiaries or branches at the end of 2015 compared to the precrisis situation.

After this extended introduction to the euro area banking sector in recent years, the following chapter moves to the question how supervision is conducted in practice as of early 2017. We will first describe the institutional setting of banking supervision in the SSM and then discuss the policy process and the individual policy instruments that are available to supervisors.

References

European Central Bank (ECB). (2007, November). *EU Banking Sector Stability*. Accessed February 16, 2017, from https://www.ecb.europa.eu/pub/pdf/other/eubankingsectorstability2007en.pdf
European Council. (2008, October). *Presidency conclusions*. Accessed from http://www.consilium.europa.eu/uedocs/cms_data/docs/pressdata/en/ec/103441.pdf
Investing.com. Accessed March 30, 2017, from https://www.investing.com/
Stolz, S., & Wedow, M. (2010, July). *Extraordinary measures in extraordinary times – public measures in support of the financial sector in the EU and the United States*. ECB Occasional Paper. Accessed from https://www.ecb.europa.eu/pub/pdf/scpops/ecbocp117.pdf

Further Reading

Blustein, P. (2016). *Laid low: Inside the crisis that overwhelmed Europe and the IMF*. CIGI Press.
European Commission. (2017). *Coping with the international financial crisis at the national level in a European context: Impact and financial sector policy responses in 2008–2015*. Accessed from https://ec.europa.eu/info/system/files/eucountries-responses-to-financial-crisis.pdf

Banking Supervision

4

Banking supervision is a shared responsibility of the ECB and national supervisory authorities in the euro area. This chapter explains how supervision is conducted within the single supervisory mechanism (SSM), which started its operations in November 2014. The first section puts the establishment of the SSM in the context of the crisis since 2007. The second section lays out the institutional setting, responsibilities, and decision-making process of the SSM. The third section provides an overview of the supervisory policy process, the main policy instruments, and their enforcement. The last section focuses on the international dimension of banking supervision, with a focus on supervisory cooperation with non-SSM countries.

The main objective of banking supervision lies in safeguarding the soundness of individual banks.[1] Supervisors take a micro-level view towards banks. In a sense, they can be thought of taking the magnifying glass and analyzing an individual institution within the euro area bank network in detail, as illustrated in Fig. 4.1. The soundness of a bank ultimately depends on the question whether its financial position is strong enough to avert default through illiquidity or insolvency. Accordingly, the supervisory perspective is forward-looking and takes many factors into account, including whether risks are adequately managed, the business model is viable, and the bank complies with applicable regulations.

The tasks of bank supervisors cover a broad range of activities:

- All banks in the euro area need to have a *license* to perform banking services. The license serves as an entry restriction to the market. Anyone that wants to set up a new bank needs to submit an application to the supervisor and prove that the new bank would meet all applicable requirements. In addition to granting new licenses, bank supervisors may also withdraw an existing license under certain circumstances.

[1]Another objective is the orderly market exit of failing banks. How this can be achieved in practice will also be discussed in this chapter.

M. Fandl, *Monetary and Financial Policy in the Euro Area*, Springer Texts in Business and Economics, https://doi.org/10.1007/978-3-319-72643-4_4

Fig. 4.1 Supervision of single banks

- Banks need to fulfill certain *liquidity requirements* that should reduce the risk of becoming illiquid. For instance, banks may be required to hold a certain amount of high-quality liquid assets to meet potential cash outflows in the near term.
- Banks also need to fulfill certain *capital requirements* that should reduce the risk of becoming insolvent. For instance, banks may be required to have a minimum amount of high-quality capital to absorb unexpected losses.
- As even banks that appear liquid and solvent may cause concerns, supervisors also need to assess the *risk exposures of banks and how they are managed*. In a similar vein, supervisors investigate whether the internal policies and processes are adequate, which type of activities the bank is engaged in, and whether the bank managers are qualified to run the bank.
- Supervisors may perform *on-site inspections* to get a first-hand impression how the above issues are addressed in practice and to demand corrective action if needed.
- Since large banks operate in many jurisdictions, supervisors also need to *coordinate with other supervisory authorities*. For instance, a bank may have a foreign subsidiary outside the euro area that affects its risk position at the consolidated level. The supervisor of the banking group thus needs to discuss with the host supervisor, i.e., the supervisor in the country in which the foreign subsidiary is located, what would be the appropriate capital level to hold against these risks.
- Lastly, supervisors need to *enforce supervisory actions*, such as specific capital requirements or corrective actions.

4.1 Single Supervisory Mechanism

The Single Supervisory Mechanism (SSM) is a part of the European Banking Union that was established in 2014. Figure 4.2 illustrates its key components.

Fig. 4.2 Banking Union

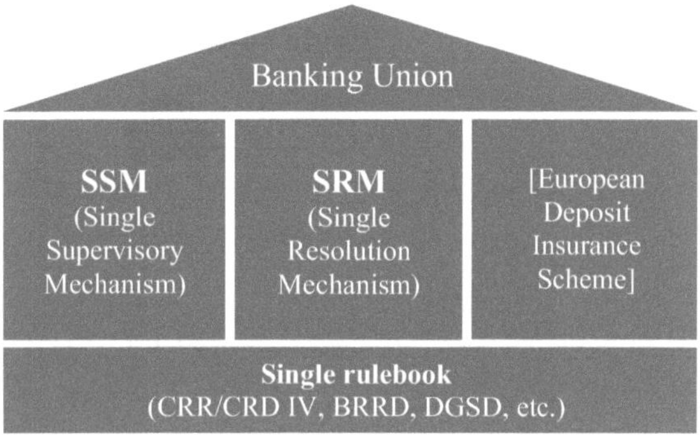

- *The foundation of the Banking Union is the Single Rulebook that is applicable in all EU member states.* It includes common capital requirements for banks and a harmonized capital definition. Both are anchored in the Capital Requirements Regulation (CRR) and the Capital Requirements Directive IV (CRD IV), which are the legal acts that transposed Basel III (see Box 4.2) in the European Union. On several issues, the CRR and CRD IV refer to technical standards that were developed by the European Banking Authority (EBA) and also considered part of the Single Rulebook. Additional elements of the Single Rulebook are common rules for early intervention and resolution of weak banks[2] as well as a harmonization of deposit guarantee schemes.[3,4]
- *The first pillar of the Banking Union is the Single Supervisory Mechanism (SSM).* It applies to the supervision of all euro area banks.
- *The second pillar is the Single Resolution Mechanism (SRM).* It provides a framework for the cross-border resolution of first- and second-tier banks in the euro area in case of their failure. The main institutions of the SRM are the Single Resolution Board and the Single Resolution Fund, which are both located in Brussels.
- *The third pillar relates to a European system of deposit insurance.* It has not been put in place by the time of writing. The EC published a proposal for a European system of deposit insurance in November 2015, which remains under discussion as of early 2017.

The SSM consists of the ECB and the national supervisory authorities of the euro area. With its establishment, the ECB assumed the responsibility of a supervisory authority for euro area banks. Prior to November 2014, the ECB did not have any active role in banking supervision. Daily supervisory tasks in the SSM are shared

[2]Through the Bank Recovery and Resolution Directive (BRRD).

[3]Through the Deposit Guarantee Scheme Directive (DGSD).

[4]An interactive single rulebook is available on the EBA website: https://www.eba.europa.eu/regulation-and-policy/single-rulebook/interactive-single-rolebook

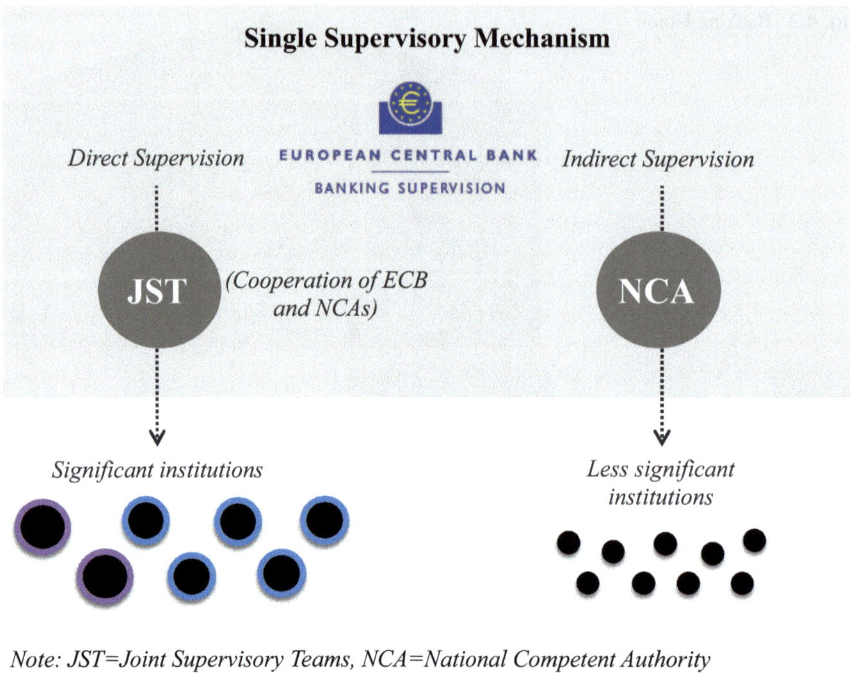

Fig. 4.3 Supervision of significant and less significant institutions in the euro area

between the ECB[5] and the supervisory authorities in euro area member states, known as the National Competent Authorities (NCAs). In some member states, the NCAs are central banks (e.g., the Netherlands). In other member states, supervisory tasks are shared between the central bank and a separate supervisory authority (e.g., Germany).

The ECB directly supervises the largest euro area banks with the support of NCAs, while NCAs have the primary responsibility for supervising smaller banks. Broadly speaking, first- and second-tier banks are supervised by the ECB and third-tier banks primarily by NCAs in the context of the SSM. Figure 4.3 illustrates the allocation of supervisory tasks for euro area banks.

- The ECB directly supervises the so-called *Significant Institutions (SIs)*. Supervision is performed through joint supervisory teams (JSTs) that are led by the ECB and comprise staff of the ECB and NCAs. One JST is established for each bank. Significant institutions are defined by their absolute and relative importance, i.e., their importance for the euro area as a whole and for the respective member states.

[5]The supervisory function of the ECB is referred to as ECB Supervision.

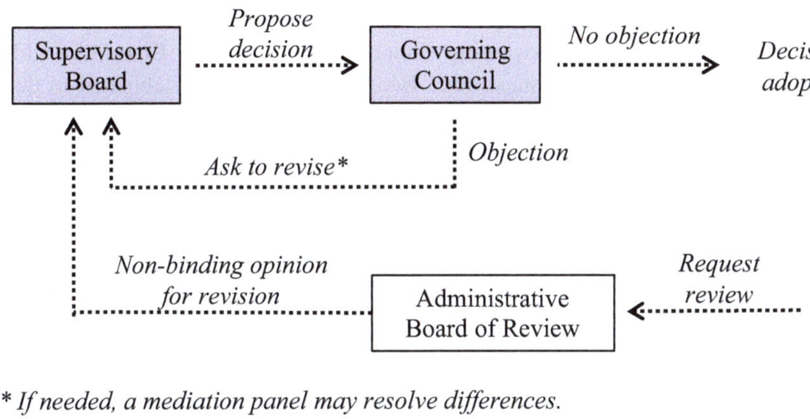

Fig. 4.4 Supervisory decision-making process for significant institutions

126 euro area banks were classified as significant institutions as of end-2016, comprising more than 80% of total assets of the banking sector.[6]

- The NCAs supervise the so-called *less significant institutions (LSIs)* based on common guidelines. The ECB oversees the supervision of the less significant institutions. If needed, it may also take over the direct responsibility for their supervision to ensure the consistent application of supervisory standards, Around 3300 euro area banks were classified as less significant institutions as of end-2016 (ECB 2017b).

The Supervisory Board of the ECB effectively takes all supervisory decisions for significant institutions. It comprises six ECB representatives, including the chair of the Supervisory Board (Danièle Nouy at the time of writing) and one senior NCA representative per SSM/euro area country. The Supervisory Board plans and carries out all supervisory tasks of the SSM. Whenever it takes a decision on an individual bank, the coordinator of the joint supervisory team provides the required analysis. All decisions of the Supervisory Board further need to be proposed to the Governing Council as the highest decision-making body of the ECB in a non-objection procedure. If the Governing Council has no objection, the decision is considered formally adopted. In case of an objection, the decision is sent back to the Supervisory Board for submission of a new draft decision. If this happens, the SSM Regulation, which provides the legal basis for the SSM, stipulates that the ECB needs to inform the European Parliament. Figure 4.4 provides a summary of the described decision-

[6]Significant institutions are euro area banks (1) with total assets above 30 billion euros, (2) with economic importance for the specific country or the EU economy as a whole, (3) that are among the three largest banks of a participating member state, (4) with total assets above 5 billion euros and a ratio of cross-border assets or liabilities in more than one other member state to its total assets above 20%, or (5) that requested or received direct assistance from the ESM.

making process. It also shows that a mediation panel is established to resolve differences of view between Governing Council and Supervisory Board. An additional body, the so-called Administrative Board of Review, is established to deal with cases in which the respective bank or concerned individuals request a review of the adopted supervisory decision. In such cases, this body is tasked with issuing a nonbinding opinion to the Supervisory Board.

The decision-making process reflects the separation principle of monetary policy and banking supervision within the ECB. With the establishment of the SSM, the Supervisory Board was created as a new body for supervisory decisions, while the Governing Council remained responsible for monetary policy decisions. The separation of the two policy functions was considered important by the architects of the SSM to avoid possible conflicts of interests. The separation does not only affect the decision-making bodies but also the supervisory business areas. The supervisory part of the ECB, which at the time of writing comprised approximately 1200 staff and was established within a short period of time, is also located in a separate building from the monetary policy part.[7] In addition, the sharing of supervisory data and documents is largely regulated within the organization.

As a general rule, the ECB performs an in-depth assessment of significant institutions before it takes over the responsibility of supervising them. If this assessment finds major weaknesses, the respective banks may for instance be asked to cover identified capital shortfalls or increase risk provisions in individual portfolios. The requirement to perform such a comprehensive assessment is set out in the SSM Regulation.

Box 4.1 ECB Comprehensive Assessment 2014

In 2014, the ECB conducted a major assessment for 130 euro area banks before it took over its supervisory responsibilities. This exercise was conducted with support by NCAs and covered 82% of the total assets of the euro area banking sector. It consisted of two parts: An asset quality review, i.e., a point-in-time assessment of bank assets, and a stress test, i.e., a forward-looking assessment of their resilience under adverse conditions. In cases where the capital ratio of a bank was found to fall below certain hurdle rates, the respective bank had to take measures to cover the identified capital shortfalls. The final results of the exercise were published in October 2014.

The comprehensive assessment showed that the capital levels of euro area banks and their resilience had been significantly strengthened since the beginning of the crisis. The identified net capital shortfall amounted to 9.5 billion euros (after capital measures taken by banks in early 2014) and was subsequently covered by the respective banks.

[7]ECB Supervision is located in the Euro Tower in the city center of Frankfurt, while most other ECB business areas are located in the new ECB Main Building, which was inaugurated in 2015.

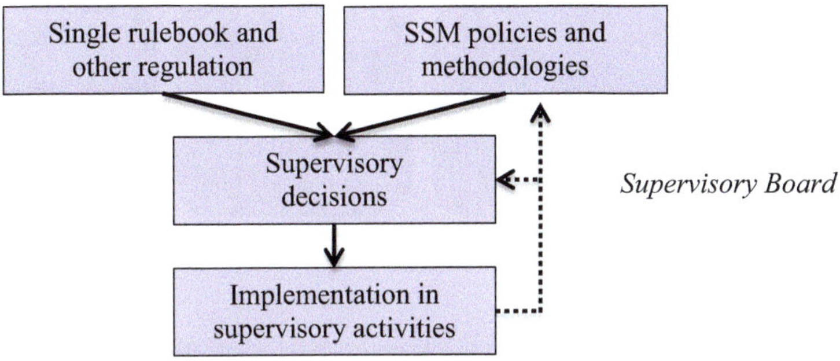

Fig. 4.5 Supervisory policy process in the euro area

The Supervisory Board also defines and communicates the supervisory priorities on an annual basis. The supervisory priorities for the respective year are published on the ECB website. For instance, the supervisory priorities of the SSM for 2016 were the analysis of bank business models with a focus on profitability drivers, credit risk with a focus on nonperforming loans and concentrations, as well as bank capital, liquidity, risk governance, and data quality. Through which supervisory policy tools these issues may be addressed by the SSM will be discussed in the next section.

4.2 Supervisory Policy

The supervisory policy process in the euro area is illustrated in Fig. 4.5. It has three main phases, similar to the monetary policy process that was described in Chap. 2.

- *The specific policies have their origin in laws and regulations, such as the Single Rulebook, or are developed within the SSM.* For instance, a policy may be set out in a technical standard or an internal methodology (e.g., on how to assess the viability of bank business models). In practice, many regulatory changes are prepared by international or European working groups and adopted by the European Commission or the European Banking Authority (EBA). Supervisors of the ECB and NCAs actively contribute to the design of these new regulations.[8]
- *The Supervisory Board decides on the supervisory policies for SSM banks, which are based on the Single Rulebook.* This does not only involve policy instruments that directly affect banks but also the methodologies and standards that need to be applied by the JSTs in the conduct of supervision.
- *The JSTs implement the policies in their daily supervisory activities.* Separate teams assess the effectiveness of the policies and provide feedback to the Supervisory Board on potential areas for improvement.

[8]Supervisors and regulators are not synonyms. Bank regulation needs to be adopted by legislative bodies, as it is the case with other laws and regulations.

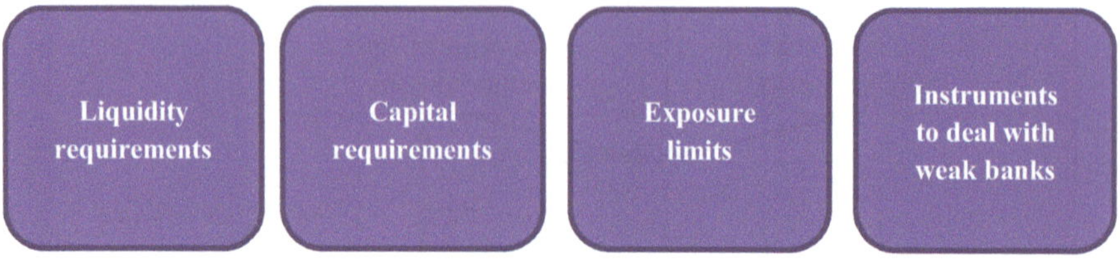

Fig. 4.6 Key instruments for banking supervision

Most policy tools in banking supervision could be grouped into liquidity requirements, capital requirements, exposure limits, and instruments to deal with weak banks (see Fig. 4.6). The following section focuses on their key characteristics. Apart from these four categories, supervisors may also apply other policy measures within the limits of applicable laws and regulations.

The liquidity and capital requirements of the SSM are based on the Basel III framework, which was developed in response to the financial crisis. Box 4.2 provides a short overview of Basel III. It introduces some key terms that facilitate the discussion of supervisory policy tools on the following pages.

Box 4.2 A Short Overview of Basel III

The Basel III framework sets international standards for liquidity and capital requirements for banks. It was developed by the Basel Committee on Banking Supervision in response to the global financial crisis (BCBS 2011). The rules were later adopted in the EU. Compared to bank regulation in the precrisis period, the Basel III framework includes more stringent liquidity and capital requirements. These requirements are gradually phased in from 2014 to 2022.[9]

1. *Liquidity regulation*

   Liquidity regulation was not a priority of regulators in the precrisis period. With the start of the financial crisis, it became clear that many banks were heavily reliant on short-term wholesale funding, which made them vulnerable to funding market stress. In addition, many banks applied overly optimistic assumptions in their liquidity management, in particular regarding funding availability during stress periods.

   In response to the crisis, Basel III introduced two liquidity requirements for banks:

   - The *liquidity coverage ratio (LCR)*, which requires banks to hold a minimum amount of high-quality liquid assets to survive a 30-day

(continued)

[9]The description of Basel III requirements follows the final rules that are applicable from 2019 onwards.

Box 4.2 (continued)

liquidity shock. It is meant to strengthen the resilience of banks in case of liquidity stress. To use a metaphor, the LCR works similar to an airbag in a car that dampens the impact of a crash.

- The *Net Stable Funding Ratio (NSFR)*, which requires banks to have a sufficient amount of stable funding—as opposed to more "flighty" sources of funding such as short-term wholesale funding—to refinance long-term operations. The main objective of the NSFR is to prevent banks from excessive maturity transformation and wholesale funding. In other words, the NSFR should limit the likelihood that banks become subject to liquidity stress, similar to cruise control in a car that should reduce the likelihood of a crash.

2. *Capital regulation*

The crisis revealed several deficiencies of capital regulation for banks. Many banks did not have sufficient high-quality capital to absorb unexpected losses during the crisis, even though most of them had been in compliance with capital requirements. Banks were also hit by risks that were not adequately captured by risk weights in capital regulation, such as securitizations or risky government bonds. Furthermore, capital regulation applied uniformly across banks, with no differentiation by size and complexity, and was not increased during the precrisis boom period.

Basel III aimed at addressing these deficiencies mainly through amendments of the minimum capital requirements. The overall capital requirement framework is based on three pillars, which were already in place in previous Basel accords. Basel I was published in 1988 and Basel II in 2004, entering into force in many euro area countries in 2008. The overall philosophy of Basel III remained largely unchanged from Basel II. Its three pillars are the following:

- *Pillar 1 sets capital requirement for specific risks.* Banks are required to have capital at least equal to 8% of their risk-weighted assets (RWAs). RWAs are determined by the bank exposure to three main risk types three main risk types: credit risk, market risk, and operational risk. For most banks, RWAs result mainly from credit risk. Two approaches are applied in determining credit risk RWAs: The standardized approach applies fixed weights that depend on criteria such as portfolio segments or external credit ratings. Alternatively, internal rating-based approaches may be used with approval by the supervisor. They allow banks to apply risk weights that depend on a number of parameters (risk exposure, probability of default, loss given default, etc.) that are (partly) estimated by the bank's internal models. In addition to the minimum capital requirement of 8% of RWAs, which was already in place before the

(continued)

Box 4.2 (continued)

crisis, Basel III introduced more stringent requirement for high-quality capital as well as three additional capital buffers, for instance to account for differences in systemic importance by banks and for situations of excessive credit growth. Basel III also introduced a simple leverage ratio as a non-risk weighted indicator of capital adequacy. At the same time, the definition of RWAs was initially left largely unchanged under Basel III. The policy section below discusses the stated elements and their interplay in more detail.

- *Pillar 2 is known as the supervisory review process.* It plays an important role in the SSM and is also discussed in the policy section below. Its overall aim is to ensure that banks have adequate capital to cover all risks they are exposed to by assessing the bank's current capital adequacy and setting bank-specific capital requirements. Hence, it complements the Pillar 1 requirements by providing a more bank-specific view on risks and capital adequacy.
- *Pillar 3 includes disclosure requirements for banks.* It aims at supporting market discipline by allowing analysts, investors, and other market participants to assess the bank's capital structure, RWAs, and other elements based on standardized definitions.

Liquidity Requirements

Liquidity regulation gained in importance following the severe liquidity strains that were observed during Phase 1 of the financial crisis. As discussed in Chap. 3, several banks faced liquidity shortages due to an excessive reliance on short-term wholesale funding, and central banks stepped in with unprecedented liquidity support. Such systemic liquidity crises had not been anticipated by the precrisis regulatory framework. The mainstream view back then was that banks would always be able to obtain sufficient liquidity from funding markets as long as they were sufficiently capitalized. The crisis developments proved this view to be insufficient, leading to an adjustment of the regulatory framework under Basel III.

Liquidity requirements are intended to ensure that banks have sufficient space to deal with liquidity risks. Liquidity risks in banks arise from three main sources:

- *Firstly, banks take deposits and need to be able to meet customer requests, such as cash withdrawals or electronic transfers.* A key characteristic of banks is that some of their liabilities include commercial bank money and other deposits that may be turned into money within a short period of time. Banks thus face the risk that many depositors may want to withdraw their deposits at the same time, creating the risk of a bank run. If a bank cannot pay out its deposits upon demand, it becomes illiquid.
- *Secondly, many banks rely on funding types that are unstable in crisis situations.* For instance, a bank may engage in short-term funding transactions with only a

few counterparties. When a crisis hits, the bank will likely run into funding difficulties because of the inability to roll over these funding transactions in the market. Overall, customer deposits proved to be rather stable during the crisis, while short-term debt instruments, such as interbank deposits, tended to be flighty.

- *Thirdly, some liquid assets on bank balance sheets may be less liquid in crisis situations compared to normal times.* Lower market liquidity means that banks cannot sell assets immediately at low cost. For instance, a bank may find it difficult to liquidate some of its security holdings in a crisis, unless it accepts high price discounts. Sometimes, other market participants are not willing to purchase the offered assets at all, and the respective market segment may dry up completely. Such developments could be observed with respect to securitizations and selected government bonds in Phase 1 and 2 of the crisis as discussed in Chap. 3.

What are the main policy tools in liquidity regulation?

- *As a first policy tool, supervisors require banks to hold a sufficiently high buffer of liquid assets to repay creditors and depositors under stressed conditions.* This is the basic idea behind the liquidity coverage ratio (LCR), which was introduced as a supervisory tool in the euro area following the transposition of Basel III.[10] The numerator of the LCR includes the bank's current holdings of high-quality liquid assets. Broadly, it covers the three types of money and other high-quality assets that can be pledged as collateral or sold quickly at a rather stable price. Such high-quality assets include for instance government bonds with high credit ratings. The denominator of the LCR are net cash outflows over a 30-day period under stress conditions. In liquidity stress situations, outflows are typically amplified (e.g., due to higher withdrawals of customer deposits), while inflows are reduced as the bank may be constrained in obtaining wholesale funding. Overall, the LCR requires that net liquidity outflows under stress conditions over a 1-month horizon need to be fully covered by available liquid assets. Should the bank witness similar funding stress in reality, the liquid asset buffer is expected to be used to cover the respective outflows. In other words, supervisors may allow the LCR to temporarily fall below 100% in stress situations.
- *As second policy tool, supervisors may require banks to have a sufficient amount of stable funding that should not dry up in times of stress.* This is the basic idea behind the net stable funding ratio (NSFR). The ratio compares available stable funding by the bank with required stable funding. Available stable funding is determined by assigning weights to bank liabilities, with higher weights for funding sources that proved stable during the crisis. For instance, the NSFR applies a higher weight to customer deposits than to short-term wholesale funding. The required amount of stable funding is determined

[10] Single Rulebook: Art. 411–412, 414, and 416–426 CRR.

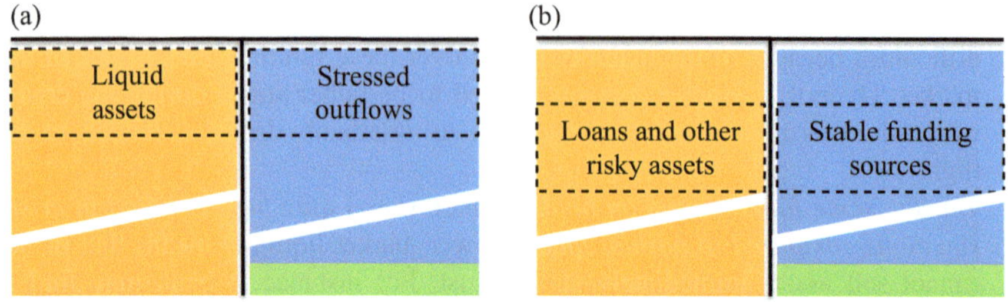

Fig. 4.7 Basic idea behind LCR and NSFR. (**a**) Sufficient buffer of liquid assets. (**b**) Stable funding

by assigning weights to bank assets, with higher weights to long-term risky assets. For instance, a higher weight applies to a 10-year mortgage loan than to a 10-year government bond.[11] Overall, the NSFR aims at ensuring that long-term risky exposures are adequately met by stable funding sources. Figure 4.7 illustrates the basic idea behind the NSFR as compared to the LCR. By the time of writing, the NSFR has not been fully implemented in the euro area yet.

- *As a third policy tool, supervisors can set bank-specific liquidity requirements to address specific liquidity risks in an individual bank.* For instance, a bank may rely on FX funding from only a few counterparties, making it difficult to obtain FX liquidity in stress situations. In such cases, the supervisor may set an LCR for the respective currency. More generally, the supervisor may design plausible bank-specific stress scenarios and estimate the respective net liquidity outflows. If they exceed the counterbalancing capacity of the bank, i.e., its liquid assets and secured funding possibilities, the supervisor may request the bank to improve its liquidity position.[12]

The SSM keeps a low profile in public communication on applicable liquidity requirements for individual banks. Several conflicting aspects surround the policy decision how transparent supervisors should be on applicable liquidity requirements and banks' compliance with them. On the one hand, creditors and investors in the bank may consider this information material, as it may influence their decision in providing funding to the bank. On the other hand, publishing information about the liquidity situation of individual banks may cause concerns by depositors and may even trigger a bank run if a bank does not comply with applicable liquidity requirements.

Liquidity requirements set by bank supervisors are not the only policy instrument that determines the minimum liquidity buffers that apply to banks. Banks are also

[11]As a caveat, the asset weights under the NSFR are not the same as the risk weights that are applied in capital regulation. The asset weights are set out in Basel III and the Single Rulebook (Art. 413, 427–428 CRR).

[12]Such liquidity stress tests are part of the liquidity element of the SREP (supervisory review and evaluation process) for euro area banks, which we discuss on the following pages.

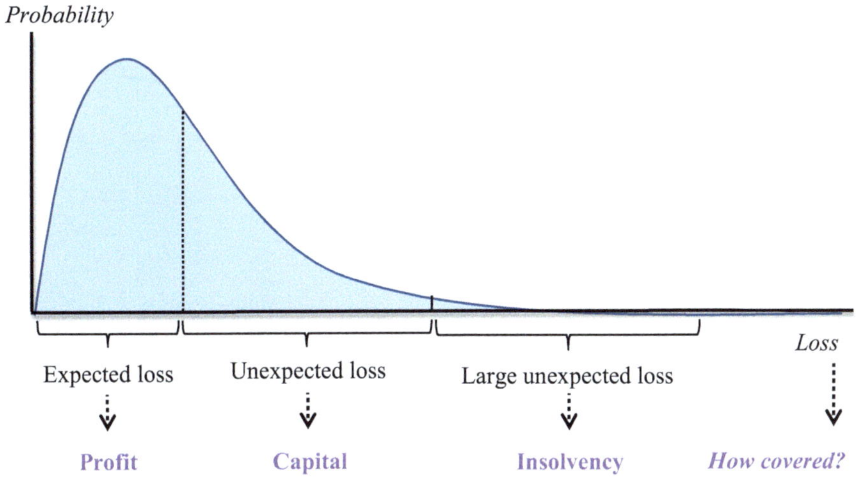

Fig. 4.8 Coverage of bank losses through profits and capital

subject to reserve requirements in the context of monetary policy. We will discuss the interaction of policy instruments in Chap. 6. Let us now turn to capital requirements as the second main policy tool for bank supervisors.

Capital Requirements

Bank operations always involve some risk of incurring losses. For instance, some borrowers may not repay their bank loans, which will likely result in a loss for the bank. At the bank level, the size of future losses is difficult to predict, yet information is available about the empirical distribution of losses across a large sample of banks, which provides a useful yardstick for setting capital regulation. The empirical loss distribution teaches us that minor losses occur regularly and may be considered the normal cost of doing business, while major losses that may threaten the existence of the bank occur less frequently. Hence, the probability distribution of bank losses is skewed, as illustrated by Fig. 4.8 in a stylized way. In the following, we will refer to the left-hand side of the distribution as expected losses, which are frequent but small, and to the right-hand side as unexpected losses, which are less frequent but potentially large.

The prime reason why banks should have capital is to be in a position to cover unexpected losses as long as they are a going concern. Capital is characterized by its ability to absorb losses. Conceptually, it is not supposed to cover all types of losses but only unexpected losses up to a certain point. Banks should be able to anticipate expected losses and incorporate them in the pricing of the products they originate (e.g., loans) or purchase (e.g., securities). For instance, banks typically charge a higher interest rate on loans to borrowers with low creditworthiness compared to borrowers with a higher ability to repay, due to the difference in credit risk and expected losses. If we aggregate all loans and view bank profitability at the portfolio level, we observe that banks typically earn a positive net interest margin, which is partly due to the stated risk premiums and partly due to other factors. These profits provide a first line of defense against losses. The second line of defense is capital,

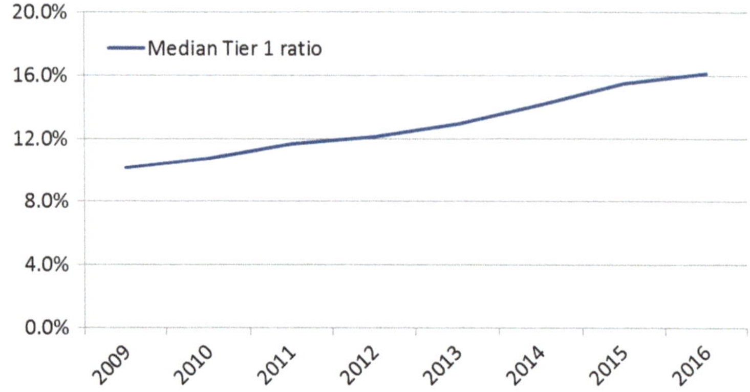

Fig. 4.9 Median Tier 1 ratio of euro area banks. Source: ECB (2017a)

which may cover unexpected losses, i.e., losses that go beyond expected losses, up to a certain point as illustrated in Fig. 4.8. If unexpected losses exceed this point, bank capital will be insufficient to cover them and the bank will be likely to fail. In other words, the bank will not be a going concern anymore.

Capital requirements are expressed as a ratio of capital to exposures. Under Basel III, the most important capital definition is Common Equity Tier 1 (CET1) capital which includes high-quality capital with undisputed loss-absorption capacity. This means that it is perpetual and ranks below all other claims in the event of insolvency. If other capital elements are added that may also absorb losses while the bank is still a going concern, the resulting capital definition is called Tier 1 capital. As regards the denominator of capital ratios, two exposure definitions are used:

- If total exposures are applied, the resulting metric is known as the leverage ratio.[13] It has a long history in banking supervision and was used in many European countries prior to the Basel Accord of 1988 (Basel I). The leverage ratio fell into oblivion during the 1990s and 2000s, but received renewed interest as a simple alternative way to assess capital adequacy of banks under Basel III.
- Risk-weighted assets (RWA) serve as an alternative measure for a bank's exposures and are widely used in capital regulation.[14] They are computed by assigning risk weights to all assets of a bank. For instance, a risk weight of 100% is applied to an unsecured loan to a BBB+ rated corporate and a risk weight of 35% to a retail loan secured by residential property. The most used capital ratio under Basel III is the CET1 ratio, which is computed as CET1 capital over RWA. Prior to Basel III, the Tier 1 ratio (Tier 1 capital over RWA) was used as the main indicator to compare capital ratios across banks. Figure 4.9 shows the

[13]This description focuses on credit risk RWAs for simplicity. The term RWA relates to the original Basel III documents by the BCBS. The EBA refers to them as Risk Exposure Amounts.

[14]A simple type of the leverage ratio is based on total assets. The leverage ratio under Basel III takes on- and off-balance sheet exposure into account.

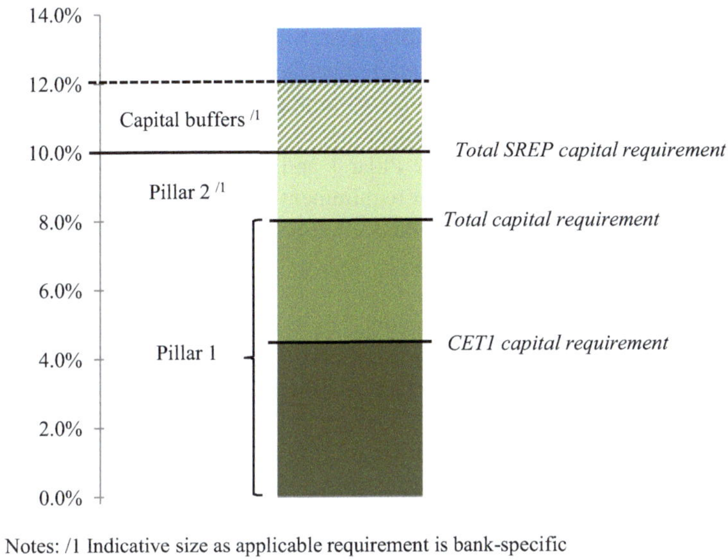

Fig. 4.10 Capital requirements for SSM banks

development of the median Tier 1 ratio for the euro area banking sector from 2009 to 2016. It increased from around 10% in 2009 to 16% by 2016.

Capital requirements for euro area banks are partly stated in regulation and partly set by the supervisor. Figure 4.10 shows the stylized capital requirements that apply to euro area banks under Pillar 1 and 2 of Basel III as transposed in the European Union by CRD IV and CRR.[15] As the figure illustrates, the requirements are stacked on top of each other, starting with Pillar 1 requirements at the bottom.

- *Under Pillar 1, the minimum CET1 ratio is 4.5% and the minimum total capital ratio is 8%.* While the CET1 ratio has to be held in CET1 capital, the remaining Pillar 1 requirement can be held in other capital instruments.[16]
- *Supervisors set an additional Pillar 2 requirement per bank, which sits on top of Pillar 1 requirements.*[17] The additional Pillar 2 requirement yields the total SREP capital requirement, which is expressed as an add-on to the minimum capital requirement. The requirement is bank-specific and determined in the supervisory review and evaluation process (SREP). In practice, the total SREP capital

[15]The chart is based on the fully-loaded Basel III requirements that apply from 2019 onwards. From 2014 to 2018, most Basel III capital requirements are gradually phased in.

[16]The minimum Tier 1 capital requirement is 6%.

[17]Putting the Pillar 2 requirement on top of the Pillar 1 requirement is the EU approach, while Basel III is silent on it. Some other countries, such as the United States, apply a parallel approach.

requirement is more relevant for banks than the minimum requirements under Pillar 1, given that it becomes binding first.

- *On top of the total SREP capital requirement, several capital buffers may apply to the respective bank.* They include the capital conservation buffer as well as macroprudential capital buffers, which will be discussed in Chap. 5. Importantly, the capital buffers differ from the Pillar 1 and 2 minimum requirements in that noncompliance with the full buffer requirement does not have the consequence of supervisory sanctions. However, banks that do not meet the capital buffers face restrictions on dividend payments.

The supervisory review and evaluation process (SREP) is the main supervisory tool to set bank-specific capital requirements in the SSM. The SREP gained in importance for first- and second-tier banks in the euro area with the creation of the Single Rulebook[18] and the SSM. Within the SSM, the ECB applies a common methodology to perform the SREP of the 129 significant institutions. In the following, we briefly explain the main elements and how the process works in practice.

The SREP consists of four main elements for which supervisors assign scores that are based on constrained judgment. This means that supervisors first assign preliminary scores that are based on hard evidence and then modify them in a constrained way based on supervisory judgment. The final scores reflect their supervisory assessment and are aggregated into the SREP decision. The four elements are the following:

- *As the first element, supervisors assess the solvency risk and capital adequacy of banks.* The ultimate purpose of the assessment lies in getting a proper understanding of the bank's risk of incurring unexpected losses and the capital needed to cover these losses. In practice, this first element is the key determinant of the total SREP capital requirement.
- *The other three elements pertain to a supervisory assessment of (1) bank-specific liquidity risk, (2) whether the business model of the bank is viable and sustainable, and (3) whether the internal governance and risk management by the bank are adequate.*[19]

The SREP assessment of solvency risk and capital adequacy is based on three pillars according to the SREP methodology. In the first pillar, the supervisor forms his own view on the risks the bank is exposed to, how the bank manages them, and how much capital the bank should hold against them. The bank does the same on a regular basis in the so-called Internal Capital Adequacy Assessment Process (ICAAP). The second pillar of the SREP is a supervisory review of the bank's ICAAP. The third pillar requires the bank and the supervisor to perform stress tests in order to test the bank's resilience should the stated risks materialize. Based on the

[18]Single Rulebook: Art. 97 CRD IV and EBA technical standards.

[19]This last element was already mentioned in the section on liquidity requirements.

results of the three pillars, the JSTs arrive at the total SREP capital requirement for the individual bank (e.g., a minimum CET1 ratio of 10% as in Fig. 4.10).

The SREP process follows the supervisory policy process that we described earlier.

- *In the first step, the ECB develops the common SREP methodology, taking into account the Single Rulebook.* This methodology is approved by the Supervisory Board and adopted after non-objection by the Governing Council. The main elements of the methodology are communicated to the supervised banks.
- *In the second step, the joint supervisory teams (JSTs) implement the common methodology for each significant institution.* The SREP is an annual exercise that starts in the first quarter and ends with final decisions in the fourth quarter. During the implementation process, supervisors from ECB and NCAs perform their analyses of the stated four elements. Thereafter, the preliminary SREP results are shared in a confidential setting with non-SSM supervisory authorities in case the respective banking group has subsidiaries in the respective country. This setting is known as supervisory colleges and will be discussed further below. In parallel to the SREP of the 126 significant institutions, which is conducted by the respective JSTs, a separate team of supervisors performs analyses across all significant institutions to cross-check the results and ensure a consistent treatment. Once the analytical process is finalized, the JSTs prepare the draft SREP decisions of the respective banks, including bank-specific policy proposals.
- *In the third step, the Supervisory Board reviews the findings and policy proposals by the JSTs and makes the final SREP decisions for each significant institution.* The decision includes an add-on to the capital requirement, which is the total SREP capital requirement mentioned above (see Fig. 4.10). The average SREP capital requirement in 2015 was approximately 10% and had to be held in CET1 capital.[20] In addition, the SSM may also set other supervisory measures in its SREP decisions, such as a higher LCR requirement or additional reporting obligations. The SREP decisions are formally communicated to the respective banks in the fourth quarter of the year and apply for the following financial year. Upon receipt of the decision, the banks have the right to be heard.

At the time of writing, the SSM did not publish the total SREP capital requirements of individual banks. Nevertheless, several banks unilaterally communicated their respective SREP capital requirements to investors and the general public. In addition to Pillar 2 requirements, the SSM introduced the so-called Pillar 2 guidance in 2016. The guidance is determined by the supervisor

[20]ECB (2016) provides an overview of the methodology as of early 2016.

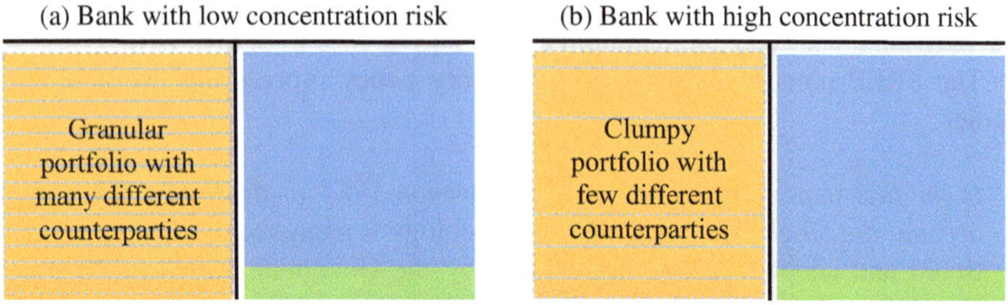

Fig. 4.11 Basic idea behind exposure limits

at a level that exceeds the total SREP capital requirement.[21] In case the bank falls short of the guidance level but fulfills the total SREP capital requirement and capital buffers, no automatic supervisory measures are triggered. However, the supervisor may use this information in requiring additional measures based on the situation of the bank.[22]

Exposure Limits

Regulators and supervisors can also impose outright limits on risk exposures of banks. Such limits may for instance prohibit banks from building up excessive exposures to an individual counterparty. Exposure limits are a more intrusive tool than capital requirements as they cap the absolute amount of exposures rather than regulating the capital to be held against them.

The most used type of exposure limits are large exposure limits that prevent banks from taking excessive concentration risks (see Fig. 4.11). If they were not in place, a bank could take very large exposures to an individual counterparty,[23] such as by providing massive loans to a single industrial company. This would be problematic as the bank could face large losses in case the respective counterparty defaults. In the worst case, the bank could not be able to absorb these losses, even if it had been in compliance with the applicable capital requirements. For this reason, large exposure limits are in place and apply to all euro area banks as part of the Single Rulebook.[24] They are determined for each bank as a percentage of its capital, with some differentiation by the type of large exposure. Stricter limits apply to exposures that are considered riskier. Some exposures are exempt from the large exposure limits, most notably sovereign exposures. At the time of writing, introducing such limits was under discussion in international fora. The issue is also relevant from the perspective of the Banking Union, which follows the objective of limiting sovereign-bank risk spillovers, as discussed earlier. Ever since the start of Phase

[21]The Pillar 2 guidance that was set for SIs in the euro area in late 2016 also incorporated the results of the 2016 EBA/SREP stress tests.

[22]See ECB (2016), page 27.

[23]In practice, large exposures limits do not apply to individual clients but to groups of connected clients (e.g., one limit applies to the exposure to a company and its subsidiaries, as their credit risk is connected).

[24]Single Rulebook: Art. 387–403 CRR.

2 of the crisis, many euro area banks have increased their exposure to the domestic sovereign, which could make the introduction of caps on sovereign exposures binding for many euro area banks, depending on the calibration.

Regulators and supervisors can also set additional exposure limits. For instance, the SSM applied a limit on domestic sovereign exposures of large Greek banks in early 2015. At the time, Greek banks had lost market access, relied heavily on central bank funding, and were already significantly exposed to the Greek State. The latter faced funding difficulties, and it was likely that banks would increase their sovereign exposure during this situation. While the decision to cap the exposure did not alleviate the strained financing situation of the Greek sovereign, it limited sovereign-bank linkages and prevented banks from a further deterioration in their funding situation. Also in other circumstances, the SSM occasionally applied exposure limits to euro area banks, for instance on specific foreign markets.

Overall, the policy instrument of exposure limits was more commonly used several decades ago than at the time of writing. Many European banks used to face restrictions by type of exposure until the 1980s. Some of these restrictions can be still seen in current bank names, such as mortgage banks or building societies. The exposure limits were gradually relaxed during the 1980s and 1990s, which allowed the respective banks to engage in other activities and expand their operations. Many credit institutions with narrowly defined business models became universal banks during the 1990s and 2000s.

Instruments to Deal with Weak Banks

In practice, supervisors are often confronted with banks that face difficulties in meeting liquidity or capital requirements or have unviable business models. For convenience, we refer to these banks as weak banks. While weak banks may still be in compliance with applicable regulations, supervisors may use additional policy tools to prevent their failure. The crisis underlined the importance of early intervention to safeguard the soundness of weak banks or to ensure their orderly exit from the market (see Fig. 4.12).

At an early stage, supervisors may require weak banks to take recovery measures. For instance, the CET1 ratio of the bank may fall below the buffer requirement due to large unexpected losses. In this situation, the supervisor may ask the bank to improve its capital position within a short period of time. More generally, supervisors require banks to prepare recovery plans that include a set of actions

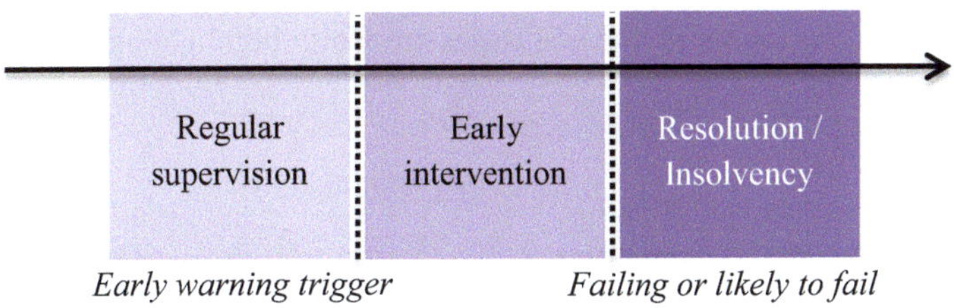

Fig. 4.12 Recovery, resolution, and insolvency of weak banks

that the bank could take to improve its financial position in case of difficulties. These plans facilitate the task of supervisors once the bank indeed faces difficulties as it allows them to demand specific actions, such as selling noncore assets, within a short period of time. If these actions prove to be insufficient, supervisors may also remove bank management, appoint a temporary administrator or require changes to the bank's operational structures.

If the financial situation of the bank deteriorates further, supervisors may at some point have to revoke its license. This step is taken once supervisors determine that the bank is failing or likely to fail. It triggers either liquidation or resolution procedures, as shown in Fig. 4.12 and described below. Both options differ in several aspects such as the distribution of losses or the use of deposit insurance. Given that the financial system is ultimately based on trust, there is widespread consensus among policymakers that the disorderly failure of a bank should be avoided as it may undermine the broader trust in the system. This does not imply, however, that the failure of banks should be avoided by all means. As argued by Tommaso Padoa-Schioppa (2000), a former member of the ECB Executive Board and one of the architects of the euro area:

> An industry where freedom to access the market is not coupled with effective mechanisms for exit from the market is not a healthy industry. Failures are not an unhealthy phenomenon, and supervisors should not be blamed for letting banks go bust, just as they should not be praised for having no failures within their jurisdiction.

Should a significant institution need to be resolved, a rather complex resolution arrangement applies. The respective procedures were put in place through the creation of the Single Resolution Mechanism in 2015. It was first applied for the resolution of Banco Popular, a Spanish SI, in June 2017.[25] Overall, reaching an effective and smooth resolution of a large euro area banks is a great challenge, in particular given the substantial coordination and burden-sharing needs involved. Cross-border resolution is even more difficult if the banking group has major operations outside the euro area.

Box 4.3 Bank Insolvency and Resolution

In the case of insolvency, the bank is put under liquidation and stops operating. Liquidation is performed under general or special insolvency procedures that apply to banks in the respective jurisdiction.[26] An insolvency administrator is appointed who oversees the liquidation of assets and the distribution of proceeds among creditors. Several issues are worth highlighting in the liquidation process:

(continued)

[25] In June 2017, the Spanish bank Banco Popular was declared "failing or likely to fail," which triggered the resolution of the bank. The bank was eventually taken over by Banco Santander.

[26] The insolvency procedure varies across countries since there is no single insolvency framework for euro area banks.

Box 4.3 (continued)

- *Insolvency implies that depositors cannot access their deposits anymore.* Nevertheless, insured depositors are paid out within a short period of time. The payout is done by the deposit guarantee scheme, of which the bank used to be a member (see Chap. 5). Uninsured depositors are treated similarly to other unsecured creditors.
- *Secured creditors receive a special treatment in insolvency.* Secured liabilities of banks typically include central bank funding (monetary policy operations and ELA) and secured market funding, such as repos or covered bonds. To satisfy the claims in insolvency, the pledged collateral is seized and liquidated. This typically leads to a higher recovery rate for secured claims compared to unsecured ones.

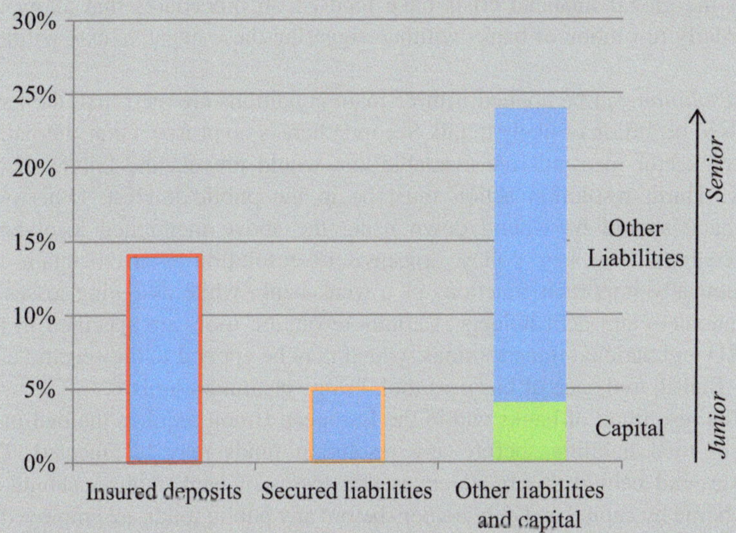

- *The proceeds from the liquidation of the remaining assets are distributed among unsecured creditors according to their rank.* Should the bank have a high degree of asset encumbrance, i.e., should many of its assets be used as collateral for secured funding operations, the recovery rate for unsecured creditors is likely to be low. The right-hand side of the above figure shows the rank of capital and remaining liabilities under liquidation. At the bottom, the figure shows going concern capital (i.e., Tier 1 capital), which is the first to absorb losses when the bank becomes insolvent.[27]

(continued)

[27]Losses of shareholders are limited to their paid in amount due to limited liability. In the nineteenth century, many European banks were based on a different system which included the unlimited liability of their shareholders and thus induced shareholders to be more cautious regarding the banks' risk exposures.

Box 4.3 (continued)

Next, losses affect gone concern capital (Tier 2 capital) and junior debt. Should these elements not be sufficient to absorb the losses in liquidation either, senior debt holders will be haircut as well. This implies that holders of senior unsecured debt and uninsured depositors will witness a nominal reduction of their claims.

- *The liquidation of a bank may lead to a significant deterioration in depositor confidence in the banking system.* Some depositors may anticipate the bank's insolvency and withdraw their deposits, which may trigger a bank run. The impact on depositor confidence is even more severe if a large bank becomes insolvent, as could be observed after the collapse of Lehman Brothers in 2008. To avoid these effects, policy efforts since the beginning of the global financial crisis have focused on procedures that allow the orderly resolution of banks without triggering these negative externalities.

Resolution can be applied if three main conditions are met: first, the bank needs to be failing or likely to fail. Second, there is no prospect that alternative private sector measures are available that would prevent the failure of the bank. Third, resolution action must be in the public interest. Otherwise, the bank should be wound down using the above mentioned insolvency proceedings. The key policy objective of resolution is to maintain the systemically important functions of a weak bank, while assigning losses to shareholders and debt holders. Various resolution tools are specified in the BRRD and national transpositions, which may be applied to the specific case (e.g. Bail-in tool, sale of business tool, bridge institution tool).[28]

The resolution of banks within the European Union requires the bail-in of 8% of total liabilities before any resolution funds may be injected. The background behind this treatment is that losses of bank failures should be first borne by capital and debt holders before any public funds are employed to support weak banks. European policymakers introduced mandatory bail-in in response to Phase 1 and 2 of the financial crisis during which many large and medium-sized banks received unprecedented public support. The purpose is thus to avoid similar situations in the future. Bail-in of liabilities was already applied in bank resolutions during Phase 3 of the crisis, such as the case of Cypriot banks in early 2013. More broadly, the bail-in regime is intended to reduce the potential for sovereign-bank spillovers, in line with the overall philosophy of the Banking Union.

In addition to bail-in, bank resolutions should be primarily funded by dedicated resolution funds rather than taxpayers going forward. Specifically, the bank resolution framework requires all euro area member states to

(continued)

[28]World Bank (2016) provides a useful introduction to resolution tools and procedures in the EU.

Box 4.3 (continued)
gradually build up national resolution funds. These funds should be sourced by bank contributions. The national resolution funds will be gradually integrated to eventually establish a Single Resolution Fund. The Single Resolution Fund should have a target volume of 1% of covered deposits by 2023 (around 55 billion euros based on covered deposits as of end-2015).

Various liability types are excluded from bail-in including customer deposits that are covered by deposit insurance. Hence, a key difference between resolution and insolvency is that the deposit guarantee system does not need to make payouts in resolution. Overall, the so-called no-creditor-worse-off principle applies in resolution, which implies that no creditor should be worse off in resolution than in case of insolvency.

Putting the Policy Tools Together

Strong and timely action by bank supervisors is needed to ensure the soundness of banks. As the crisis showed, many banks tend to operate with limited liquidity and capital buffers compared to their risk exposures. These characteristics make them vulnerable to adverse developments. As a consequence, liquidity and capital requirements were significantly tightened in response to Phase 1 of the crisis. Ever since that time, supervisors have also become more intrusive in the analysis of bank business models and the request for restructuring measures. Overall, the crisis showed that supervisors need to liquidation or demand corrective action and intervene in weak banks up to the point when the resolution of an unviable bank is triggered. Short-term pain may sometimes be preferable to long-term agony and externalities for the system as a whole. In this context, the establishment of the SSM has created an opportunity for a new type of banking supervision in the euro area, based on common standards and perhaps also a less special treatment for banks that are considered national champions in their respective countries.

4.3 International Dimension

The establishment of the SSM also has implications for the international dimension of banking supervision. Many significant institutions have exposures outside the euro area through cross-border lending, branches or subsidiaries. Figure 4.13 shows the foreign exposure of ten large euro area banking sectors by geographies, which amounted to 5.7 trillion euros as of end-2015. In addition, 8 of the 30 globally systemically important banks on the list of the FSB (2016) are headquartered in the euro area (see Table 4.1). Due to the significant foreign exposures and global interconnectedness, cooperation between the SSM and other supervisory authorities and standard-setting bodies plays a key role for effective banking supervision in the euro area.

Fig. 4.13 Foreign exposure of euro area banks (end-2015). Source: BIS (2017). Note: Total claims of BIS-reporting euro area banks (Austria, Belgium, Germany, Spain, Finland, France, Greece, Italy, the Netherlands and Portugal) to counterparts outside the euro area

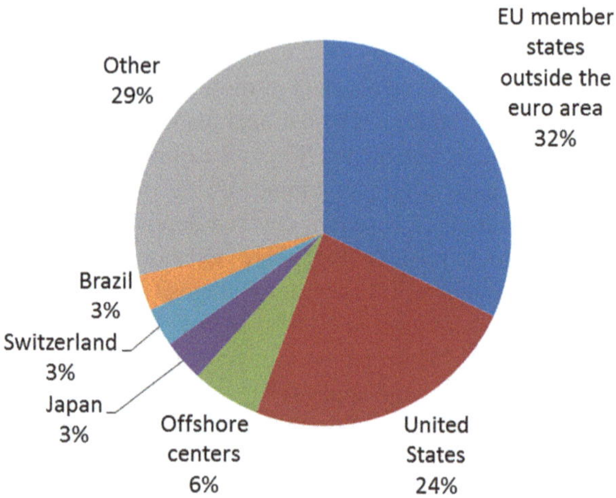

Table 4.1 List of globally systemically important banks[a]

United States	Euro area	China	Japan	Other
Bank of America Bank of New York Mellon Citigroup Goldman Sachs JP Morgan Chase Morgan Stanley State Street Wells Fargo	BNP Paribas Crédit Agricole Deutsche Bank Groupe BPCE ING Bank Santander Société Générale Unicredit Group	Agricultural Bank of China Bank of China China Construction Bank Industrial and Commercial Bank of China	Mitsubishi UFJ Mizuho Sumitomo Mitsui	Barclays Crédit Suisse HSBC Nordea Royal Bank of Scotland Standard Chartered UBS

Source: FSB (2016)
[a]As of November 2016

The SSM and Other European Countries
Within the European Union, bank regulation is largely harmonized. As the Single Rulebook applies to all EU member states, supervisory policy tools are similar across jurisdictions, while their application may vary between SSM and non-SSM countries. For instance, the Bank of England applies a different methodology for determining the total SREP capital requirement than the ECB, yet its SREP decisions need to be made in compliance with the CRR/CRD IV as well. Furthermore, all EU member states contribute to the development of the Single Rulebook. The ECB and the NCAs of euro area countries interact with stakeholders of other countries in the respective European fora (e.g., EBA working groups) regarding changes in regulation.

Supervisory colleges are established to facilitate the cooperation between the SSM and other supervisory authorities in the context of cross-border banking groups. As an example, an Italian bank may operate subsidiaries in SSM countries, other EU member states and third countries. While the ECB is the consolidating supervisor for the banking group as a whole, it can only carry out its supervisory tasks if it has access to information on the foreign subsidiaries and can engage with the respective host supervisors. For instance, the ECB may require exposure data for foreign subsidiaries and information on supervisory findings by the host supervisor to be in a position to assess the capital and liquidity risks of the banking group. Supervisory colleges are established for each cross-border banking group as a vehicle for such international cooperation and coordination. In practice, they involve regular teleconferences, meetings and information exchange among supervisory authorities. The ECB acts as the consolidating supervisor for significant institutions and chairs many of the supervisory colleges.

EU member states that are not part of the euro area may also request to join the SSM. If the request is accepted, the country enters into close cooperation with the ECB regarding banking supervision, but remains autonomous with respect to monetary policy.[29] So far no country has applied for close cooperation with the SSM. Should a country decide to apply, the criteria involved require, among others, a strong commitment of supervisory authorities to cooperate and a comprehensive assessment for all new significant institutions (ECB 2014).

The SSM and Other Parts of the World

The relationship between the SSM and other parts of the world is mainly characterized by the interaction with standard-setting bodies. Three sets of global standards are particularly relevant for banking supervision in the euro area:

- *Basel III as the global standard for bank capital and liquidity regulation, which is set by the Basel Committee on Banking Supervision (BCBS).* This committee is hosted by the BIS in Basel. Euro area members are the ECB as well as Belgium, France, Germany, Italy, the Netherlands and Spain.
- *Basel Core Principles for Effective Banking Supervision (BCP) as the global standard for banking supervision, which is also set by the BCBS.* The Basel Core Principles serve as the basis for assessments of banking supervisory practices by the International Monetary Fund (IMF) in individual countries. These assessments are typically done within the context of the IMF Financial Sector Assessment Program (FSAP), which we will discuss in Chap. 5.
- *International financial reporting standards (IFRS) as the global reporting standards, which are set by the International Accounting Standards Board (IASB).* The IASB is located in London as a private non-profit organization that comprises industry experts. IFRS need to be transposed into EU law in order to become applicable for euro area banks. Unlike other standards stated above, IFRS

[29]European countries outside the EU are not allowed to join the SSM.

are subject to constant changes, which are reported on the IASB website. One major change that affects euro area banks in 2018 is the introduction of IFRS 9, which is the new reporting standard for financial instruments.

Box 4.4 Banking Supervision in Practice

Imagine you are the JST coordinator of a medium-sized banking group in the euro area. The bank has the following characteristics:

- The bank is focused on corporate and SME business in five euro area countries. It also operates local subsidiaries in South-Eastern Europe (retail/corporate) and London (investment banking, funding). The bank is exploring a possible market entry in Turkey.
- Performance in recent years was characterized by weak profitability, a gradual reduction in total assets and a significant increase in the NPL ratio, in particular in the SME loan portfolio. Provision coverage improved following the ECB Comprehensive Assessment 2014, which the bank narrowly passed. In 2015, net interest income continued to decline, operating expenses slightly increased and trading income was negative.
- The banking group is funded by customer deposits (50%), wholesale markets (30%) and the Eurosystem (20%). Market funding is mostly short-term and in major currencies (EUR, USD). Liquidity lines to foreign subsidiaries were stable at 10% of the parent bank's total assets in recent years.

Questions:

1. What are the main risks the bank is exposed to? Which areas would you recommend for the next on-site inspection?

The bank is mainly exposed to three risks: (1) credit risk, as reflected by the high NPL ratio, SME loans and international exposure, (2) weak profitability, as indicated by declining net interest income—the main income source of the described bank, increasing operating expenses and credit risk costs, and (3) funding risks, linked to the high reliance on short-term wholesale funding and central bank funding, as well as the high maturity transformation inherent in the bank's business model. Credit or funding risks may warrant an on-site inspection regarding risk management.

2. Which policy instruments do you have available to address the risks and ensure the soundness of the bank?

All requirements of the Single Rulebook apply to the stated bank. Additional instruments may be applied based on the annual SREP of the bank. The

(continued)

Box 4.4 (continued)
SREP decision includes, among others, the bank-specific Pillar 2 capital or liquidity requirements, as well as the Pillar 2 guidance.

3. Which institutions or bodies do you need to involve in setting the overall SREP capital requirement of the banking group?

You will need to involve the Supervisory Board as well as supervisory colleges due to local subsidiaries in non-SSM countries.

4. How has the establishment of the SSM changed the way the banking group is supervised?

The main supervisory responsibility moved from NCAs in the individual member states, including the NCA in the bank's parent country as former consolidating supervisor, to ECB Supervision. The Supervisory Board takes all supervisory decisions for the banking group. A Joint Supervisory Team (JST) was created that consists of the ECB and the five NCAs. In addition, supervision follows harmonized standards, most notably as regards the SREP, which needs to follow the SSM methodology.

Questions for Consideration

- What are the lessons learned from banking supervision in the pre-crisis period?
- Which policy instruments can the SSM apply to reduce the potential for risk spillovers between sovereigns and banks in the euro area?
- How can supervisors speed up the process of resolving nonperforming loans?
- To which extent should supervisors interfere in business decisions of banks?
- How could the complexity of capital regulation be reduced?
- How should the too-big-to-fail (TBTF) issue be addressed?
- Which institution should assess if supervisors do too little or too much to ensure the soundness of banks?
- How can central banks manage the reputational risks arising from supervisory tasks?
- Should banking supervision be institutionally separated from monetary policy?
- How transparent should supervisors be on their policy decisions and risk assessment?

References

Bank for International Settlements (BIS). (2017). *Consolidated banking statistics. Total claims of domestic banks from ten BIS-reporting euro area banking sectors to counterparts outside the euro area on an immediate counterparty basis*. Accessed February 16, 2017, from http://stats.bis.org/

Basel Committee on Banking Supervision (BCBS). (2011). *Basel III: A global regulatory framework for more resilient banks and banking systems*. Accessed from http://www.bis.org/publ/bcbs189.pdf

European Central Bank (ECB). (2014). *Guide to banking supervision*. Accessed from https://www.bankingsupervision.europa.eu/ecb/pub/pdf/ssmguidebankingsupervision201411.en.pdf

ECB. (2014). *ECB Governing Council decision of 31 January 2014*. Accessed from https://www.ecb.europa.eu/pub/pdf/other/en_dec_2014_05_fen.pdf?5105e4c768e886be0f5844b03a868418

ECB. (2016). *SSM SREP methodology booklet*. Accessed from https://www.bankingsupervision.europa.eu/ecb/pub/pdf/ssm_srep_methodology_booklet.en.pdf

ECB. (2017a). *Report on financial structures*. Accessed November 14, 2017, from https://www.ecb.europa.eu/pub/pdf/other/reportonfinancialstructures201710.en.pdf

ECB. (2017b). *LSI supervision with the SSM*. Accessed from https://www.bankingsupervision.europa.eu/ecb/pub/ssm.reportlsisupervision2017.en.pdf

Financial Stability Board (FSB). (2016). *2016 list of global systemically important banks (GSIBs)*. Accessed from http://www.fsb.org/wp-content/uploads/2016-list-of-global-systemically-importantbanks-G-SIBs.pdf

Padoa-Schioppa, T. (2000). *Speech at the Belgian Financial Forum on 10 February 2000*. Accessed from https://www.ecb.europa.eu/press/key/date/2000/html/sp000210_content.en.html

Further Reading

Bank of England. (2013). *Bank capital and liquidity*. Quarterly Bulletin 2013 Q3. Accessed from http://www.bankofengland.co.uk/publications/Documents/quarterlybulletin/2013/qb130302.pdf

Haldane, A., & Madouros, V. (2012, August). *The dog and the frisbee*. Speech at the Federal Reserve Bank of Kansas City 366th Economic Policy Symposion, Jackson Hole. Accessed from http://www.bis.org/review/r120905a.pdf

Veron, N. (2015). *Europe's Radical Banking Union*. Bruegel Essay and Lecture Series. Accessed from http://bruegel.org/wp-content/uploads/imported/publications/essay_NV_CMU.pdf

World Bank. (2016, November). *Understanding bank recovery and resolution in the EU: A guidebook to the BRRD*. Accessed from http://documents.worldbank.org/curated/100781485375368909/pdf/112266-REVISED-PUBLIC-0317-FinSAC-BRRD-Guidebook.pdf

Zhou, J., et al. (2012). *From bail-out to bail-in: Mandatory debt restructuring of systemic financial institutions*. IMF Staff Discussion Note 12/03. Accessed from http://www.imf.org/external/pubs/ft/sdn/2012/sdn1203.pdf

Financial Stability 5

Financial stability is a shared objective of the ECB, national central banks, national authorities, and other institutions in the euro area. This chapter explains the activities that are pursued to safeguard the stability of the financial system. The first section defines systemic risk and explores how it can be measured. The second section discusses the policy process and instruments available with a focus on macroprudential measures, financial safety nets, and crisis management. The third section puts the policy area in an international context.

Financial stability is a critical condition for the smooth functioning of the economy. Its relevance is most visible during crisis episodes that can be very costly, not only for financial institutions but also for individuals, businesses, and governments. For instance, the economic and financial crisis since 2007 resulted in the deepest recession in Europe since the Second World War, high unemployment, unprecedented public support for banks, and financial assistance to crisis countries. Other historical examples prove the point that financial crises tend to be rather costly, from emerging markets (Mexico 1994, Asian crisis 1997, Russia 1998) to advanced economies (Nordic countries 1990s). An obvious question is, therefore, which types of policies may be pursued to reduce the likelihood or costs of financial crises. This leads us to financial stability policy, which complements the functions of monetary policy and banking supervision that were discussed in Chaps. 2 and 4.

The main objective of the policy area lies in ensuring the stable provision of credit and financial services even under conditions of stress. Stable provision in this context refers to the minimization of supply-side restrictions rather than a predefined scope of provided credit and services. For instance, customers should be able to use payment services, such as electronic payments, even after the breakdown of parts of the financial infrastructure or the insolvency of a large bank. The stable provision of financial services even under conditions of stress is typically at the core of financial

M. Fandl, *Monetary and Financial Policy in the Euro Area*, Springer Texts in Business and Economics, https://doi.org/10.1007/978-3-319-72643-4_5

stability definitions.[1] In line with this ultimate objective, central banks aim at containing systemic risk and ensuring that the financial system is sufficiently resilient to shocks. The aim is to reduce the likelihood that stress conditions emerge and to dampen the impact should the system experience stress.

Five questions guide the activities of central banks in the field of financial stability:

1. What are the main *sources* of systemic risk?
2. What is the *likelihood* that the identified risks materialize?
3. What would be the *impact* of particular risk events?
4. Which *policies* are needed to address these concerns?
5. Are *financial safety nets* and *crisis management mechanisms* adequate?

Proper analysis is a prerequisite for taking adequate policy action. Hence, we start the discussion with the three questions that relate to analysis. As a first step, we need to define what systemic risk means and how it can be measured.

5.1 Systemic Risk Assessment

Systemic risk is the risk that the stable provision of financial services is disrupted by an impairment of parts of the financial system. From a policy perspective, it is useful to differentiate the time and cross-sectional dimension of systemic risk:

- *Financial imbalances may build up over time but can unravel quickly.* For instance, an economy may witness a period of excessive credit growth with credit rising faster than income for an extended period of time. At some point, the period of excessive credit growth comes to a halt and dynamics reverse. This point is typically followed by payment difficulties of individuals or businesses, and losses by financial institutions, which may have a systemic dimension. Other examples of financial imbalances are the buildup of excessive leverage, maturity mismatches, or large common exposures that make financial institutions vulnerable to shocks.
- *Risks may also propagate within the system at a given point in time.* For instance, the default of a systemically important bank has contagious effects on other financial institutions due to their direct and indirect linkages (such as exposures via money or bond market transactions). The collapse of Lehman Brothers in 2008 serves as a good example for contagion within the financial system.

[1]These definitions vary slightly across the euro area, yet the differences do not matter much in practice. As of early 2017, the ECB defined financial stability as *"a state whereby the build-up of systemic risk is prevented. Systemic risk can best be described as the risk that the provision of necessary financial products and services by the financial system will be impaired to a point where economic growth and welfare may be materially affected."* (https://www.ecb.europa.eu/ecb/tasks/stability/html/index.en.html, accessed on 15 February 2017).

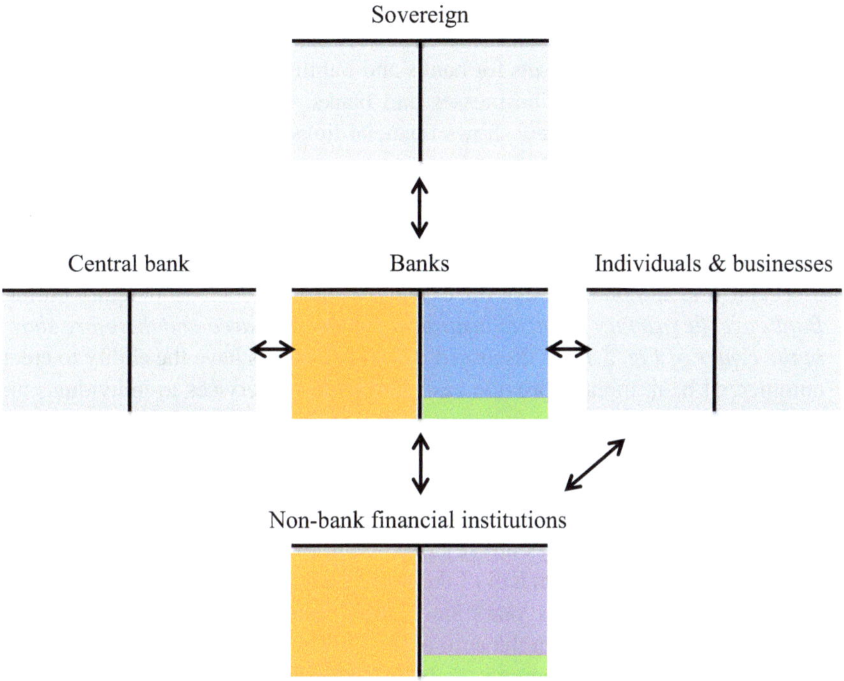

Fig. 5.1 Schematic overview of the financial system

Liquidity shocks are another example for the cross-sectional dimension of systemic risk. A sudden loss in confidence may cause a freeze on funding markets that forces banks to liquidate assets at fire sale prices. These transactions may dampen asset prices and result in valuation losses across the system. Such developments could be observed in the US subprime mortgage crisis of 2007.

Banking supervision alone would not be sufficient to address such systemic risks. As discussed in Chap. 4, the ultimate objective of banking supervision lies in ensuring the soundness of individual banks. Financial stability has a broader perspective by focusing on the capability of the system as a whole to perform its core functions even under conditions of stress. Effective banking supervision is a necessary but not a sufficient condition to this aim. Bank supervisors typically have a single-bank view and may miss the buildup of common risk exposures across the system. At the same time, some issues such as risk under-provisioning in small banks may be relevant for supervisors but not for financial stability.

While banking supervision takes a micro-level view, financial stability takes a macro-level view. Figure 5.1 provides a simplified overview of the macro-level view on the financial system. It consists of the central bank, banks, nonbank financial institutions, businesses, individuals, and the sovereign. From a systemic risk perspective, there are several aspects worth highlighting:

- *The main sectors of the economy are presented in Fig. 5.1 by their aggregate balance sheets.* Some assets of one sector are liabilities of another sector. For instance, bank loans are assets for banks and liabilities for borrowers. Banknotes are assets for individuals, businesses and banks, and liabilities for the central bank. The balance sheet view shows financial linkages between the sectors, also known as inter-sectoral linkages.
- *The balance sheet view is useful to analyze the development of financial conditions in the respective sectors over time.* For instance, the evolution of balance sheets may show the buildup of leverage, currency mismatches between assets/income and liabilities, or the evolution of liquid assets and equity buffers.
- *Banks are the primary financial institutions in the euro area and therefore shown in the center of Fig. 5.1.* As discussed in Chap. 1, banks have the ability to create commercial bank money, provide cash and payment services to individuals and businesses, and transmit the monetary policy stance through operations with the central bank. Bank operations further benefit from the existence of two financial safety nets: the deposit guarantee scheme and emergency liquidity assistance (ELA). These safety nets are not available to other financial institutions or businesses. Moreover, banks are key players on financial markets and their total assets account for more than half of the entire financial sector in the euro area. As demonstrated by the crisis years since 2007, banks are the main source and amplifier of systemic risk in the euro area.
- *Nonbank financial institutions include insurance companies, real money investors, and shadow banks.* These institutions vary significantly with respect to their liability structure. While some are rather leveraged, such as insurance companies or defined-benefit pension plans,[2] other institutions such as asset managers mostly invest funds that are not linked to specific payouts but rather have equity character. The latter type of nonbank financial institutions bears little solvency risk, given that any losses they incur are translated into losses for investors. By contrast, losses incurred by more leveraged institutions can give rise to solvency risks. Should the institutions eventually be brought down by the size of their losses, their default impacts their liability holders (e.g., holders of insurance policies), while it is unlikely to cause major stability risks. Nevertheless, they need to be monitored from a systemic risk perspective, given that, for instance, financial linkages between nonbank financial institutions and banks may serve as channels for risk propagation during crisis times. Activities of nonbank financial institutions are also relevant for financial stability due to their potential impact on the market liquidity of financial instruments and associated systemic effects. For instance, suppose that investment funds engage in fire sales of residential mortgage backed securities during a crisis. Such situation would not only have an adverse impact on the market price and liquidity of these instruments but it may also lead to valuation losses by other holders of such securities and increase liquidity risk across the system.

[2]These institutions mainly invest funds that are linked to specific payouts, such as insurance or pension payments.

- *Individuals and businesses constitute the core of what is sometimes referred to as the real economy.* Almost all of them have relationships with one or several banks. Some also use services by nonbank financial institutions, for instance when taking out insurance or investing in mutual funds. Just like other agents in the economy, individuals and businesses may face a high debt burden, limited liquidity buffers or equity positions, and may default on their obligations. While the bankruptcy of individuals and most nonfinancial businesses is not a systemic event that may threaten financial stability, a proper analysis of the real economy is crucial to assess macro-financial risks. Even though a default of a single borrower is usually not a systemic event, the simultaneous default of many borrowers certainly impairs bank balance sheets and creates systemic risk.
- *The sovereign sector includes the central government, which issues debt liabilities such as government bonds.* Traditionally, the government in an advanced economy was seen as a safe haven from a systemic risk perspective. This view changed with the sovereign debt crisis. In some cases, large holdings of government bonds by banks proved to be an amplifier for risk spillovers from the sovereign to the banking sector. Apart from banks, central banks have also increased their holdings of government bonds during the crisis, in particular following the launch of the Public Sector Purchase Program (PSPP) in 2014 (see Chap. 2).

In addition to the conditions in these five sectors and their subsectors, systemic risk may result from cross-border linkages, external conditions, financial markets, and infrastructure. For instance, the assets and liabilities of a sector may reflect transactions with foreign counterparts, which may act as channels for risk spillovers during crises. As an example, a bank may have foreign subsidiaries, and an insurance company may hold foreign government bonds. Should the subsidiaries incur large losses and government bonds lose in value, the financial position of the bank and insurance company could deteriorate and give rise to systemic risk. In addition, external conditions such as a low interest rate environment may contribute to the build-up of systemic risk, as it may incentivize financial institutions to use leverage and search for yield by making investments with expected high return and risk. Bank regulation, another external factor, may also impact the behavior of financial institutions in a way that leads to the emergence of systemic risk. One example is the treatment of highly related US subprime securitizations prior to financial crisis, which contributed to the build-up of large holdings by some European banks and valuation losses during the global financial crisis. Another example is the growth of the shadow banking sector during the crisis, among others as a means to circumvent tightened bank regulation. It is also worth noting that Fig. 5.1 does not capture other sources of systemic risk such as systemically relevant financial markets or infrastructure. Central banks perform an oversight function on these parts, primarily for reasons of financial stability. Despite this function, events such as the "Flash Crash" of May 2010, when major US stock markets collapsed within an hour for no specific

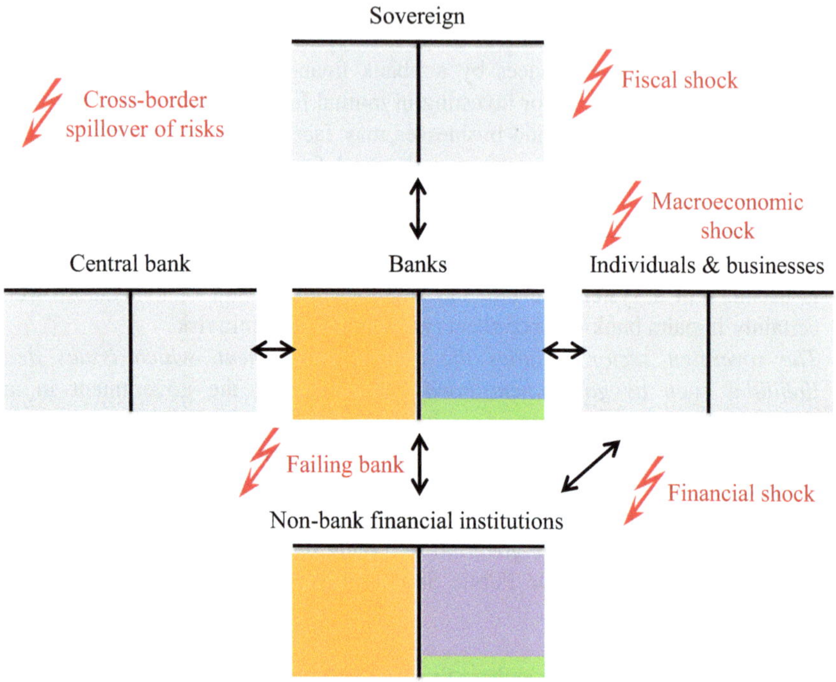

Fig. 5.2 Sources of shocks across the financial system

reason at first sight, suggest that financial infrastructure and algorithmic trading can serve as another source of systemic risk that is still not widely understood.[3]

Shock events that trigger the manifestation of systemic risk may originate from different parts of the financial system. Figure 5.2 provides an overview of the main sources. They include:

1. *Macro-economic shocks* (such as a drop in domestic demand caused by a sudden deterioration in consumer or business confidence)
2. *Financial shocks* (such as a sudden change in commodity prices or FX rates)
3. *Fiscal shocks* (such as an unexpected strong increase in the budget deficit)
4. *Shocks within the banking system* (such as the collapse of a systemically important bank)
5. *Cross-border spillover of risks* (such as a reversal of risk premiums on global financial markets, leading to an increase in funding costs).

[3]Ensuring the smooth functioning of payment systems is also done for reasons of monetary policy, given its importance for the monetary transmission mechanism and maintaining public trust in the currency.

The likelihood of such shocks to occur is difficult to assess. Various methods can be applied, for instance based on historical observations or probability distributions. In practice, the task involves a significant degree of expert judgment. Some analysts also apply early-warning models, for instance to identify the buildup of asset price bubbles. Such bubbles occur when an asset price deviates from its fundamental value for an extended period of time, for instance in case of a credit-fueled increase in real estate prices. Experience with early-warning models is mixed, partly due to difficulties with indicator selection and model risk. Models may also yield signals that are difficult to rely on as the basis for policy decisions in the build-up phase of the bubble as they may be interpreted differently by analysts and policymakers involved. Only once a bubble has burst, it is easy to detect the bubble, but then it is also too late for preventive policy action.

Once analysts have developed a view on key risks and vulnerabilities, the next step is to assess the resilience of financial institutions to shocks. This task requires access to granular data on risk exposures of financial institutions, i.e., their exposure to direct risk factors (such as credit risk, market risk, or liquidity risk) and indirect risk factors (such as real estate prices or FX-induced credit risk in the case of foreign currency loans). Particular attention needs to be paid to common risk exposures across the system. For instance, many banks may be exposed to an overheated sector of the economy, such as the construction sector in boom years.

Box 5.1 Basics of Stress Testing

Stress tests are the main analytical tool applied in the euro area to assess the impact of shocks to the financial system. The topic has become popular in the financial and regulatory industry in recent years. This box briefly explains the main purpose and steps of a stress test. It uses a solvency stress test for the banking sector as the example. This type of stress test is used to find out whether banks are resilient to a given set of shocks that affect their solvency.

- *The starting point is the balance sheet of a bank, based on current data (see left-hand side of the first figure).* Let us suppose the bank in question has a CET1 ratio of 10% and that most current data is end-2016.
- *In a first step, we conduct an analysis of the bank's development under a baseline scenario.* This scenario corresponds to the expected economic development, which is for instance based on a recent economic forecast, such as the IMF World Economic Outlook. We assume this scenario to take hold in the next period and project the various P&L items of the bank under these conditions. In the current example, we estimate that the bank would generate a pre-provision profit of 2 million euros and loan losses of 1 million euros, resulting in a net profit of 1 million euros. These profits strengthen the bank's capital position at the end of the year, which is shown in the projected balance sheet on the right-hand side. If we assume for simplicity

(continued)

Box 5.1 (continued)

that the bank does not pay taxes or dividends, the net profit would increase the CET1 capital from 10 million euros to 11 million euros by the end of 2017. Accordingly, the CET1 ratio is estimated to increase from 10% (end-2016) to approximately 11% (end-2017) under the baseline scenario.

- *In a second step, we analyze the bank's development under an adverse scenario.* This is essentially a what-if analysis. We investigate what would be the impact on the bank's balance sheet if the economic and financial system were subject to a shock. The shock needs to be a severe but still plausible event. A meteorite destroying the City of London would be a very severe event, but not really plausible. A strong macroeconomic downturn in the euro area may be a better candidate in terms of severity and plausibility. Once the adverse scenario has been established, we project the various P&L items of the bank under the corresponding conditions. In the current example, we estimate that the bank would generate a pre-provision profit of 1 million euros and face loan losses of 3 million euros, resulting in a net loss of 2 million euros. These losses reduce the bank's capital position at the end of the year (see right-hand side of the figure). CET1 capital decreases from 10 million euros to 8 million euros. Accordingly, the CET1 ratio is estimated to decrease from 10% (end-2016) to approximately 8% (end-2017) under the adverse scenario.
- *The two steps can be repeated for other years.* To do this, we use the projected balance sheets under baseline and adverse scenario as of end-2017 as the basis to estimate the impact of the respective scenario in future periods (2018 and 2019). As can be seen from the figure, the projected P&Ls always constitute the link between the respective year-end balance sheets. Once these calculation steps are done, the development of the CET1 ratio under baseline and adverse scenario can be plotted, as illustrated in the second figure. In the example, we estimate that the CET1 ratio increases to 12.5% by end-2019 under the baseline scenario and decreases to 6% by end-2019 under the adverse scenario.

(continued)

Box 5.1 (continued)

Baseline scenario

Bank

CET1 ratio = 10%

P&L

Interest income	4
Interest expenses	-2
Pre-provision income	2
Loan losses	-1
Net income	1

Bank

CET1 ratio ~11%

Adverse scenario

P&L

Interest income	4
Interest expenses	-3
Pre-provision income	1
Loan losses	-3
Net income	-2

Bank

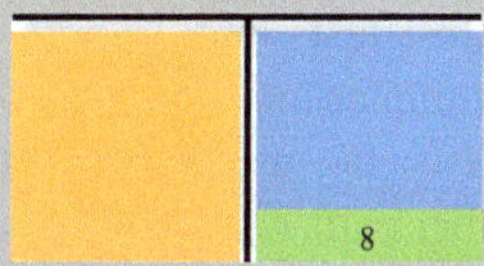

CET1 ratio ~8%

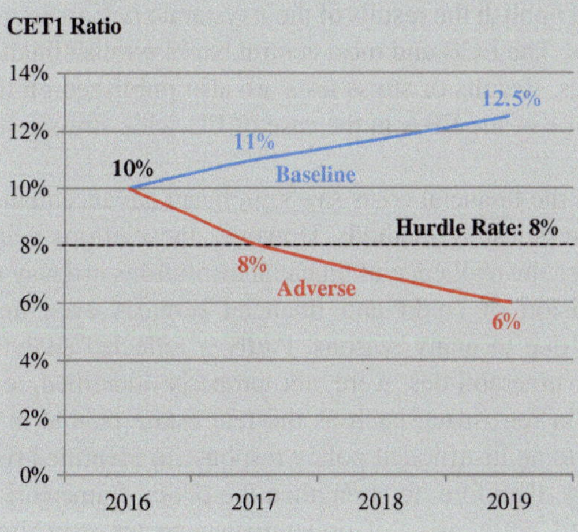

(continued)

Box 5.1 (continued)

- *The application of a reasonable hurdle rate allows us to assess the resilience of the bank under the adverse scenario.* We may for instance define a hurdle rate of 8% in advance. The bank in the example does not meet the hurdle rate during the adverse scenario, as its CET1 ratio is estimated to fall below it in the years 2018 and 2019. Hence, the bank failed the stress test. As a follow-up action, the bank may be asked to strengthen its current capital position to be able to withstand the assumed shock in the adverse scenario with a CET1 ratio of at least 8%. Specifically, the bank may be required to increase its CET1 capital by the capital shortfall in the adverse scenario, i.e., the maximum difference between hurdle rate and CET1 ratio under the adverse scenario.

Stress tests may also be performed for other risks and institutions. Common examples are stress tests for bank solvency, liquidity, or contagion. During the crisis, the use of stress tests has also broadened from the banking sector to other parts of the financial sector, such as insurance companies, pension funds, and central counterparties (CCPs).[4]

Central banks in the euro area publish the results of their systemic risk assessment and stress tests on a regular basis. The ECB and most central banks publish financial stability reports on their websites. Results of stress tests are also published on their websites, including on the website of the EBA in the case of EU-wide stress testing exercises.

The years prior to the start of the financial crisis saw significant advancements in systemic risk assessment and stress testing methods. However, these efforts neither prevented the crisis nor strengthen the resilience of financial institutions in a way that could ensure the "stable provision of credit and financial services even under conditions of stress." This was due to many reasons. Partly it reflected analytical deficiencies. Many risks and vulnerabilities were not properly identified, even though they appeared obvious in retrospect, such as the real estate bubble in the United States. Partly it was due to an insufficient policy response to identified risks. A key lesson from the crisis was, therefore, to strengthen the policy framework, in order to increase the ability and willingness of policymakers to act in a timely manner. These efforts gave rise to a new policy area known as macroprudential policy. It should complement the microprudential function of banking supervision and make the system more stable and resilient.

[4]European stress testing exercises were conducted for insurance companies, occupational pension funds, and CCPs by EIPOA and ESMA, respectively.

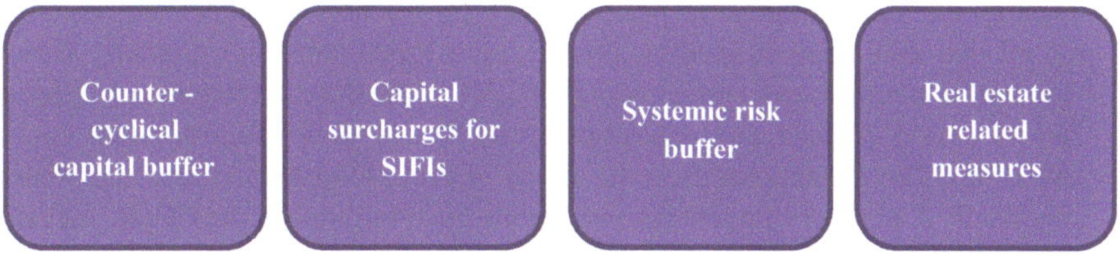

Fig. 5.3 Key tools for macroprudential policy

5.2 Macroprudential Policy

Macroprudential policy is pursued with the primary aim to address the build-up of systemic risk and manage 'soft landings' when risks materialize.[5] The policy area is an offspring of the financial crisis since 2007, yet some of its elements were already used under different headings in the past. An example for a macroprudential measure is the countercyclical capital buffer. It requires banks to build up an additional capital buffer in times of strong credit growth. The buffer is released in times of crisis and allows banks to absorb additional losses without impairing their ability to provide credit to the economy.

Macroprudential measures reach from soft to hard instruments. In the case of soft measures, the policymaker expresses an opinion or recommendation that is not coupled with a comply-or-explain mechanism. An example is the warning of the macroprudential authority that a certain market segment, such as commercial real estate, is overheating. In the case of hard measures, the policymaker has direct control over the calibration of a macroprudential tool. An example is the countercyclical capital buffer that the authority sets at a certain level. Semi-hard measures are between the two and comprise formal recommendations that are coupled with a comply-or-explain mechanism.

The macroprudential toolkit includes the following main policy instruments, as illustrated in Fig. 5.3:

- *Countercyclical capital buffer (CCyB):* The CCyB addresses the time dimension of systemic risk by addressing the buildup of systemic vulnerabilities. It is considered to be a balance sheet measure as it influences the bank balance sheet by requesting an additional capital buffer for certain exposures. The level of the buffer varies over time, depending on the situation as assessed by the

[5]As of early 2017, the ECB defined the aim of macroprudential policy as (1) to "*prevent the excessive build-up of risk, resulting from external factors and market failures, to smoothen the financial cycle (time dimension)*," (2) to "*make the financial sector more resilient and limit contagion effects (cross-section dimension)*," and (3) to "*encourage a system-wide perspective in financial regulation to create the right set of incentives for market participants (structural dimension)*" (see https://www.ecb.europa.eu/ecb/tasks/stability/html/index.en.html, accessed on 15 February 2017).

macroprudential authority. In practice, each jurisdiction calculates the required CCyB that shall apply to credit exposures in its jurisdiction on a quarterly basis. The buffer is subject to an upper bound of 2.5% in the Basel III framework. Banks have 1 year to get their capital position above the CCyB before restrictions come into effect. The restrictions affect the ability of banks to make dividend and bonus payments. A number of countries worldwide have introduced the CCyB, including all countries in the euro area.

- *Capital surcharge for systemically important banks:* This instrument addresses the cross-sectional dimension of systemic risk by requiring a higher loss-absorption capacity for banks whose failure may threaten systemic stability. The Basel Committee on Banking Supervision (BCBS) and the Financial Stability Board (FSB) have developed a methodology to measure global and domestic systemically relevant institutions. The capital surcharge for individual banks depends on a score that is calculated based on the methodology as transposed in each member state. Positive surcharges are known as the G-SII buffer for global banks and the O-SII buffer for other systemically important banks, following the terminology of the Single Rulebook. G-SII buffers are phased in from January 2016 onwards and apply to first-tier banks of the likes of Deutsche Bank or BNP Paribas (see Table 4.1). Most euro area countries have also announced O-SII buffers for selected second-tier banks and given indications from which date they will apply to the respective banks.
- *Systemic risk buffer (SRB):* This buffer may be set for specific systemic risks in the jurisdiction, for instance related to cross-border spillover risks.[6] It applies in conjunction with G-SII and O-SII buffers. For an individual bank, this means that the higher of the capital surcharges and the SRB applies.
- *Real estate related measures* can take various forms. They cover balance sheet measures, such as higher risk weights for mortgage loans, as well as instruments that directly influence the terms and conditions of lending transactions. The latter category includes, among others, limits on loan-to-value (LTV) ratios and on debt servicing as a percentage of borrowers' income.

A practical challenge for policymakers is the limited experience with these instruments. Several aspects are subject to current research, in particular their effectiveness in reaching the intended objectives, their transmission mechanism, the time lag between policy announcements, implementation, and effectiveness, their interaction when applied in parallel with other instruments, and cross-country spillovers. Insights on these issues can be gained by analytical work on impact assessments and by experience once the instruments are applied.

The SSM Regulation assigns macroprudential responsibilities to both national authorities and the ECB, who are thus jointly responsible for macroprudential policy.

[6]Not all euro area countries have established a legal basis to apply the systemic risk buffer.

- *At the national level, one authority in each country is assigned with a macroprudential mandate.* Three models are common across EU member states: The mandate may be assigned to (1) the central bank (e.g., in the Czech Republic), (2) a designated committee within the central bank (e.g., in the United Kingdom), or (3) a designated committee outside the central bank (e.g., in Germany). In some cases, the decision-making powers are separated from execution powers. For instance, many countries have established a financial stability committee that comprises representatives of the central bank, supervisory authority, ministry of finance, and other stakeholders. These committees monitor systemic risks and take decisions on macroprudential policy in the form of recommendations, which are addressed to the national supervisory authority. The latter is responsible for the implementation of the decided measure (e.g., to set the CCyB at the certain level).
- *Due to the strong financial linkages which characterize euro area countries, there is a need for macroprudential authorities to exchange information among each other.* For this reason, notification requirements are in place, which involve national authorities and the ECB.
- *At the level of the euro area, the SSM Regulation gives the ECB the power to tighten certain macroprudential measures.* For instance, the ECB may apply higher requirements for capital buffers at the level of an individual jurisdiction than those that are applied by the respective NCA (ECB 2016). This power is confined to tools that are specified in the Single Rulebook, while all other tools remain a national competence. In practice, this means that the balance sheet tools described above (e.g., the CCyB or capital surcharges for systemically important institutions) are in the ECB top-up competence, while measures that directly influence business transactions (e.g., limits on LTV ratios) are not. The macroprudential powers of the ECB were introduced at the time of the establishment of the SSM in late 2014.

The macroprudential policy process is illustrated in Fig. 5.4. The selection and calibration of policy instruments need to be preceded by the identification and assessment of systemic risks. Once instruments are implemented, they need to be evaluated on a regular basis and adjusted as needed. All steps of the policy process should be underpinned by appropriate analysis. Some common analytical tools that correspond to the respective policy steps are shown on the right-hand side of Fig. 5.4. A common practical challenge lies in the existence of data gaps, which sometimes restrict the ability to perform deeper analysis and develop an adequate policy response. For instance, it is impossible to calibrate limits to LTV ratios in the absence of LTV data. Identifying and closing data gaps for macroprudential analysis are, therefore, important tasks that are closely linked to the policy process.

In general, policy implementation can be based on rules, judgement, or a combination, known as constrained judgement. Central banks have some experience with rules-based decision making from their monetary and FX policy responsibilities, as discussed in Chap. 2. Specifically, central banks set policy rates to keep inflation below a certain level or to maintain a peg to another currency (in the case of a fixed

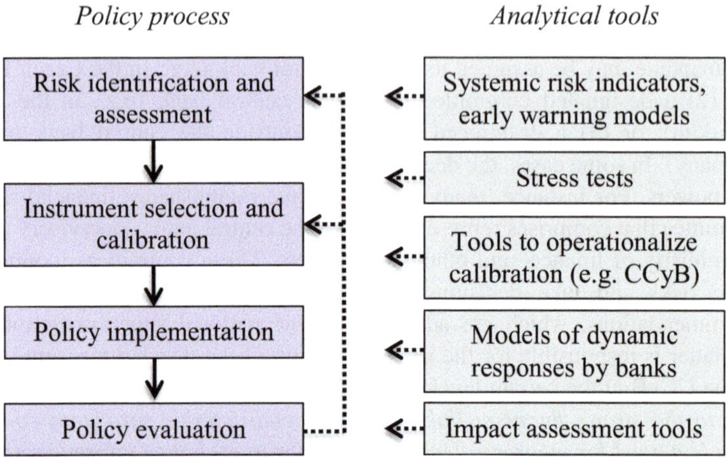

Fig. 5.4 Macroprudential policy process

exchange rate regime). The main advantage of rules-based policy lies in time-consistent decisions. It may also give the authority additional credibility, provided that the rules allow the achievment of well-defined targets (e.g., price stability or a fixed exchange rate). A major drawback of rules-based policy is its non-reaction to model errors or unexpected structural changes. In the case of macroprudential policy, it is further very difficult to define simple decision rules due to the multitude of indicators, tools, and limited experience with their application. At the same time, a purely judgement-based approach has drawbacks as well, such as limited predictability, susceptibility to regulatory capture and lobbying pressure, as well as inaction bias. The prevailing consensus is, therefore, to go for the middle ground, which is known as constrained judgement.

In practice the inaction bias is a key challenge in the field of macroprudential policy. Policy initiatives in boom times such as increasing the countercyclical capital buffer requirement may face resistance from several fronts: The financial industry (which profits from the boom), politics (which likes booming economies), unions (for the same reasons), borrowers (who like cheap loans), financial media (because this time is different), and almost everyone else (because optimism prevails). In times of weak growth, policy initiatives may be criticized as being premature and to threaten the recovery of the economy. This may result in a wait-and-see attitude and delays in policy implementation. Given the inaction bias, it is important for macroprudential authorities to have a strong mandate, an adequate toolkit and, most importantly, the courage to take policy decisions, even if there is strong resistance.

Macroprudential measures in euro area countries have so far focused on the real estate market, the SRB, and buffers for systemically important institutions. An overview is presented in Table 5.1 for the situation as of 3 July 2017. In general, macroprudential measures tend to focus on flows (such as credit growth) rather than

Table 5.1 Macroprudential measures in the euro area as of 3 July 2017

Country	CCyB	G-SII buffer	O-SII buffer	Systemic risk buffer	Real estate-related measures
Austria	√ (0%)		√(7 banks, 0.25–0.5%)	√(12 banks, 0.5–1%)	
Belgium	√ (0%)		√(8 banks, 0.5–1%)		Additional risk weight for real estate-related exposure
Cyprus	√ (0%)		√(6 banks, 0%)		LTV limit; debt service to income limit
Estonia	√ (0%)		√(2 banks, 2%)	√(all banks, 1%)	LTV limit; debt service to income limit; maximum maturity restriction for real estate-related exposure
Finland	√ (0%)		√(3 banks, 0.5–2%)		LTV limit; risk weight floor for real estate-related exposure
France	√ (0%)	√(4 banks, 0.5-1%)	√(6 banks, 0.125–0.75%)		
Germany	√ (0%)	√(1 bank, 1%)	√(14 banks, 0.16–0.66%)		
Greece	√ (0%)		√(4 banks, 0%)		
Ireland	√ (0%)		√(7 banks, 0%)		LTV limit; loan to income limit; additional risk weight for commercial real estate-related exposure
Italy	√ (0%)	√(1 bank, 0.5%)	√(3 banks, 0%)		
Latvia	√ (0%)		√(6 banks, 0%)		LTV limit
Lithuania	√ (0%)		√(4 banks, 0.5–2%)		LTV limit; debt service to income limit; maximum maturity restriction for real estate-related exposure
Luxembourg	√ (0%)		√(6 banks, 0.25–0.5%)		Additional risk weight for high-LTV loans
Malta	√ (0%)		√(3 banks, 0.25–1%)		
Netherlands	√ (0%)	√(1 bank, 0.5%)	√(5 banks, 0.5–1%)	√(3 banks, 1.5%)	LTV limit; debt service to income limit

(continued)

Table 5.1 (continued)

Country	CCyB	G-SII buffer	O-SII buffer	Systemic risk buffer	Real estate-related measures
Portugal	√ (0%)		√(6 banks, 0%)		
Slovakia	√ (0.5%)		√(5 banks, 1–2%)	√(4 banks, 1%)	LTV limit; debt service to income limit; maximum maturity restriction for real estate-related exposure
Slovenia	√ (0%)		√(8 banks, 0%)		
Spain	√ (0%)	√(1 bank, 0.5%)	√(6 banks, 0.125–0.5%)		

Source: ECB (2017), ESRB (2017)

stock problems (such as high NPL levels). This feature limits their usefulness in environments that are characterized by high debt levels and crisis legacies hampering the economic recovery.

Appropriate monetary policy, banking supervision, and fiscal policy are important elements to enhance the effectiveness of macroprudential policy. The objectives of these other policy areas can at times conflict with financial stability, as we will discuss in Chap. 6. This calls for some coordination among policy areas. Furthermore, the goals and scope of macroprudential policy need to be clearly defined, also vis-à-vis other policy areas and it should not be overburdened with objectives it cannot achieve. As argued by Tommaso Padoa-Schioppa (2010) a fomer member of the ECB executive board:

> *The conclusion is that macroprudential regulation is a fundamental innovation, extremely positive, maybe the most significant brick that has been so far brought to the task of reconstructing a more viable system, but it is just one brick and not the reconstruction.*

Financial Safety Nets and Crisis Management

Apart from macroprudential policy in the narrow sense, financial stability policy includes two additional elements the adequacy of financial safety nets and crisis management arrangements. These policies, which are illustrated in Fig. 5.5 in a stylized manner, may be seen as preparatory measures to effectively deal with crisis situations and safeguard financial stability. As we will point out below, they also have an effect on the behavior of financial institutions in normal times. Overall, these policies are pursued for financial stability reasons, but they are also closely related to other policy areas such as monetary policy, banking supervision, bank resolution, and public finance.

Fig. 5.5 Financial safety nets and crisis management

Financial safety nets cover emergency liquidity assistance (ELA) and deposit insurance. They are referred to as safety nets as they are intended to be used only in emergency situations.

- *ELA can be used when a solvent bank faces temporary liquidity problems.* We already discussed ELA in Chap. 2 as it involves the provision of CBM to banks, similar to monetary policy operations. The history of ELA goes back to the nineteenth century when it was first applied by the Bank of England.[7]
- *Deposit insurance is activated when banks have insufficient liquidity to meet withdrawals of covered deposits.* The mechanics are as follows: All banks in the euro area need to be part of a deposit guarantee scheme (DGS). Deposit insurance covers only a limited amount per depositor, which is harmonized at 100k euros in all euro area countries. These deposits are known as covered deposits. In cases where many bank customers want to withdraw their deposits from a single bank, for instance because they do not consider the bank as safe anymore, the bank may run out of liquidity and close down. This would leave bank customers with no access to their deposits. In such cases, deposit insurance is activated and a third party pays out the covered deposits to all customers of the respective bank. These payments are made by the DGS, which is in turn funded from contributions of all its member banks. The bank contributions to the DGS can be either ex ante (paid in) or ex post (only paid in when the need arises). Hence, in a sense, the DGS acts as a type of insurance company for bank deposits. The idea of deposit insurance goes back to the 1930s when it was first applied in the United States following the Great Depression.

[7]The idea of ELA goes back to the famous 1873 book "Lombard Street: A Description of the Money Market" by Walter Bagehot.

Both safety nets are national competences in the euro area but share some common elements. National deposit guarantee schemes in the euro area were harmonized with the Deposit Guarantee Scheme Directive (DGSD) of 2014 as part of the Single Rulebook. Specifically, the DGSD harmonized the coverage (100k euros per depositor), payout time (gradually reduced to 7 days by 2024), and funding type (gradual move to ex-ante funding with a target volume of 0.8% of covered deposits within 10 years and risk-dependent contributions by banks). The DGSD aims at gradually loosening of the link between sovereigns and DGS. Instead, it envisages deposit guarantee schemes that are backed by a dedicated fund, sourced from regular bank contributions.

While financial safety nets contribute to the public confidence in the stability of banks, their existence also has unintended effects that may increase their riskiness. The expectation of external support in case of stress may create moral hazard as it may encourage banks to take higher risks and fund their activities with lower levels of capital and liquidity than they would otherwise. Moreover, these expectations also have the consequence that depositors and investors do not discipline banks sufficiently. This reduces the funding costs of banks and exacerbates their incentive to take on more risk.

Authorities can engage in several activities to enhance their preparedness for crisis situations should they occur. Most importantly, the roles and responsibilities of all institutions involved, such as the ministry of finance, central bank, supervisory authority, and DGS, need to be clarified. Furthermore, processes need to be in place, for instance for coordinated public communication to support public confidence. Standing arrangements for crisis situations that comprise all relevant stakeholders play an important role for the exchange of information, coordination needs, and fast decision-making. Some euro area countries have performed crisis simulation exercises to test these procedures and remove obstacles to effective crisis resolution.

The initial stage of a financial crisis is typically focused on efforts to contain systemic risks and adverse confidence effects. As an example, a euro area country may experience a banking crisis due to a deep economic recession, high stock of NPLs, and concerns about bank solvency. Policy efforts will first aim at addressing the weakest banks, for instance through stress tests to identify additional capital needs, supervisory actions to improve NPL resolution, and perhaps providing ELA to solvent banks, if requested and conditions are met. Some banks may also need to be resolved or liquidated. Public communication will aim at assuring the public that the banking system and customer deposits are safe.

If national authorities do not manage to contain the crisis, they may also seek external financial assistance. When the euro area was established, this option was not foreseen. Instead the no-bail-out clause was added to the Treaty, which excluded external financial assistance in an attempt to discipline national fiscal policy in the monetary union. However, no other arrangements were considered how the euro area would deal with member states experiencing a major economic or financial crisis. Monetary policy could not be used for this purpose anymore and no central financial backstop was put in place. As a consequence, the first sovereign debt crisis in the euro area, experienced by Greece in 2009/2010, was followed by long discussions among European policymakers and an ad hoc response in the form of the first Greek Program. More than 7 years later, euro area countries that experience a major crisis have the option to approach the ESM to request financial assistance. If an agreement on the terms and conditions can be reached, a country program is set up for a defined period of time, which provides temporary financing to the country, with appropriate conditionality. Programs allow crisis countries to focus on economic adjustment and restoring financial stability. Several euro area member states used the option of EU/IMF Programs during the crisis, partly due to risk spillovers between the sovereign and banks as discussed in Chap. 3.

In severe crisis situations, authorities may also consider the application of other policy tools as a last resort. These tools include bank holidays and capital controls. Both impose restrictions on economic agents as regards their ability to withdraw or transfer deposits and other financial assets. Given that such restrictions run counter the objective of a monetary union that is based on the free movement of capital, they need to be duly justified by extraordinary circumstances that threaten financial stability.

- *The declaration of bank holidays means that bank branches remain closed and customers have restricted access to their deposits.* For instance, when bank holidays were declared in Greece in June 2015, depositors could only withdraw a maximum of 60 euros per day from ATMs. The measure was preceded by the massive outflow of deposits over several months and taken in light of an imminent bank run.
- *Capital controls are imposed in extraordinary situations by national authorities to restrict the outflow of deposits from the country.* This was for instance done by Iceland in 2008, Cyprus in 2013, and Greece in 2015. Among others, capital controls restrict electronic transfers from domestic bank accounts to bank accounts abroad. Special committees are put in place to evaluate the purpose of each transfer application and approve a limited amount of transactions, for instance to pay for the import of medical supplies.[8] Deposit withdrawals are also restricted, similar to the case of bank holidays, and special attention is paid at border controls to prevent banknote flight. Due to the detrimental effect of capital controls on depositors' confidence and payment culture, it takes several years to fully relax them once they have been introduced. On the positive side, capital controls can contribute to the short-term stabilization of the funding situation in banks and prevent their imminent failure due to illiquidity.

[8]Under capital controls, electronic transactions between bank accounts within the national system usually remain unrestricted.

5.3 International Dimension

The macroprudential toolkit in the euro area is mainly set out in the Single Rulebook. Most of these tools were originally developed by the Basel Committee on Banking Supervision (BCBS) as part of Basel III (BCBS 2011) and then transposed into the Capital Requirement Directive (CRD IV) and Capital Requirements Regulation (CRR). The Single Rulebook determines the main features of macroprudential instruments, such as the countercyclical capital buffer (CCyB) or the capital surcharges for systemically important banks. While the main features are harmonized, their application and calibration is done for individual jurisdictions. For instance, a CCyB requirement of 1% may be set only for exposures in Slovakia. Other tools such as loan-to-value (LTV) limits are not part of the Single Rulebook, but based on laws and regulations at the national level.

Extensive information exchange and discussions among macroprudential policymakers take place within the European Union. The main structures for this purpose are the European Systemic Risk Board (ESRB), which includes all EU countries (see Box 5.2), and the Macroprudential Forum (MPF), which only includes euro area countries. The MPF brings together micro- and macroprudential perspectives on the euro area banking sector. It is composed of the Governing Council and the Supervisory Board of the ECB. The MPF is supported by the Financial Stability Committee (FSC), which includes the ECB and central bank representatives of the euro area countries.

Box 5.2 European Systemic Risk Board (ESRB)

The ESRB was set up in 2010 to provide an EU-wide platform for information exchange and policy coordination by macroprudential policymakers. It involves central banks and supervisory authorities from all 28 EU member states as well as several European institutions.[9] The decision-making body is the ESRB General Board, which is chaired by the ECB President. The ESRB secretariat is located at the ECB premises.

Apart from facilitating information exchange and joint analytical work, the ESRB provides guidelines for the conduct of macroprudential policy to national authorities in the form of recommendations and decisions, which are published on its website.[10] These guidelines are coupled with a comply-or-explain mechanism, as the ESRB itself does not have direct powers to set macroprudential policy. To provide an example, the ESRB issued a recommendation in 2013 regarding the adoption of legal mandates for macroprudential authorities in EU member states. This recommendation

(continued)

[9]EC, ECB, EBA, EIOPA, ESMA, and Economic and Financial Committee (EFC). Iceland, Liechtenstein and Norway were observers in the ESRB at the time of writing (early 2017).

[10]https://www.esrb.europa.eu/

Box 5.2 (continued)
required national authorities to put in place a legal and institution framework that would enable them to effectively conduct macroprudential policy.

The ESRB operates substructures in the form of committees and working groups that involve representatives from central banks and supervisory authorities of the 28 EU member states. In the context of these substructures, the ESRB has prepared and issued several flagship publications to support decision-makers, such as the ESRB Handbook on how to use macroprudential instruments for the banking sector (ESRB 2014).

Outside the European context, several international institutions are involved in analyzing financial stability, hosting discussions of policymakers, and recommending policies to promote financial stability. The leading institution in this respect is the IMF.

- *The IMF engages in multilateral surveillance of its 189 member states, including the countries of the euro area.* The IMF publishes on a semiannual basis the Global Financial Stability Report, which also covers developments and risks in the euro area. The IMF further produces spillover reports and shares results of early warning exercises with representatives of its member states on a confidential basis at the IMF Spring and Annual Meetings. These meetings provide a forum for global policymakers in the field of monetary and financial policy to discuss topical financial stability issues. For instance, the IMF Spring Meeting in April 2016 discussed among others the situation in Greece, commodity prices, the emerging market slowdown, and the incomplete balance sheet repair of European banks.
- *The IMF also performs bilateral surveillance activities of its member states and their financial systems.* This is done as part of so-called Article IV consultations,[11] which are performed on a 12-month cycle for euro area member states, and Financial Sector Assessment Programs (FSAPs), which are performed occasionally. While Art. IV consultations cover all policy areas (including nonfinancial issues such as labor market policy), FSAPs are focused in-depth assessments of a country's financial sector. They cover all areas discussed in this chapter, from risk identification and stress testing to macroprudential policy and the adequacy of financial safety nets and crisis management. The IMF performs FSAPs for around 15 countries every year. Countries with financial sectors that are considered as globally systemically relevant are obliged to

[11]Article IV refers to the Articles of Agreement of the IMF, which all member states have committed to adhere to.

undergo mandatory FSAPs at least every 5 years.[12] FSAPs also include an assessment of supervisory practices based on international standards, such as the Basel Core Principles for Effective Banking Supervision.

- *Lastly, international discussions on financial stability issues and related policies also take place in Basel.* The Financial Stability Board (FSB), the Bank for International Settlements (BIS), and the Committee on the Global Financial System (CGFS) are all involved in the monitoring and assessment of financial stability developments. They also make policy recommendations, which are, however, not directly addressed to individual countries or the euro area as a whole.

Questions for Consideration

- How can the assessment of systemic risks be improved?
- Which policies are needed to safeguard financial stability?
- Can financial crises be avoided or are they inevitable?
- Which factors contribute to effective macroprudential policy?
- How can the consistent application of macroprudential instruments across the euro area be ensured?
- Should policymakers interfere in the structure of the financial system?
- What can policymakers do to prevent the collapse of a too-big-to-fail bank?
- Should the Banking Union be complemented by single financial safety net (e.g. European deposite insurance or centralization of ELA)?
- Is there a need for a central fiscal authority in the euro area to support financial stability?
- How can the institutional complexity of financial stability policy in Europe be reduced?
- How can unintended financial stability risks that result from financial regulation be mitigated?
- Should the macroprudential authority directly interfere in the composition of bank credit and, if yes, what are the benefits and risks?

References

Basel Committee on Banking Supervision (BCBS). (2011). *Basel III: A global regulatory framework for more resilient banks and banking systems*. http://www.bis.org/publ/bcbs189.pdf

European Central Bank (ECB). (2016, March). The ECB's macroprudential policy framework. *Macroprudential Bulletin Issue 1/2016*. https://www.ecb.europa.eu/pub/pdf/other/ccbmp201603.en.pdf

[12]This requirement applies to 10 countries of the euro area: Austria, Belgium, Finland, France, Germany, Ireland, Italy, Luxembourg, the Netherlands, and Spain.

European Central Bank (ECB). (2017). *Macroprudential measures in the euro area as of 3 July 2017*. Accessed August 15, 2017, from https://www.ecb.europa.eu/pub/fsr/html/measures.en.html

European Systemic Risk Board (ESRB). (2014). *ESRB handbook on operationalising macro-prudential policy in the banking sector*. https://www.esrb.europa.eu/pub/pdf/other/140303_esrb_handbook_mp.en.pdf

European Systemic Risk Board (ESRB). (2017). *Other macroprudential measures*. Accessed August 15, 2017, from https://www.esrb.europa.eu/national_policy/other/html/index.en.html

Padoa-Schioppa, T. (2010, September). Keynote address at the IMF conference "Macro-prudential regulatory policies: The new road to financial stability?" http://www.tommasopadoaschioppa.eu/wp-content/uploads/2010/10/speech_TOMMASO-PADOA-1.pdf

Further Reading

Blancher, N., et al. (2013). *Systemic risk monitoring ("SysMo") toolkit – A user guide*. IMF Working Paper 13/168. http://www.imf.org/external/pubs/ft/wp/2013/wp13168.pdf

Constancio, V. (2016, April). *Principles of macroprudential policy*. Speech at the ECB-IMF Conference on Macroprudential Policy, Frankfurt am Main. https://www.ecb.europa.eu/press/key/date/2016/html/sp160426.en.html

European Systemic Risk Board (ESRB). (2014). *Flagship report on macro-prudential policy in the banking sector*. https://www.esrb.europa.eu/pub/pdf/other/140303_flagship_report.pdf

International Monetary Fund (IMF). (2013a). *Key aspects of macroprudential policy*. https://www.imf.org/external/np/pp/eng/2013/061013b.pdf

International Monetary Fund (IMF). (2013b). *Key aspects of macroprudential policy – Background paper*. http://www.imf.org/external/np/pp/eng/2013/061013c.pdf

International Monetary Fund (IMF). (2014). *Staff guidance note on macroprudential policy*. http://www.imf.org/external/np/pp/eng/2014/110614.pdf

Policy Interaction

6

The three policy functions of monetary policy, banking supervision, and financial stability are interrelated in many ways. This chapter focuses on the intended and unintended policy interaction in the implementation of monetary and financial policy in the euro area. The first section summarizes the main characteristics of the three policy functions, based on the discussion in previous chapters. The second section analyzes their interaction, coordination, and possible frictions. It also provides case studies to illustrate the challenges of policy coordination in practice.

6.1 Main Characteristics of the Three Policy Functions

Monetary policy was the main policy function of the ECB when the euro area was established. This was in line with international trends in central banking during that time. The 1990s and early 2000s were a time when central banks in advanced economies were focused on monetary policy, which was believed to contribute both to price stability and macroeconomic stability—the latter under the assumption that national fiscal policies remained disciplined as well. The primary objective of monetary policy in the euro area is price stability. The ECB applies a quantitative definition of price stability by aiming at an annual inflation rate in the euro area of below but close to 2% in the medium term. The main instruments are standard measures (such as MROs or LTROs) and nonstandard measures (such as asset purchases). Monetary policy is decided by the ECB for the euro area as a whole, with the Governing Council as the sole decision-making body.

Banking supervision is a new policy function of the ECB since the establishment of the SSM in 2014. Previously, the policy function used to be a national competence. It clearly increased in importance with the financial crisis that also revealed weaknesses in supervisory practices. In the SSM, decisions on supervisory policy are proposed by the Supervisory Board and adopted by the Governing Council through non-objection procedure. For significant institutions (i.e., first- and second-tier banks), banking supervision is performed jointly by the ECB and national competent authorities.

M. Fandl, *Monetary and Financial Policy in the Euro Area*, Springer Texts in Business and Economics, https://doi.org/10.1007/978-3-319-72643-4_6

For LSIs (third-tier banks), supervision remains in the competence of national authorities, with indirect supervision by the ECB. The primary objective of banking supervision is to safeguard the soundness of individual banks. The main instruments are liquidity regulation, capital regulation, exposure limits, and instruments to deal with weak banks, such as early intervention measures. The main decision-making bodies are the Supervisory Board and national competent authorities for LSIs. Decisions of the Supervisory Board require a non-objection of the Governing Council to be adopted.

Financial stability became an important topic for central banks in the early 2000s. The precrisis period was characterized by large growth in the euro area financial system relative to GDP, cross-border integration, and increasing complexity, for instance due to risk transfers through securitizations or derivatives. The policy function was in the spotlight during the initial stage of the global financial crisis. The development of a legal and institutional policy framework for financial stability as a separate policy area has its origin in this period. Its primary objective lies in safeguarding the stability of the financial system as a whole, i.e., to make sure the system remains capable of fulfilling its economic functions even under stress. Banking supervision is a necessary but not a sufficient condition for financial stability, as it does not capture issues such as sectoral debt accumulation, risk concentrations, asset price bubbles, or systemically important functions of banks. Policy instruments are mainly of preventive nature, such as (most of) macroprudential policy, but also include financial safety nets and crisis management tools.

The primary objectives of the three policy functions do not include apparent trade-offs but can be seen as mutually reinforcing. For instance, financial stability requires effective banking supervision. Price stability is a precondition for financial stability in the medium term. Banking crises may undermine the ability of central banks to maintain price stability. At the same time, there is a hierarchy among the three policy functions. Price stability is the primary objective of central banks in the euro area, while financial stability is a subordinated objective. Banking supervision is a separate objective as reflected by the separation of monetary policy and banking supervision tasks within the ECB.

Table 6.1 provides a summary overview of the primary objectives, instruments, and allocation of competences for the three policy areas. The three policy functions vary significantly as regards transparency, independence, and accountability. The treatment of these issues is shown in Table 6.2.

Monetary policy decisions are communicated in the form of press releases and press conferences with the ECB President. Minutes of policy meetings and the underlying analysis of policy decisions are published shortly thereafter, the latter in the Economic Bulletin on the ECB website. In addition, indicators and other statistics that may be relevant for policy decisions, such as the use of the deposit facility or the development of monetary aggregates, are also made available on the website. At the same time, a more restrictive transparency regime is in place for ELA decisions.

Table 6.1 Three policy areas: objectives, instruments, competence

	Monetary policy	Banking supervision	Financial stability
Primary objective	Price stability	Safeguarding the soundness of individual banks	Stability of the financial system as a whole
Main instruments	Standard measures (MROs, LTROs, standing facilities, reserve requirements) Nonstandard measures (asset purchases, forward guidance)	Liquidity requirements Capital requirements Exposure limits Instruments to deal with weak banks	Macroprudential policy (counter-cyclical capital buffer, etc.) Financial safety nets Crisis management
Competence	ECB	SSM	National ECB/SSM
Decision-making body	Governing Council	Supervisory Board/ Governing Council; NCA for LSIs	National arrangement ECB/SSM

Table 6.2 Three policy areas: transparency, independence, accountability

	Monetary policy	Banking supervision	Financial stability
Transparency			
– Policy decisions	Public	Individual bank	Public
– Minutes	√	–	–/√[a]
– Underlying analysis	√	–	√
– Statistics	√	–[b]	√
Envisaged government involvement	–	–	National: √ ECB/SSM: –
Accountability	European Parliament	National: Parliaments ECB Supervision: European Parliament	National: Parliaments ECB/SSM: European Parliament

[a]Only published in some countries
[b]Only selected publications

Banking supervision decisions are only communicated to the respective banks. The supervisory process does not include any external communication after policy meetings neither regarding policy decisions, minutes, nor underlying analysis. Similarly, only selected indicators and other statistics on European banks are made available on the websites of ECB supervision or NCAs, or in publications such as the Annual Report of ECB Supervision. Two reasons for the limited transparency are the confidentiality of supervisory information and the potential impact of the communication on sensitive single bank issues. For instance, the results of on-site inspections constitute sensitive information that may affect the public confidence in the respective bank. Overall, supervisory authorities in the euro area tend to follow a restrictive stance as regards the availability of single-bank information and often do not publically comment on policy decisions.

In the field of financial stability, macroprudential policy decisions are communicated to the public. This is usually done through press releases or on the websites of macroprudential authorities. The ECB also publishes statements after meetings of the Macroprudential Forum when needed.[1] A few countries, such as Ireland, have also started to publish minutes of policy meetings, yet this practice is more the exception than the norm at the time of writing. Some analysis behind policy decisions is also made available in most countries. The ECB and most national central banks in the euro area publish financial stability reports on a regular basis, which summarize analytical findings and provide guidance for their policy stance.

The independence of central banks implies that government entities should not be involved in their tasks regarding monetary and financial policy. This is particularly the case for monetary policy and banking supervision, which are exclusively the responsibility of central banks or national supervisory authorities. For financial stability policies, institutional arrangements in most countries in the euro area give the government an active role in the decision-making process, for instance by the participation of representatives of the ministry of finance in financial stability committees or similar macroprudential bodies. As regards the macroprudential role of the ECB, national governments are not involved, in line with its independence.

While independence provides protection for policymakers from political interference, they also need to be accountable for their decisions.

- *The accountability of monetary policy in the euro area mostly regards the relationships of the ECB vis-à-vis the European Parliament (EP) and European citizens.* Hearings with the ECB President take place in plenary sessions of the EP and with the Economic and Monetary Affairs Committee several times a year. In these occasions, the President explains recent monetary policy decisions and answers to questions by the Members of the EP. Written questions may also be submitted to the ECB. The questions and answers are then published on the websites of the ECB and the EP.
- *The accountability of banking supervision is vis-à-vis the EP and national parliaments.* Similarly to monetary policy, the Chair of the ECB Supervisory Board is invited to hearings in the EP on a quarterly basis. In these hearings, the Chair explains the current supervisory priorities and other topical issues of the SSM and answers to questions. National supervisory authorities are also accountable to the respective national parliaments.
- *Financial stability policy is a shared policy competence, and therefore the accountability frameworks vary across the public institutions involved.* At the national level, central banks and supervisory authorities involved in macroprudential

[1]This practice started in December 2016: https://www.ecb.europa.eu/press/pr/date/2016/html/pr161215_1.en.html

policy are primarily accountable to national parliaments. At the European level, the ECB is accountable to the EP for the use of its macroprudential mandate. By the time of writing, the ECB has not used its powers to top up policy instruments at the national level, which may be done for instance by setting a higher countercyclical capital buffer in an individual jurisdiction.

6.2 Policy Interaction

The conduct of monetary policy, banking supervision, and financial stability policy gives rise to crossover effects that have an impact on the respective policy functions. Crossover effects can take various forms:

- *The application of policy instrument A may influence the objective of policy area B.* For instance, large-scale asset purchases for monetary policy purposes may under certain conditions create asset price bubbles and give rise to financial stability concerns.
- *The application of policy instrument A may restrict the ability to apply policy instrument B.* For instance, high capital requirements set by bank supervisors may make it more difficult to perform countercyclical macroprudential policy.
- *The optimal level of policy instrument A may depend on policy instrument B.* In other words, the calibration of policy instrument A to reach policy objective A may take into account the application of policy instruments in areas B and C. For instance, the decision to use the systemic risk buffer may take the monetary policy stance and applicable microprudential policies into account.
- *In practice, it may not always be clear-cut if policy instrument A is exclusively in the realm of policy area A or if it can also be applied as an instrument for policy area B.* For instance, capital surcharges for systemically important institutions could be claimed by both macroprudential policy and banking supervision as being within their area of competence.[2]

The interaction of the three policy functions raises the question to which extent they should be coordinated. Coordination can take different forms and may be either explicit or implicit:

- *In the case of minimal coordination, the three policy functions are fulfilled independently of each other by different policymakers.* Each policy area applies instruments from its own toolkit without communication with other areas. Nevertheless, some information about the conduct of the various policies will be publically available, in particular regarding monetary policy. Hence, even without direct communication, policymakers may take information about the

[2]The SSM Framework Regulation assigns capital surcharges for systemically important institutions as a macroprudential policy tool.

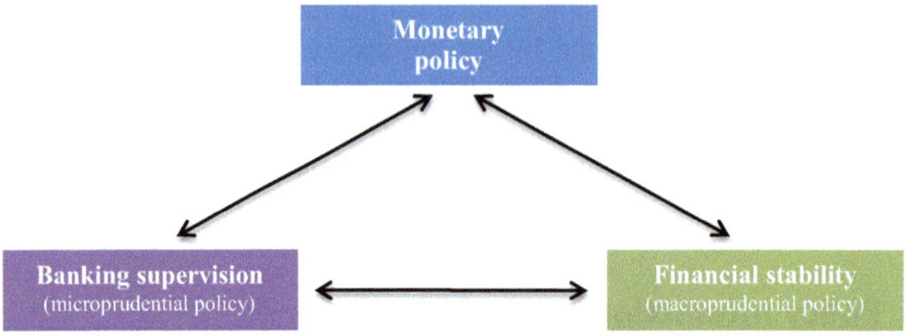

Fig. 6.1 Policy interaction

conduct of other policies into consideration when deciding on their policy instruments. This is known as implicit coordination. For instance, bank supervisors may consider the current monetary policy stance when deciding on the application of supervisory instruments.

- *In the case of maximum coordination, the three policy functions engage in regular information exchange, discussions of crosscutting themes, and may have overlapping decision-making bodies.* For instance, the Bank of England has three committees for monetary policy, banking supervision, and financial stability policy with overlapping participation. This means that several members of one committee are also members of another committee, and some are even members of all three committees.[3] Such level of interaction is easier to establish if the competences for the three policy functions are allocated to the same institution and apply to the same jurisdiction.

As macroprudential policy is a rather new field, the literature on policy interaction and possible coordination between monetary policy, banking supervision, and financial stability policy is still at an early stage.[4] The following sections investigate these relationships one by one (see Fig. 6.1), starting with the interaction of monetary policy and financial stability.

Monetary Policy and Financial Stability

Central banks are key players in monetary policy and financial stability in the euro area. They are exclusively responsible for monetary policy and have a leading role in decision-making bodies for macroprudential policy in most countries. In many member states, Governors or Vice Governors of national central banks participate

[3]The Governor of the Bank of England and the head of the financial stability department participate in all three committees (MPC, FPC, PRA).

[4]Many economics textbooks focus on another type of policy coordination, between monetary and fiscal policy. This relationship is undeniably important for the dynamics of economies in the short- to medium term, yet it is outside the scope of this book.

in financial stability committees as well as in the Governing Council of the ECB. At the European level, the Governing Council is involved in monetary policy and macroprudential policy decisions of the ECB. This overlap in decision-making bodies facilitates policy coordination in normal times. In crisis situations, macroprudential policy is not sufficient to safeguard financial stability. As a consequence, it is not surprising that ministries of finance are also involved in financial stability committees or similar bodies at the national level.

Both policy functions can be used for countercyclical policy. For instance, the central bank may tighten monetary policy when the economy experiences strong growth and inflation, and loosen it when it is in recession. Similarly, the macroprudential authority may require a higher countercyclical capital buffer from banks in times of strong credit growth and release it during crisis episodes. Unlike monetary policy, such measures can be more targeted, for instance to a certain jurisdiction or market segment (e.g. commercial real estate). For the effective conduct of such countercyclical policy, it is important that policymakers tighten policy sufficiently in normal times to have room for maneuver during severe crises when standard policy tools can be quickly exploited.

Monetary policy affects financial stability in many ways:

- *Accommodative monetary policy during a financial crisis provides liquidity support to the banking sector and thereby supports financial stability.* The monetary policy response during the global financial crisis serves as a good example. In general, financial crises are likely to coincide with an economic downturn and limited price level pressure, which allows monetary policy to take an accommodative stance without jeopardizing price stability. In short, this crossover effect is supportive for financial stability.
- *Persistent low official rates or large asset purchases by central banks compress net interest margins by banks and other financial institutions and may induce search for yield behavior.* Both effects may give rise to additional risks in individual institutions and the system as a whole. In such environment, policymakers may consider the application of macroprudential policy, for instance to prevent the emergence of credit-fueled asset price bubbles. Overall, this crossover effect from monetary policy to financial stability is a negative one.
- *High and unstable inflation has an adverse impact on businesses and individuals, and indirectly on banks and financial stability.* Such developments can be observed in high-inflation countries outside the euro area, such as Turkey. Maintaining price stability in broad terms instead supports financial stability.

There are different views regarding the application of monetary policy instruments for financial stability purposes. To use a practical example, suppose that Riksbank, the Swedish central bank, identifies the buildup of an asset price bubble in the real estate market. The question then is whether it should only apply macroprudential policy instruments to prevent a further growth of the bubble or whether it should use a combination of monetary and macroprudential policy.

- Before the financial crisis, when macroprudential policy was largely inexistent, the prevailing view in central banking was that monetary policy should not aim at addressing asset price bubbles. Instead, it was considered best that central banks wait for the asset price bubble to burst and "mop up" afterwards—to use the famous words of A. Greenspan, the former chairman of the US Federal Reserve System.
- When the financial crisis hit, the Bank for International Settlements (BIS) drew the lesson that it would be preferable for central banks to "lean against the wind" through all available means, including monetary policy.
- The current position of the ECB is that asset price developments should be taken into account in the conduct of monetary policy, yet there should be a clear focus on price stability. Financial stability concerns should be primarily addressed by macroprudential instruments. Only in some specific situations, monetary policy could play a role, although a risk of damaging the central bank's credibility remains. The IMF and the Bank of England share broadly similar views on this issue.[5]

Turning to the other side of the relation, financial instability clearly undermines the ability of central banks to maintain price stability. For instance, the breakdown of large-value payment systems would make it impossible for central banks to perform monetary policy operations. Broader crisis developments, such as the drying up of the interbank market, also impact the demand for CBM or the deposit facility. Such developments may further impair the transmission mechanism, through which monetary policy is transmitted to the economy, as could be observed during the sovereign debt crisis.

Little is known about the impact of macroprudential policy on price stability. This is due to the relatively recent emergence of macroprudential policy and the limited experience on the effectiveness and transmission mechanism of policy instruments. Potential causal relationships, which require further analysis, may run through credit growth or the resilience of banks. For instance, measures such as an LTV cap may have an impact on credit growth, which in turn influences aggregate demand and price developments. Measures such as the countercyclical capital buffer may also strengthen the resilience of banks, thereby ensuring that the transmission mechanism for monetary policy operations remains intact during crisis times.

Financial safety nets support the conduct of monetary policy. Both deposit insurance and ELA enhance the public confidence in banks and commercial bank money. In situations in which the DGS is weakened, for instance because of large payouts following the failure of a medium-sized bank, individuals are less likely to keep savings in banks, leading to a shift in money demand from commercial bank money to cash. Against this background, monetary policy has a genuine interest in ensuring that the DGSs in all countries of the euro area remain a credible and functional safety net at all times.

---

[5]The view of the Bank of England at the time of writing was that monetary policy would be a last line of defense against asset price bubbles, after all available instruments of macroprudential policy have been exploited.

Banking Supervision and Financial Stability

Among the three policy functions, the objectives of banking supervision and financial stability are the closest to each other. As already discussed, banking supervision has a micro-level view on individual institutions, while financial stability has a macro-level view on the system as a whole. Effective banking supervision is a necessary but not a sufficient condition for financial stability. Simply relying on the micro-level perspective may for instance miss debt accumulations, risk concentrations, asset price booms, the emergence of shadow banks outside the regulatory perimeter, or the development of new markets that amplify losses during crises, such as the CDS market in the run-up to the global financial crisis.

While the objectives of both areas should be aligned in most situations, there are cases in which they reach different policy conclusions.

- *One example is capital regulation during a crisis.* Suppose that an overall SREP capital requirement of 11% applies to Portuguese banks when the country enters a major economic and financial crisis. Banks face significant unexpected losses, which erode their capital base. The CET1 ratio of banks quickly approaches the SREP capital requirement. What should policymakers do in this situation? The macroprudential authority may favor a relaxation of the capital requirement, arguing that capital is held to absorb unexpected losses in such situations. However, bank supervisors may have a preference to maintain the existing SREP requirement to make sure they remain sound and argue that risks even increased for the respective banks.
- *Another example in the liquidity crisis of a banking group in the euro area.* An Austrian banking group may operate subsidiaries in Slovakia and Slovenia. Suppose the Slovak subsidiary of the bank is a net provider of intragroup funding vis-à-vis the Austrian parent, while the Slovenian subsidiary is a net receiver of intragroup funding (see Fig. 6.2). Now assume that the banking group enters a major financial crisis and the parent bank faces difficulties in obtaining wholesale funding. In this situation, the Austrian bank will aim at using the liquidity surplus by its Slovak subsidiary to cover liquidity shortfalls elsewhere in the group.

  The macroprudential authority in Slovakia may get concerned about cross-border contagion effects of the crisis. It may thus consider the implementation of measures to ring-fence liquidity in the Slovak subsidiary, for instance by setting a

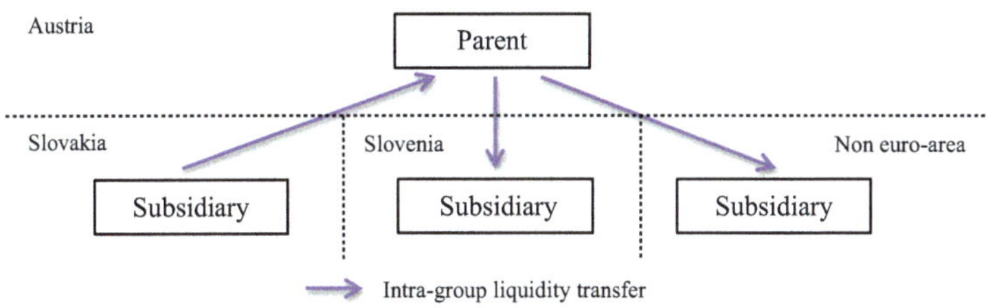

Fig. 6.2 Liquidity transfers in a banking group

lower exposure limit to the Austrian parent. The main objective of the measure would be to safeguard financial stability in Slovakia. However, the measure would also worsen the ability of the Austrian banking group to manage its group liquidity in the crisis situation.

Against this background, bank supervisors would most likely have a different view than the macroprudential authority. Instead of focusing on the situation in Slovakia, the ECB as the competent supervisory authority has the perspective on the euro area as a whole. Hence, it may be concerned about the impact of ring-fencing measures on the soundness of the Austrian banking group.

The proximity of the two policy functions may also give rise to frictions in practice. For instance, banking supervisors may not always agree with some financial stability analyses and misunderstand it as a criticism of their activities. In addition, restrictions on the sharing of confidential supervisory data may make cooperation challenging. Moreover, the border between the two policy functions may sometimes be unclear, for instance as regards the interplay between micro- and macroprudential capital requirements.

Policy coordination between the two areas is important for effective micro- and macroprudential supervision. Coordination can be facilitated by information exchange on risk assessment and policy priorities. Macroprudential policymakers further need to ensure that the supervisory perspective is heard before they take decisions. For instance, at the level of the ECB, the Supervisory Board is involved in macroprudential policy through joint meetings of the Governing Council and the Supervisory Board in the Macroprudential Forum.

Monetary Policy and Banking Supervision

The relationship between monetary policy and banking supervision in the euro area is characterized by the separation principle. It means that the two policy functions are fully separated, thus allowing no explicit policy coordination. The separation principle was introduced with the establishment of the SSM.

The interaction of the two policy functions tends to be more developed in case of weak banks or crisis countries. For instance, ELA provision requires a solvency assessment of the competent supervisory authority. Another example are supervisory exposure limits (e.g., limits to the domestic sovereign exposure of Greek banks), which may affect the collateral pool of individual institutions for monetary policy operations or ELA.

Monetary policy affects banking supervision mainly through the impact on the liquidity and profitability of banks. For instance, a bank may lose its counterparty status for monetary policy operations, which may trigger supervisory consequences or even a failing-or-likely-to-fail determination. Another example are asset purchases by central banks that provide additional liquidity to banks and may have positive effects on the market value of security holdings.

Banking supervision also impacts the conduct of monetary policy in many ways. For instance, higher capital or liquidity requirements may influence credit supply by banks. Given that most commercial bank money is created through new credit, capital and liquidity regulation indirectly also affects the growth of monetary aggregates. Moreover, monetary policy requires that banks are financial sound and solvent, which creates a direct link to the objective of banking supervision.

Box 6.1 Case Studies

The following case studies have been prepared for course instructors. The objective of the case studies is to illustrate the policy interaction of monetary policy, banking supervision, and financial stability in the euro area. They are intended for about 20 participants.

Participants need to be split into six groups.

- *Policymaker for monetary policy.* You are the sole decision-maker for monetary policy in the euro area. The policy framework described in Chap. 2 applies.
- *Policymaker for banking supervision:* You supervise all banks and are solely responsible for supervisory actions. The policy framework described in Chap. 4 applies.
- *Policymaker for financial stability:* You have a key role for financial stability in the respective member state. You cannot decide on your own but need the approval by the ministry of finance in order to take any policy action. You may request information from the policymakers for banking supervision and monetary policy. The policy framework described in Chap. 5 applies.
- *Ministry of finance:* You are responsible for the public finances of your country. All further assumptions are at your discretion.
- *Bank:* Your shareholders expect a high return on equity. All further assumptions are at your discretion.
- *Individual:* You are employed at a company in the respective country and are currently thinking of applying for a loan at the bank in order to purchase a house. All further assumptions are at your discretion.

(continued)

Box 6.1 (continued)

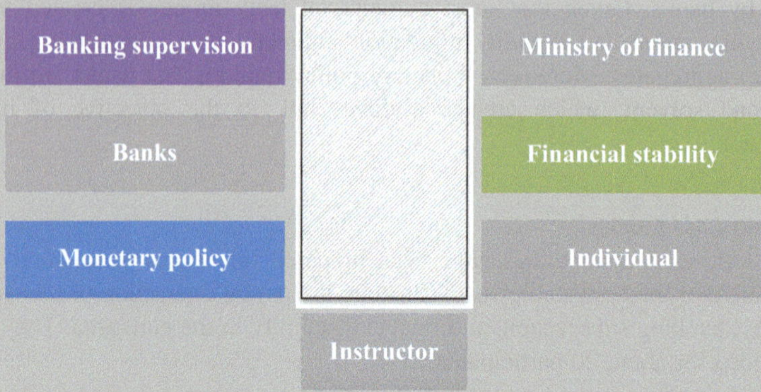

The description of the case studies establishes the initial state of the economy, the financial system, and the policies currently in place. All subsequent developments, effects of policy decisions, and other developments are in the hands of the instructor, who has a similar function as the game master in role-playing games.

The case study is performed in rounds, with the following procedure in each round:

- The instructor describes the developments since the last round.
- Groups decide independently on their actions for the next round.
- Participants are informed about the actions taken by all groups.
- The four policymakers (for monetary policy, banking supervision, financial stability, and fiscal policy) may communicate and coordinate their actions for the next round. Any agreements are nonbinding for subsequent actions of policymakers. At the same time, banks and individuals have the possibility to raise a limited number of questions to the four policymakers in each round.

Case 1: Renewed Sovereign Debt Crisis in a Euro Area Member State

Economy: Real GDP growth has been sluggish since the Great Recession. The economy is experiencing slight deflation. Unemployment has remained high at levels above 15%. Real wage growth has remained flat. Debt levels in the public and private sectors are elevated. Many businesses and individuals have difficulties to service their debt. House prices declined by 20% over the past 5 years. The decline has bottomed out over the last year.

(continued)

Banking sector: The banking sector has only four banks as a result of past consolidation in the sector. Three banks have low capital ratios and face difficulties in obtaining liquidity from the market. All banks have high exposures to the domestic sovereign. The nonperforming loan ratio stands at 25% and has remained relatively stable over the past year. Recently, market rumors emerged regarding funding difficulties in one bank, which led to a loss in depositor confidence. Customers have started to withdraw their deposits from the bank, despite being subject to deposit insurance. Deposit flight is currently increasing and there is a significant risk of a bank run, which may also affect other banks due to confidence effects.[6]

Nonbank financial institutions: The nonbank financial sector is relatively small. It mainly consists of insurance companies and pension funds, which are partly owned by domestic banks. Insurance companies are heavily invested in domestic government bonds.

Current policies:

- *Monetary policy:* Official interest rates have been close to zero for many years. The extended asset purchase program by the central bank has been gradually reduced over the past year. Market participants expect it to be discontinued in the next monetary policy meeting. As the four banks in the country do not have sufficient collateral for monetary policy operations, they are reliant on ELA. The provision of ELA has continuously increased and currently stands at approx. 50% of GDP.
- *Banking supervision:* All requirements of the Single Rulebook apply to the banks of the country. An on-site inspection in the largest bank has recently shown major deficiencies in risk management and the documentation of loan transactions. An EU-wide stress testing exercise is planned for the next year. Two small banks have been resolved over the past year, with performing assets and customer deposits being assumed by one of the four banks.
- *Macroprudential policy:* No macroprudential measures are currently in place, except for a minor capital surcharge for the two largest banks (O-SII buffer of 0.5%) that has been announced to increase to 1% next year.
- *Fiscal policy:* Public debt is about 120% of GDP. The country has notorious difficulties in complying with the Stability and Growth Pact and envisages a budget deficit of 3% this year. Yields on 5Y domestic government bonds have increased from 4% to 5% in recent weeks.

[6]Mervyn King, the former Governor of the Bank of England, noted in the aftermath of Northern Rock: "*It is not rational to start a bank run but rational to participate in one once it has started.*"

Case 2: Booming Economy in the Euro Area

Economy: The overall euro area economy experiences a slight economic recovery. The country in question has been the best performing member state in terms of real GDP growth over the past 3 years, with annual growth rates of approx. 5%. Growth is supported by a surge in exports to non-euro area countries. Unemployment has fallen from 15% to 7% within 3 years. Commercial real estate prices have increased by 25% last year. House prices have risen by approx. 15% last year and by 20% in big cities. The strong increase in house prices has sparked a public debate about the affordability of housing, in particular for young people.

Banking sector: The nonperforming loan ratio has fallen from 9% to 3% over the last few years. Low interest rates have encouraged banks to search for high-return investments with manageable risk. Some banks have identified commercial real estate as an attractive investment opportunity. After initial loans to commercial real estate projects, collateral values have increased and more projects have come to the market. The boom in commercial real estate is amplified by the availability of credit at low costs. Overall credit growth has been close to 10% over the last year.

Nonbank financial institutions: The sector has experienced strong growth in recent years in all segments, from insurance companies, asset managers, and mutual funds to shadow banks.

Current policies:

- *Monetary policy:* The marginal refinancing rate in the euro area stands at 1%. The extended asset purchase program was discontinued 2 years ago. The reserve requirements are unchanged compared to 2017.
- *Banking supervision:* All requirements of the Single Rulebook apply to the banks of the country. SREP capital requirements for banks in the country are between 10% and 13%. Recent supervisory analysis showed deficiencies in the assessment and management of risks from commercial real estate in at least two banks.
- *Macroprudential policy:* A countercyclical capital buffer requirement of 1% was introduced 1 year ago. In addition, capital surcharges for the three largest banks apply (1% each).
- *Fiscal policy:* The public debt to GDP ratio stands at 90%. A balanced budget was recorded last year. The government has recently introduced a subsidy for first-time buyers of residential real estate.

Further Reading

Coeuré, B. (2013, February). *Monetary policy and banking supervision*. Speech at Goethe University, Frankfurt. https://www.ecb.europa.eu/press/key/date/2013/html/sp130207.en.html

International Monetary Fund (IMF) (2013) The interaction of monetary and macroprudential policies. http://www.imf.org/external/np/pp/eng/2013/012913.pdf

Epilogue

Crisis developments over the past 10 years have resulted in profound changes in the way monetary and financial policy is conducted in the euro area. Among others, the decade has seen expansionary monetary policy through standard and nonstandard measures, unprecedented financial assistance to euro area member states and banks experiencing severe stress, extensive regulatory reform, and the establishment of the European Banking Union with a Single Supervisory Mechanism for all euro area banks. This book provided an overview of the main developments and sketched out the policy framework for monetary policy, banking supervision, and financial stability that was in place as of early 2017.

The myriad of changes in the policy framework can be difficult to follow for people that do not work in this field. Some areas have become very complex—capital regulation being the prime example—and acronyms are extensively used in all three policy areas. Unfortunately, the pace of changes in practice has not been matched by the pace of adjustments in standard textbooks for university students during the past decade. At the time of writing, many economics and business curricula at European universities still do not cover issues related to monetary and financial policy in much detail.

Nonetheless, the stated policy areas are highly relevant, as they affect economies and citizens in many important ways. In this respect, they would deserve much wider awareness and broader discussion than is currently the case. This textbook only provided an introduction to monetary and financial policy in the euro area. Readers are encouraged to dig deeper and develop well-argued opinions about these policies and ideas for possible alternatives. Every aspect of monetary policy, banking supervision, and financial stability that has been described in the six chapters of this book is eventually a policy choice and can be different in the future.

M. Fandl, *Monetary and Financial Policy in the Euro Area*, Springer Texts in Business and Economics, https://doi.org/10.1007/978-3-319-72643-4

Annex

Annex A: Basic Structure of the European Union

The European Union comprises 28 member states, including the 19 countries that form the euro area. The non-euro area member states of the EU are Bulgaria, Croatia, the Czech Republic, Denmark, Hungary, Poland, Romania, Sweden, and the United Kingdom.[1] The objectives of the European Union and its *modus operandi* are set out in the Treaties of Rome (1957) and Maastricht (1992) with subsequent amendments.

Four European institutions constitute the political center of the European Union. The competences of these institutions complement the tasks and decision-making powers of national authorities and parliaments in the 28 member states.

- The *European Council* comprises the heads of state or government of the 28 EU countries. It provides the general political directions and priorities for the European Union but has no dedicated executive or legislative functions. Meetings take place in Brussels at least four times per year and are chaired by the President of the European Council. The members of the European Council elect the President for a term of 2.5 years (Donald Tusk at the time of writing). Meetings of the European Council may also take place in euro area composition and are referred to as Euro Summits.
- The *European Commission* (EC) is the executive branch of the European Union. It is located in Brussels and Luxembourg and comprises a staff of approximately 23,000. The EC includes 28 commissioners including the President of the European Commission (Jean-Claude Juncker at the time of writing). It has two main functions: Firstly, it executes EU law, ranging from the common agricultural policy to competition policy. Secondly, it proposes new EU law such as Directives. The EC has the exclusive right to make legislative proposals on EU law.

[1]Following a referendum on 23 June 2016, the UK government invoked the procedures of Art. 50 of the Treaty of the European Union on 28 March 2017, initiating the withdrawal process of the UK from the EU.

M. Fandl, *Monetary and Financial Policy in the Euro Area*, Springer Texts in Business and Economics, https://doi.org/10.1007/978-3-319-72643-4

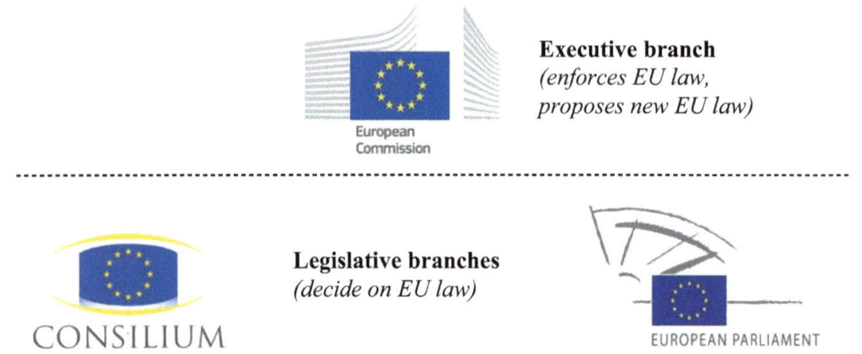

Fig. A.1 EU institutions with executive and legislative powers

- The *European Parliament* (EP) is the first chamber of the legislative branch of the European Union. It is composed of 751 members (MEPs), which are directly elected in pan-European elections every 5 years. Plenary sessions take place in Brussels or Strasbourg. All legislative proposals by the EC need to be discussed in the EP, which may adopt them with simple majority. In addition to plenary sessions, the EP operates parliamentary committees that consist of various MEPs. They support the EC in initiating legislation in the respective policy area. For monetary and financial policy, the relevant committee is the Economic and Monetary Affairs (ECON) Committee.
- The *Council of Ministers* (Council) is the second chamber of the legislative branch of the European Union, as illustrated in Fig. A.1. It is composed of the national ministers of the 28 member states, which meet in 10 different configurations depending on the policy area (foreign affairs, environment, etc.). Ministers of finance and economy meet once a month for meetings of the Economic and Financial Affairs Council (ECOFIN). All new EU legislation in this policy area (such as the CRD IV or the BRRD) needs to be adopted by the ECOFIN with qualified majority in order to enter into force, provided it was also passed by the EP. In addition to its legislative powers, the ECOFIN serves as a forum for discussions on economic policy across member states.

EU law in the field of financial sector policy can take the form of directives or regulations. Both are prepared and proposed by the EC. To enter into force, they need to be adopted by the EP and Council. Once adopted, EU directives need to be transposed into national law within a certain period of time. For instance, the CRD IV had to be transposed in all 28 EU countries. National adoption also implies that there is some degree of national discretion in the way the directive is transposed. By contrast, EU regulations (such as the CRR) are directly applicable in all member states and do not require the involvement of national parliaments. This choice of legislative instrument eliminates the potential for national discretion.

Decisions on monetary policy in the European Union are taken by central banks independently of the abovementioned executive and legislative European institutions. The independence of central banks is anchored in Article 130 of the Treaty. It comprises the European Central Bank (ECB) and the national central banks of the 28 EU member states. In line with their independence, the ECB and the national central banks are accountable to European citizens and parliaments.

An additional body, the Eurogroup, has gained importance for economic and financial policy in euro area countries as a result of the sovereign debt crisis. The Eurogroup includes the ministers of finance of the 19 euro area countries. It is an informal body that focuses on issues related to economic and financial policy in the currency union.[2] Regular meetings take place on a monthly basis, typically on the evening before the ECOFIN. They are chaired by the President of the Eurogroup that is elected among its members for a period of 2.5 years (Jeroen Dijsselbloem at the time of writing). The Eurogroup gained in political importance during the sovereign debt crisis and in the course of the EU/IMF Programs in several euro area member states. In the Program context, the Eurogroup takes note of progress made in the respective country, based on reviews by the Troika of EC, ECB, and IMF, and assesses whether the conditions for disbursements under EU Programs are met.

Annex B: Basics of Accounting

The balance sheet is a snapshot of an entity's assets, liabilities, and equity at a certain point in time. Assets are shown on the left-hand side, while liabilities and equity are recorded on the right-hand side of the balance sheet. Assets are essentially everything the entity owns (e.g., property, equipment, accounts receivable). Liabilities are everything the entity owes (e.g., accounts payable, bank loans that need to be repaid upon maturity). Equity is the residual between assets and liabilities. Together, liabilities and equity reflect the sources of funds. Assets indicate the use of funds. By convention, the two sides of the balance sheet are referred to as the asset and liability sides. The balance sheet always refers to a point in time, for instance the financial situation of the entity as of end-2016.

The income statement shows the entity's revenues and expenses during a certain period of time. It is usually presented in column format, starting with operating revenues and expenses, followed by nonoperating items and taxes during the period. Adding up all positive and negative items leads to net income after taxes, the bottom line of the income statement. This line item indicates the profit or loss the entity generated during the period (e.g., the year 2016). Conceptually, it also provides the

[2]ECOFIN and Eurogroup meetings are typically preceded by meetings of committees that consist of high-ranking officials in national ministries of finance. The two committees that mirror the ECOFIN and Eurogroup country compositions are the Economic and Financial Committee (EFC) and the Eurogroup Working Group (EWG).

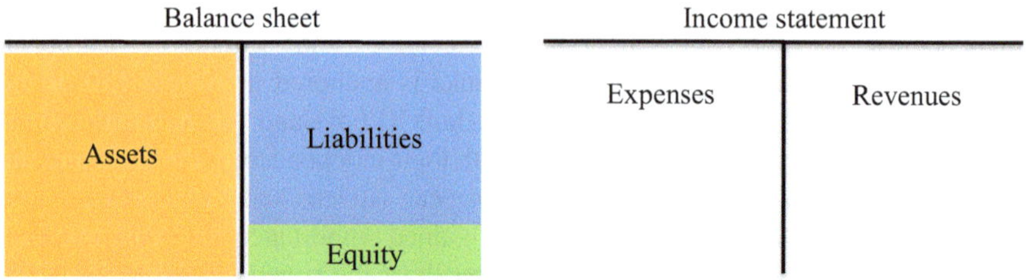

Fig. B.1 Structure of balance sheet and income statement

link between the income statement and the balance sheet of the entity, given that the net income also enters the equity section of the balance sheet at the end of the period. If the entity generated a net profit after taxes, its equity increases by the same amount. If the entity pays a dividend, equity decreases again. Otherwise, profits are retained and strengthen the equity position.

All transactions of the entity have to be recorded via double-entry bookkeeping. Entities are obliged to record their sales revenues, the payment of salaries, the interest received on securities held, or more generally all transactions or events that affect their financial position. This is done by applying the method of double-entry bookkeeping, which requires entities to make two booking entries for each transaction. The method is crucial to understand how transactions affect the balance sheet and income statement.

- The main components of the balance sheet and income statement (i.e., assets, liabilities, equity, expenses, and revenues) consist of many accounts and are structured as illustrated in Fig. B.1. Assets and expenses are on the left-hand side, while liabilities, equity, and revenues are on the right-hand side. As a general rule, the sum of the left-hand side and the right-hand side needs to match at all times.
- In any transaction, the same amount needs to be added or deducted from the accounts on the left and right-hand side. This ensures that the stated overall balance is maintained. Whether a transaction affects only accounts on the balance sheet, the income statement, or both depends on the nature of the transaction as the following examples illustrate.
- Suppose the entity receives rent from a property it owns. This transaction increases its cash position (an asset) and its revenues by the same amount. Doing so does not change the balance of the two sides. The additional revenues boosted the entity's performance in the given period.
- Now suppose the entity needs to pay taxes. The transaction reduces its cash position (an asset) and adds to its expenses. Decreasing assets and increasing expenses by the same amount again maintains the balance of the two sides. The entity's net income after taxes has decreased due to the tax payment.

- Lastly suppose the entity grants a loan to a customer. This transaction creates a claim against the customer (an asset) and reduces the cash position (another asset). Again, the overall balance is maintained. However, unlike in the previous examples, this transaction did not affect the entity's performance but only the structure of its assets.

Several indicators for the entity's liquidity, solvency, performance, and risks can be computed based on the balance sheet and income statement. For instance, the net income after taxes divided by total equity indicates the return on equity for the given period. Computing it for several entities allows useful comparisons, irrespective of the entities' size. An investor may, for example, find it useful to know that company A produced a return on equity of 8% in 2016, while its competitor B only generated a return of 2%. Another example is the current ratio, which is calculated as current assets divided by current liabilities. It provides information on the entity's liquidity position. Many other indicators can be calculated and are used by businesses, external analysts, investors, creditors, and other institutions.

Generally accepted reporting standards are applied to ensure that entities record transactions and other changes to their financial position in a comparable manner. Most large and other capital-market-oriented businesses in the euro area apply a globally known set of reporting standards known as IFRS (International Financial Reporting Standards). IFRS have been developed by a standard setting body located in London and are intended to serve as a global benchmark for recording business transactions. With the rise of economic and financial globalization in the 1990s and early 2000s, their use and importance have risen substantially. At the same time, the trend reduced the relevance of national accounting standards that were commonly used in the past and are still applied today by smaller and less capital-market-oriented businesses in the euro area.

Finally, financial statements need to be audited by an independent external party on a regular basis. The main purpose of the external audit is to assess whether the entity's financial statements (i.e., its balance sheet, income statement, and some other elements) are in material compliance with the applicable reporting standards. Auditors then make this assessment available to the general public. In the euro area, most businesses are required to have their financial statements audited at least once a year. The audit statements can usually be found in the companies' annual reports, which are often published on company websites.

Annex C: Basics of Corporate Finance

A key question in corporate finance is how to finance investments. For instance, a business may want to invest in new equipment (e.g., a new tractor for a farmer) and consider various forms of financing. Two main forms are debt and equity financing, i.e., for instance to obtain a bank loan or to use own funds.

- Debt comprises borrowed funds that need to be repaid at some point. Related to this characteristic, it does not give ownership rights to its holder. Compensation of debt can be either fixed or variable. An example for variable compensation is a floating-rate bank loan whose interest rate is linked to a market rate.
- Equity does not have a repayment date. In its purest form, it comprises shares in the ownership of the business. This means that the shareholder can influence major decisions, such as the selection of management, through voting rights that he or she can exercise in shareholder assemblies. The compensation of equity is known as dividend payments. Unlike interest, dividends are only paid in profit years and upon discretion of the business. After the end of each year, the business decides how much of its annual profit it distributes as dividends. Retained profits increase the equity base of the business and allow the financing of new investment. Similarly, newly raised equity can be used for this purpose. Another important characteristic of equity is that it is the first item on the liability side to absorb losses. This is also the reason why the required return on equity is typically higher than for debt. The ability to absorb losses means that in loss years, the business does not pay dividends and a part of equity is written down. If losses are large and equity is insufficient to cover them, the business becomes insolvent. In such cases, the shareholders do not get anything back from their equity investment. If the business is a limited liability company, the loss for shareholders is limited to their initial investment. In other words, they are not required to provide additional funds to satisfy debt holders.

Limited liability provides an incentive for businesses to use leverage in order to increase the return on equity. Leverage refers to the proportion of debt versus equity financing. As long as the business is able to generate higher returns than what it has to pay as compensation to debt holders, it has a financial incentive to use more debt financing in order to increase the return on equity for its shareholders. This is known as the leverage effect. The shareholder gets the upside (higher compensation in profit years), while enjoying limited liability in the downside when the business becomes insolvent as a result of large losses. The flipside of the leverage effect is that the risk of becoming insolvent increases with higher leverage, given that more reliance on debt financing limits the capacity of the business to absorb losses.

The choice between debt and equity financing is also determined by the respective costs of the two funding sources. The costs do not only depend on the suppliers of the respective funds (such as the interest the bank charges to provide the loan) but they are also influenced by the tax treatment. The tax regimes of euro area countries provide a favorable treatment of debt compared to equity, given that interest payments are tax-deductible while dividend payments are not. This treatment makes debt a less expensive funding source for businesses than it what would be in the situation of equal treatment of debt and equity.

Annex D: Basics of Credit Risk

In debt relationships, the borrower sometimes does not meet his payment obligations to the lender. The associated risk is known as credit risk. This annex provides a short introduction to credit risk from the perspective of the lender, which is typically a bank.

When providing a loan, the bank assesses the credit risk associated with the respective borrower and the terms of the transaction. This assessment leads to an internal rating for the envisaged loan. It also influences the pricing of the transaction, as the expected loss should be considered in the pricing of the loan, when deciding on the offered interest rate. A higher interest rate will be charged for borrowers with low creditworthiness than for borrowers with higher debt servicing capacity. For instance, an unemployed person with limited savings will have to pay a higher interest rate for a 100k euro loan than an employed person with a stable income and moderate expenses.

As long as the borrower makes the contractual payments to the bank, credit risk does not materialize. However, there may be times when the borrower misses a payment. This can be due to many reasons, including when the borrower simply forgets to make the payment on time. Should the borrower be in arrears for more than a certain period of time—typically 90 days—the borrower is assumed to have a persistent problem as regards his ability or willingness to pay. From this point onwards, the loan is considered as nonperforming.

The definition of nonperforming loans (NPLs) varies across the euro area. In 2014, the European Banking Authority (EBA) issued a harmonized definition of nonperforming exposures (NPEs) that is applicable in all euro area countries. The definition of NPEs is broader than NPLs as it also includes new forborne loans. These are nonperforming loans that have been recently restructured by the respective bank. For instance, the bank may restructure a loan by agreeing with the borrower on a different repayment schedule. For 1 year, such forborne loans are still considered nonperforming. Afterwards the loan is reclassified as performing, provided that the borrower complies with the revised payment plan.

When the bank realizes it will make a loss on a loan, it needs to set aside a risk provision. Such provision reduces the value of its assets and creates an expense that impacts the bank's net income of the year. While the contractual claim against the borrower does not change by the provision, the net value of the loan for accounting purposes is written down. For example, a bank may observe that a construction company gets into difficulties and becomes delinquent on its loan. The loan thus turns nonperforming and the bank estimates that it will eventually lose 50% on the loan. Hence, it will make a provision of 50% of the outstanding loan balance. If the likelihood of recovering a part of the loan becomes very low, the bank may also write off the loan, by which a part of it disappears from its balance sheet.

The extent to which NPLs are covered by risk provisions is known as the coverage ratio. It can be calculated for entire portfolios, for instance the loan book of the bank. Other versions of the coverage ratio take the level of collateralization into account on top of risk provisions. In case a secured loan becomes

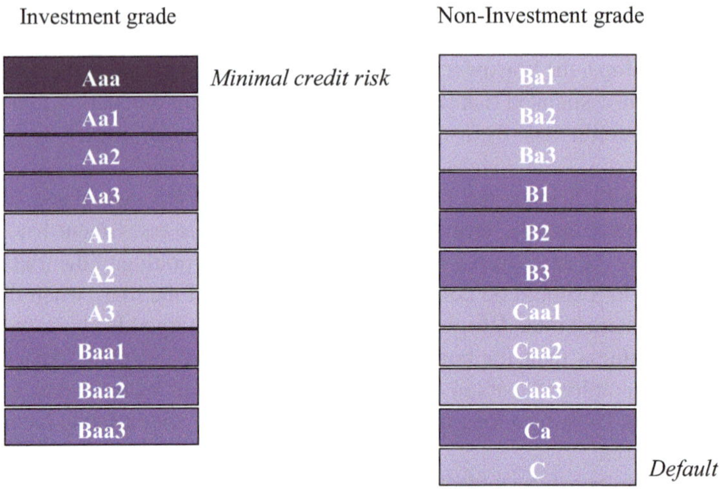

Fig. D.1 Moody's rating scale

nonperforming, the bank has the advantage compared to an unsecured loan that it can take recourse to the provided collateral in order to satisfy the claim. This reduces its loss upon the default of the borrower and therefore lowers the expected loss.

In addition to loan portfolios, the bank may also hold securities that are associated with credit risk, such as corporate bonds. Given that securities, unlike loans, are tradable financial instruments, many market participants consider them as potential investments and will want to know the associated credit risk. Against this background, specialist firms known as rating agencies provide external assessments of the creditworthiness of bond issuers or the credit risk of specific bond issuances. These ratings are mainly paid by the issuers themselves, which raises concerns about a potential conflict of interest. Nevertheless, external ratings, such as those provided by Moody's, Standard & Poor's, or Fitch Ratings, are commonly used by banks and other investors. Ratings range from minimum credit risk to the outright default of the issuer. The rating scale of Moody's is illustrated in Fig. D.1. It includes two main categories, known as investment grade and non-investment grade. On average, the yield of bonds broadly correlates with the external rating, i.e., higher quality bonds tend to be associated with a low yield, while riskier bonds tend to offer higher yields.

Annex E: Simplified Eurosystem Balance Sheet

The central bank balance sheet can provide useful insights into the functioning of the monetary and financial system. This annex provides a short introduction to the Eurosystem balance sheet in a simplified manner. The balance sheet witnessed significant change in terms of size and composition ever since the onset of the global financial crisis. Its size increased from 1.5 trillion euros (end-2007) to 3.6 trillion

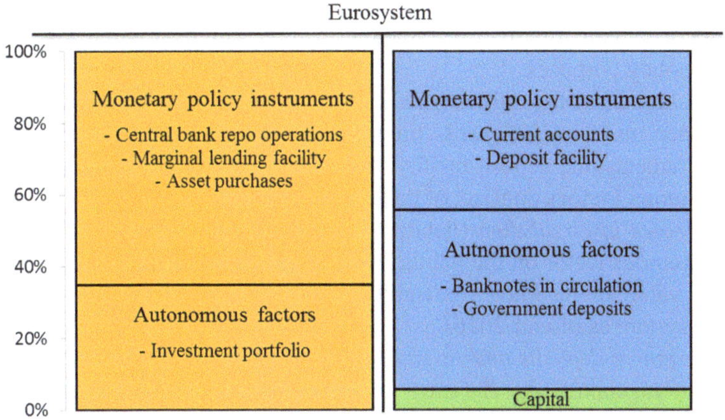

Fig. E.1 Simplified Eurosystem balance sheet

euros (end-2016), mainly driven by additional liquidity provided to the banking sector. Total assets experienced a strong expansion in the initial phases of the crisis (2008 to mid-2012), followed by a gradual reduction until late 2014, and another marked increase due to asset purchases conducted by the Eurosystem from late 2014 until the time of writing (early 2017).

The central bank is the monopoly supplier of two types of money. It issues banknotes and provides central bank money (CBM) to the banking sector. As discussed in Chaps. 1 and 2, banks use CBM to meet minimum reserve requirements, make interbank payments, and keep excess reserves as a liquidity buffer. The two types of money are shown on the liability side of the central bank balance sheet.[3] Chapter 2 explains how the central bank steers the amount of CBM it provides to the banking system in the context of monetary policy. By contrast, the amount of banknotes in the system mainly depends on the demand for banknotes by individuals, businesses, and banks. Due to the limited ability of the central bank to steer the demand for banknotes, they are considered an "autonomous factor" in the context of central bank liquidity management.

The simplified Eurosystem balance sheet consists of three main components, as illustrated in Fig. E.1:[4,5]

- **Monetary policy instruments:** Liquidity-providing operations are shown on the asset side and liquidity-absorbing operations on the liability side.[6]

[3]See Fig. 1.7 in Chap. 1.

[4]FX liquidity providing operations are sometimes mentioned as a fourth category.

[5]The Eurosystem publishes its balance sheet on its website on a weekly basis.

[6]Chapter 2 provides a detailed description of the respective policy instruments.

- *Liquidity-providing instruments* include short- and long-term central bank repo operations, the marginal lending facility, and asset purchases for monetary policy purposes.
- *Liquidity-absorbing instruments* include current accounts, which banks for instance use for interbank transactions and to meet minimum reserve requirements, the deposit facility, and other liquidity-absorbing operations.

• **Autonomous factors** consists of three main elements:
  - *Banknotes in circulation* (liability side): Banknotes are typically the largest autonomous factor on the liability side of the central bank balance sheet. The total value of banknotes covered roughly a third of the liabilities of the Eurosystem as of end-2016.
  - *Government deposits and residual items* (liability side): The central bank has little or no control over the extent of these elements. It is also worth noting that governments, unlike individuals and nonfinancial businesses, are allowed to have accounts at the central bank.
  - *Investment portfolio* (asset side): Investments of the Eurosystem include FX reserves, domestic assets, gold, and some other assets such as IMF Special Drawing Rights.[7]

• **Capital** as the residual between assets and liabilities.

Central banks are always net providers of liquidity to the banking system. Monetary policy instruments on the asset side, therefore, always exceed those on the liability side, as illustrated in the figure above. This also implies that net autonomous factors are always a liability for the central bank. In other words, the total value of banknotes in circulation, government deposits, and residual items is larger than the investment portfolio.

Lastly, the Eurosystem balance sheet only shows assets and liabilities vis-à-vis third parties, such as banks or the holders of banknotes. Claims and liabilities between central banks within the Eurosystem are netted and not shown in the consolidated balance sheet.[8]

[7]Chapter 2 provides more details.

[8]There are different views in the literature regarding the usefulness of analyzing claims across the members of the Eurosystem. The respective discussion focuses on so-called Target 2 balances of various national central banks within the Eurosystem. Target 2 imbalances showed a strong increase from 2010 to mid-2012, followed by a gradual reduction until late 2014 and another increase until the time of writing (early 2017).

Index

M. Fandl, *Monetary and Financial Policy in the Euro Area*, Springer Texts in Business and Economics, https://doi.org/10.1007/978-3-319-72643-4

MIX
Papier aus verantwortungsvollen Quellen
Paper from responsible sources
FSC® C105338

If you have any concerns about our products,
you can contact us on
ProductSafety@springernature.com

In case Publisher is established outside the EU,
the EU authorized representative is:
Springer Nature Customer Service Center GmbH
Europaplatz 3, 69115 Heidelberg, Germany

Printed by Libri Plureos GmbH
in Hamburg, Germany